Police Culture

Police culture has for over half a century attracted interest from academics, students, policy-makers, police institutions and the general public. However, the literature of this area has proven to be diverse, sprawling and prone to contradiction, leading to an enthralling yet intricate body of knowledge that, whilst continuing to provoke interest and debate, has largely escaped any wider commentary.

This book provides a comprehensive overview of the area of police culture primarily by situating it in the context of the literature of organizational culture. From this starting point, the idea of police culture is developed as an occupationally situated response to the uniqueness of the police role and one in which our understanding is, at times, hindered by the challenges of definitional, operational and analytical concerns. The book then charts the development of our understanding of the concept, through traditional explanations to the contemporary, highlighting in turn the tensions that exist between the elements of continuity in the police world and those of change.

Police Culture: Themes and Concepts draws on research from the 1950s to the twenty-first century from the UK, USA and elsewhere to show how the historical trajectory of police work from its early origins through to the late modern present has imbued it with a complexity that is undermined by deterministic explanations that seek to simplify the social world of the police officer. This book will be of interest to academics, practitioners and students studying the sociology of policing.

Tom Cockcroft is Senior Lecturer in the Department of Law and Criminal Justice Studies, Canterbury Christ Church University, UK. His areas of publishing and research interest are criminal justice, policing and occupational culture.

Police Culture

Themes and concepts

Tom Cockcroft

Routledge
Taylor & Francis Group

LONDON AND NEW YORK

First published 2013
by Routledge
2 Park Square, Milton Park, Abingdon, Oxon, OX14 4RN

Simultaneously published in the USA and Canada
by Routledge
711 Third Avenue, New York, NY 10017

Routledge is an imprint of the Taylor & Francis Group, an informa business

British Library Cataloguing in Publication Data
A catalogue record for this book is available from the British Library

Library of Congress Cataloging in Publication Data
    Cockcroft, Tom.
    Police culture : themes and concepts / Tom Cockcroft.—1st ed.
    p. cm.
    Includes bibliographical references.
    1. Police—Social aspects. I. Title.
    HV7921.P555 2012
    306.2'8—dc23
    2012010327

ISBN 13: 978–0–415–50257–3 hbk
ISBN 13: 978–0–415–50259–7 pbk
ISBN 13: 978–0–203–10115–5 ebk

Typeset in Times New Roman by Swales & Willis Ltd, Exeter, Devon

ed and bound in Great Britain by the MPG Books Group

For Ulanda and Tegan
with love.

Contents

Acknowledgements

The writing of this book has been made an altogether easier process through a wide range of support. I am very grateful to have been granted study leave by Canterbury Christ Church University for three months in the academic year 2010/2011, and colleagues from the Department of Law and Criminal Justice Studies have been a valued source of ideas, advice and friendship. Iain Beattie's encyclopedic knowledge of obscure pieces of police research has proved an invaluable resource for several years now, and I thank him for his willingness to share it so generously. On the publishing side, Nicola Hartley at Routledge patiently coaxed me towards my deadline and was incredibly helpful throughout. The ongoing encouragement of my parents Keith Cockcroft and Jane Hopkins and brother Graham has, likewise, been greatly appreciated. Whilst many friends and loved ones have helped to sustain my enthusiasm over the year or so when I actually wrote the book, some deserve a less perfunctory mention. Ged Denton has proved a relentless source of friendship and laughter since our misspent youth. The greatest acknowledgements, however, must go to my wife Ulanda and my daughter Tegan. I received the book's contract the same week that we learned of Ulanda's pregnancy, and the writing process has been punctuated by all those things in life that really matter. For my absences, both physical and mental, I thank you for your patience and support.

Introduction

This book is about police culture, a subject which, as broadly criminological concepts go, remains something of an anomaly. As Westmarland (2008) notes, whilst essentially an academic term, it has become widely accepted as a means of referring to what are generally considered problematic areas of policing and police behaviour. Despite having significance for academics, policy-makers, practitioners and members of the public alike, the cultural elements of police work and police institutions have failed to attract significant attention in any ordered way. Whilst scholastic work into police culture has generated a number of monographs, and an even larger number of academic papers spanning a period of over 50 years, there has been little attention paid to providing some kind of overview of the area. This is not particularly surprising. The subject area of police cultural studies (if it can be called that) is, at one level, loosely held together by a multitude of definitions, methodologies, disciplinary orientations and focuses. In part, its fragmented nature parallels that of McLaughlin and Muncie's (2006) depiction of criminology as a cross-disciplinary endeavour where the lack of a common language has led to a vibrant academic community from a variety of intellectual foundations. This, in turn, has meant that the subject area of police culture has benefited from the insights of a wide array of perspectives and intellectual orientations focused upon a relatively narrow range of issues.

Somewhat ironically, and despite the broad and flexible parameters of the subject area, recent years have seen commentary move towards a more critical appraisal of the state of this academic subject area. In particular, there is a hint that the area is, in some respects, trading on past glories rather than developing new intellectual ground. Whilst this is not wholly justified, especially in the light of more recent work, the ceaseless politicization of policing and the emergence of new police scandals against the backdrop of a changing society lend weight to calls for a reinvigoration of what is becoming an ever more complex set of concepts. Whilst this book in no way should be seen as advocating what McLaughlin and Muncie (2006, p. xiii) suggest as a 'discursive unification' of the subject area, what it does aim to do is to highlight its origins, its development and the practical, conceptual and analytic challenges that have become associated with it over recent decades.

As has already been suggested, the literature and research of police culture, owing to the expansiveness of the term, represent an incredibly extensive body of work. One substantial challenge is to provide an appropriately broad assessment of the cultural elements of themes common to this subject area such as discretion, gender, ethnicity and corruption and which amount to substantive subject areas in their own right. To overcome this, the book makes no attempt or claim to present an exhaustive coverage of all the individual contributions made in this field. Instead, I have adopted an approach that I hope will serve not just to identify many of the key pieces of work and their importance but also to assess their influence and their relevance. Indeed, reflecting on the chapters of this book as I come to the end of the writing process, I am struck by the fact that, to me at least, the book is about the balance of change and continuity. Crucially, such changes refer not just to the police institution, their policies, processes and the means by which officers navigate these, but also to the people who constitute the societies that the police serve and the relationships that, at different times, draw the two sides together or apart. At a more removed level, this balance is also explored with reference to the more general social changes associated with late modernity, which signify a whole range of conceptual challenges for traditional visions of police culture.

If one compares the work of Banton (1964), one of the first systematic studies of this subject area, with one of the most recent (by Loftus, 2009), differences and similarities quickly emerge. Banton's work is an incredibly illuminating account of the state of policing (in both American and Scottish contexts) and its treatment by sociologists during the 1960s. His research could be considered to have been driven by fundamentally different motivations to more contemporary work not least in respect of its acknowledgement that policing, at that time, had been subjected to insufficient academic scrutiny. However, perhaps the fundamental difference relates to his suggestion that policing merited attention on account of its status as being a 'successful' institution. Given the orientation of later works, one might reflect on the extent to which sociological dissections of police work have been, for the most part, essentially negative rather than positive evaluations of police culture and practice. At the same time, Banton's work identified a number of issues that would go on to become persistent themes in later pieces of research, if not those that immediately followed it. Indeed, his work can be considered quite prophetic not least in respect of its identification of the evolution of different policing styles and cultures in different locations, the impact of population changes, the rise of consumerism, the growth of information technology, shifting conceptions of class, nostalgic depictions of 'golden ages' of policing and the importance of the police relationship with the public.

Loftus's work, published 45 years after Banton's, provides a fitting comparison by acknowledging the present state of police cultural studies. Whilst Loftus notes that police culture, and the way we conceptualize it, is going through a period of change, she also highlights a potential schism in the orientation and form that our explanations and descriptions take. To some, therefore, police culture is a phenomenon that through targeted action can be addressed and subsequently modified. These approaches are fundamentally reformist and exemplify a means of addressing the manifestations of police culture without really engaging too explicitly with the subtleties of the culture itself. On the other hand, argues Loftus, a series of different explanations have been used to present a much more complex conception of the nature and properties of police culture and one that is predicated upon differences in culture and behaviour rather than similarity. To such writers the idea of police *culture* has been replaced by one of police *cultures*. These essentially different sets of explanations have meant that traditional ideas of police culture have generally fallen out of favour, leading to a variety of ideas about what police culture is, how it works and how best to investigate it. In what some might consider a telling affirmation of the cyclical nature of many intellectual ideas, Loftus, whilst acknowledging the contribution made by those authors who emphasize difference above continuity at a cultural level, makes a persuasive case to argue that there is sufficient universality between police cultures for us to address them in the singular. One of the largest challenges that faces us, and one that is made explicit by Loftus's work, is that culture impacts broadly and at many levels within a police context. Whilst management initiatives to implement cultural change may be deemed successful by virtue of them causing a change in expressed behaviour, it might be premature to hail these as successful instances of cultural change. Cultural artefacts or manifestations and underlying cultural beliefs are, as organizational theorists like Schein make clear, essentially different. 'Evidence' of cultural change being driven by new initiatives may therefore be misleading and may represent behavioural but not necessarily attitudinal change. Furthermore, such changes may be driven by external pressures such as the recognition of formerly marginalized groups. When one focuses on less politicized dimensions, such as class, we find that little effort has been made by police institutions to address these at the structural level let alone the behavioural or attitudinal.

Police culture was, and continues to be, a complex issue and, after 48 years, the following passage from Banton's work remains exceptionally germane:

> Were I to aim at a really complete description and analysis of the policeman's role I fear that I should commit myself to a lifetime's labour. One of the difficulties is that the police service is a little world of its own in which almost everything is related to everything else and it is impossible to isolate a single aspect for separate examination.
>
> (1964, p. xii)

For a book aiming to explore the themes and concepts associated with police culture, therefore, the challenge is of conveying a sense of discrete and identifiable concepts without losing track of the less tangible themes that nevertheless have a primary role in explaining the complexities of culture. Given that all these variables are open to analysis at a number of levels and from a variety of perspectives, any attempt to isolate them would amount to an act of gross over-simplification. To avoid such an eventuality I have attempted to create an account that highlights the components of the cultural world, and the ideas that we use to explain them, but which ultimately makes no wholesale attempt to extricate them for the purpose of 'examination'. The interrelatedness to which Banton refers is essentially where the power of the culture of the police resides and, for better or worse, I have attempted to keep this intact.

1 Organizational and occupational cultures

Introduction

Any analysis of police occupational culture, arguably, begins not with a review of the literature of policing and police studies but with an acknowledgement of the literature of organizational culture. It is perhaps fair to say that research into the area of police culture has largely been driven by the work of sociologists and criminologists seeking answers to immediate issues of police behaviour. This approach has undoubtedly generated a wealth of knowledge regarding the police, their behaviour and their values. However, reviews of the literature often leave one with the impression that, to some police scholars, our understanding of police culture, police behaviour and the relationship between the two can be understood solely through knowledge generated within those two subject areas (although writers such as Chan, 1997, can be seen as an exception to this generalization). By starting with a broad overview of the literature of organizational management and the conceptual challenges associated with it, we can unravel some of the wider themes relating to organizations, the cultural factors inherent to them and the behavioural and attitudinal responses that they encourage.

What is organizational culture?

To Johnson, Koh and Killough (2009) organizational culture refers to the values shared by colleagues in an organization and which become manifest through the occupational practices within that environment. Numerous factors can influence the direction and intensity of the cultural dynamics of organizations, and these can be internal or external to the organization. Internal factors can include the size, function, structure, technology and goals of the organization, and external factors can include the qualities of the industry or sector that they operate within as well as societal and national cultures.

Schein (2004) begins by addressing the meaning of the word 'culture' and shows how, over the years, it has popularly been used to denote the level of an individual's sophistication, to describe the traditions that communities engage in and which become embedded historically and, also, to represent the context-specific principles and values that inform the way that people think and behave. Fundamental to the complexity of the term 'culture', in a social scientific sense, is the fact that despite being an abstract and non-tangible concept it has real and perceivable impacts across a range of organizational and occupational life. In turn, this idea of culture as lacking in physical substance but significant in its role as a stimulus to certain behaviours and beliefs has become commonly accepted. To Schein (2004), 'culture', within the context of understanding organizations and occupations, refers to a sharing of beliefs or a consensus of values. These shared social artefacts are not to be considered as synonymous with a particular group's culture but as manifestations of it and represent the variables through which we try to observe and identify the culture. The importance of this point is not to be underestimated, as it reminds us of the need to differentiate between culture as a concept and those behaviours and attitudes that are displayed by human actors as a result of it.

Culture (according to Schein, 2004) can be broadly understood in terms of the following categories: 'observed behavioural regularities when people interact'; 'group norms'; 'espoused values'; 'formal philosophy'; 'rules of the game'; 'climate'; 'embedded skills'; 'habits of thinking, mental models, and linguistic paradigms'; 'shared meanings'; 'root metaphors or integrating symbols'; and 'formal rituals and celebrations'. However, the above categories are interlinked with concepts that group members share but which cannot strictly be considered as a 'culture' and, to Schein, the term 'culture' is important in that it is more flexible and fluid than the above explanatory categories. Therefore, to fully understand culture, we need to contextualize the above categories of sharing in terms of 'critical elements' of 'structural stability', 'depth', 'breadth' and 'patterning' or 'integration' (2004, p. 14). 'Structural stability' refers to the inherent resilience of cultural dynamics. This is not to say that cultures cannot change, but that their strength lies not just in their definitional powers (in terms of bringing meaning to people's lives) but in their ability to remain *in situ* regardless of the turnover in membership of group members. 'Depth' is an important attribute of cultures, as culture, as we have already noted, lacks a physical dimension and impacts largely at an unconscious level. The essence of culture, therefore, is 'hidden' underneath its more visible manifestations. 'Breadth' represents the all-encompassing nature of culture and the way it influences an organization's internal hierarchy, its task orientation and its relationship to the environments that it operates within. Fundamental to many ideas of culture is that it is broad enough to impact significantly upon all areas of organizational life. Finally, 'patterning or integration' refers to the way in which cultures draw together the various manifestations of themselves into a meaningful whole. Thus, both horizontally and vertically, the culture equates to more than the sum of its parts and draws, in terms of depth, from the observable manifestations of cultural life down to unconscious and intangible constructs. Likewise, its breadth encapsulates all aspects of organizational life from conventions of presentation and language to the nature of relationships with colleagues and client groups. Such integration (both vertically through the concept of 'depth' and horizontally through that of 'breadth') is paramount to the notion of culture, as its very pervasiveness is what makes it meaningful to individuals.

It is upon these principles that Schein defines culture as:

a pattern of shared basic assumptions that was learned by a group as it solved its problems of external adaptation and internal integration, that has worked well enough to be considered valid and, therefore, to be taught to new members as the correct way to perceive, think, and feel in relation to those problems.

(Schein, 2004, p. 17)

Buono *et al.* lend further clarity to the concept by noting that:

Organizational culture tends to be unique to a particular organization, composed of an objective and subjective dimension, and concerned with tradition and the nature of shared beliefs and expectations about organizational life. It is a powerful determinant of individual and group behaviour. Organizational culture affects practically all aspects of organizational life from the way in which people interact with each other, perform their work and dress, to the types of decisions made in a firm, its organizational policies and procedures, and strategy considerations.

(cited in Schraeder, Tears and Jordan, 2005, p. 493)

Different levels of culture

We can understand culture at a number of different levels and can differentiate between these levels in respect of their visibility to the observer. A failure to understand the intricate layers of cultural phenomena is probably one of the key reasons why we find defining culture difficult. Accordingly, we have to differentiate between the explicit physical expressions of culture and the 'deeply embedded, unconscious, basic assumptions' (Schein, 2004, p. 25) that represent its purest, most abstracted form.

Schein goes on to define three levels of culture: 'artefacts'; 'espoused beliefs and values'; and 'underlying assumptions'. 'Artefacts' represent those perceptible phenomena associated with the cultural group and include traditions, ceremonies, folklore, explicitly articulated values, language, products and modes of dress and address. These, the most visible manifestations of the culture, are also the most difficult for those from outside the culture to interpret or to make sense of without prolonged exposure to the group. 'Espoused beliefs and values' represent conscious and explicitly articulated philosophies that will lead to some observable phenomena at the 'artefact' level. Those beliefs and values that 'work' for group members and which provide meaning to their social experience may, over time, become embedded at the deeper level of 'underlying assumption'. Complexities may arise at this level in terms of some beliefs and values that might seem to hold conflicting purposes. Sometimes these apparent ambiguities may emerge owing to the fact that some values are at the level of rhetoric (as opposed to tested or learnt behaviour) or may be regarded as aspirational rather than justificational. 'Underlying assumptions' represent those espoused beliefs and values that through repeated and successful use or testing have changed in status from conjecture to reality. Once these assumptions have been ascribed this status, their validity is guaranteed and consensus is reached regarding their value. Such assumptions are internalized at an unconscious level and are embedded sufficiently to negate, in most cases, debate regarding their worth or 'correctness'.

Cultural typologies

Typologies have a particular function to play in helping us to understand the non-tangible elements associated with organizational culture. In other words, basic experience has little, if any, implicit meaning and understanding arises only as we develop conceptual categories through language learning. This process of applying systems of language to our experiences represents our cultural education, and we continue to develop these cultural categories as we enter new cultural environments. Individuals working in particular organizations or roles build conceptual categories that help them to understand the different types of phenomena that they experience, and these conceptual categories can be drawn from existing cultural distinctions represented through language or, alternatively, new phrases can be developed to distinguish these differences in meaning.

New cultural categories and their accompanying additions to our language serve three key roles. First, they allow us greater clarity or understanding of a particular observed occurrence; second, they help us to understand the constitution of that occurrence by developing hypotheses that explain its existence; and, finally, they allow us to predict how other occurrences (as yet unwitnessed) might appear. Schein provides a number of examples of such interorganizational typologies. For example, he draws on the work of Etzioni (1975) that distinguished between three different types of organization – coercive, utilitarian and normative – which denote varying amounts of interplay between two factors: the economic control of the employee and employee commitment to the goals of the organization. Similarly, Schein (2004) highlights the work of Goffee and Jones (1998) that differentiated between 'fragmented', 'mercenary', 'communal' and 'networked' cultures on the basis of the levels of solidarity and sociability that were present in organizations. This is not to suggest, however, that the social world of a particular organization has to be rooted within one set of cultural ideas, and Schein does draw attention to intra-organizational typologies which highlight cultural differences in the workplace and which are produced through distinctions between different roles or statuses within the organization. To Schein, the most obvious of these distinctions is that of the cultural division between management and workers. There are, however, more nuanced divisions within organizations such as those that exist between operator cultures (which focus on the performance of core tasks), engineering cultures (which focus on the development of commodities and systems) and executive cultures (which focus on financial matters within the organization). The extent to which such typologies can and should be employed is debatable. Although Schein differentiates between 'integrated', 'differentiated' and 'fragmented' cultures in terms of the varying degrees to which organizations subscribe to a particular set of cultural assumptions, questions can be raised regarding the usefulness of the concept of culture when it is subject to such differentiation. We appear, therefore, to be confronted with an apparent variety of cultures that threatens, at times, to undermine the idea that culture reflects a coherent degree of shared values.

At this point, it might appear that organizational culture is, although nuanced, a relatively straightforward subject. Specific social and operational forces impact on people who belong to certain organizational groups (and sometimes become differentiated through further stratification within these organizational groups), and these forces can be evidenced in three different ways – at the level of 'artefact', 'espoused beliefs' and 'views and underlying assumptions'. We can then adopt or develop broad conceptual categories known as 'typologies' to facilitate our understanding of the cultural behaviours that we observe.

Martin (2002), noting the contested nature of culture played out in the academic world, describes a number of tensions that arise when attempting to make sense of organizational culture and how these impact on the ways we frame research into it. In doing so she draws attention to the 'culture wars' that have arisen in the area of cultural research and which refer to arguments surrounding ideas of the nature and properties of culture. These reflect fundamental intellectual tensions that have surfaced within the social sciences in recent years and will be described in the following sections.

Researching culture

Objectivity and subjectivity

Much research in the area of organizational behaviour is premised upon the notion that the world we live in will reveal its true and objective nature through sustained investigation with suitable methodologies. This relatively unproblematic rendering of the relationship between social phenomena and the use of social science methodology tends to mask some entrenched problems and, consequently, poses some challenging questions for those undertaking research into organizational cultures. At a fundamental level, we are faced with the challenge of subjecting the focus of our research, culture, to empirical scrutiny. Culture, after all, is an abstract concept, an elusive entity that is experienced as much as witnessed. Thus we face the very real danger that we merely confuse some of the manifestations of a group culture as the physical embodiment of the culture. Although this issue will be explored at greater length later in this book, it is important to note that this apparent reification of culture into mere artefacts influences not just how we physically research organizational culture, but also how we interpret the knowledge that it generates.

Academic opinion is divided in respect of this debate over subjectivity. Martin (2002) charts the different positions in respect of this, showing how opinions are positioned on an axis stretching from the purely objective to the purely subjective and notes how debate revolves around the degree of subjectivity which one should acknowledge within this process. She goes on to outline the key differences between strong subjective and moderate subjective positions in respect of this by drawing on the work of Sahlins (1995) and Stablein (1996). For Sahlins, objective reality or realities do not exist, and members of a cultural world subjectively interpret the realities that they experience. To highlight this, Sahlins (cited in Martin, 2002) shows how, for example, different national cultures have developed and internalized different cultural understandings regarding particular types of animal meat and its suitability for human consumption. Consequently, the same 'reality' leads to a wide variation in cultural responses, leading Sahlins to conclude that events or experiences themselves do not lead to cultural experience, because, quite simply, such events and experiences take place against a backdrop of existing symbols and meanings. The relationship, therefore, between stimulus and response is, in the case of the relationship between 'reality' and cultural reaction, unreliable. Sahlins's views, however, might be considered a little uncompromising to some cultural researchers, with many adopting more moderate views of the subjective standpoint. Writers like Stablein (1996), for example, propose a reading of the subjective position which stresses that subjectivity is subject to restraining influences and that these operate at a collective as opposed to an individual level. Such an approach can be conceptualized as being essentially founded upon the principles underpinning the work of Berger and Luckmann (1967), which highlighted the importance of socially constructed reality in restricting the cultural judgements that are made.

Etic and emic research

A further distinction, between etic and emic research, mirrors the above issues regarding subjectivity in our understanding of cultural phenomena. More specifically, it refers to the issue of subjectivity in developing categories of what is to be considered meaningful in a cultural research context. In etic research, categories of analysis are informed from existing literature and theory and are imposed on the research by the researcher. In emic research, researchers adopt, as far as is possible, an insider perspective that focuses on categories that are seen as important to those being studied. These strategies are usually adopted when investigating cultural practices that might be considered alien to us as researchers and draw parallels with Weber's (1949) *verstehende* sociology, which, according to Spradley (1980), highlights the need to avoid 'the pre-definition of what is to be considered relevant' (p. 24). This approach therefore proposes that we should assess phenomena in relation to their own 'cultural significance' rather than in relation to our own values. Ultimately, however, to successfully distinguish between the etic and the emic positions might be an impossible aspiration. The two approaches, although portrayed as diametrically opposed, are more intertwined than first appearances might suggest, and the most appropriate position may be concerned with finding a suitable balance between the two.

Generalizable and context-specific knowledge

The distinction between generalizable and context-specific knowledge refers to differing conceptions both of the nature of cultures and of the way we research them. Researchers who subscribe to the idea of generalizable knowledge in the field of culture see the purpose of cultural research as being the fundamental means by which we build theories to explain cultural dynamics in more than one setting. In other words, for some, the primary purpose of conducting research is to develop knowledge that can be used to explain cultural phenomena in other settings and thus to develop universals that can then be used to predict how culture will 'play out' in other situations. On the other hand, however, some cultural researchers seek not to generate transferable generalizable knowledge but merely to develop 'thick description' (Martin, 2002, p. 43) regarding a particular culture. Most proponents of this 'case study' approach premise their support for such a method on the assumption that each culture is unique and, therefore, that the search for 'cultural universals' is superfluous. Indeed, as in the case of policing, many organizations and occupations may view their social worlds and cultural dynamics as unlike any other. One of the reasons which makes the cultural uniqueness position so attractive is that some would suggest that a particular situation or context could give rise to a number of cultural consequences. That is, a number of different cultural responses could have emerged to make sense of a particular situation negating the idea of generalization between cultures. This position seeks, therefore, 'an appreciation of contextually specific knowledge rather than an understanding that emerges from the process of abstraction and generalization across cases' (Martin, 2002, p. 41). In many respects, this tension between the two positions echoes traditional differences between ideographic (based on a solitary example) and nomothetic research (which seeks to develop generalizable and universal rules regarding phenomena through exploring samples composed of numerous cases). Martin (2002) helps to clarify the differences between the two approaches as follows. Generalizable research treats culture as a variable, whereas context-specific treats it as a metaphor. Generalizable research seeks to use information to predict effects, whereas context-specific research seeks textured information as an end in itself. Generalizable research generates 'thin' description, and context-specific generates 'thick' description (Martin, 2002, p. 43).

'Focus' and 'breadth'

Associated to the point concerning generalizable and context-specific knowledge is that of different approaches to 'focus' and 'breadth' in research. Some researchers focus on a limited number of cultural manifestations or artefacts when investigating a culture, whereas others draw on a wider range. Once again, this difference broadly reflects differences between ideographic and nomothetic stances, with ideographic work tending to focus on a broader range of conceptual categories. Nomothetic approaches may focus on variations within a single specific cultural manifestation between, for example, different organizations or groups.

Level of depth

Similarly, Martin (2002) reiterates Schein's notion that cultures have three distinct levels: 'artefacts'; 'values'; and 'basic assumptions'. The existence of these distinct and differentiated levels of understanding have implications for cultural researchers, the most important being which level of culture one should seek to explore. Traditional ethnographic approaches would work towards a level of understanding that equated with the basic assumption level and which produced thick description, whereas more quantitative approaches would work at the level of artefact or values and produce thin description. Schein's approach suggests that research into deeper levels of cultural meaning (such as that of the basic assumption) reveals a more profound level of understanding of a culture than research that deals with artefacts or values. Opinion on this topic is divided, and Martin (2002) advocates a more flexible approach by suggesting that the different levels of cultural manifestation outlined by Schein reflect different types, rather than depths, of cultural manifestations.

Ideational and materialistic approaches

It is important to note that further definitional divisions occur within the study of organizational culture depending on whether one adopts an ideational or materialistic approach, with the former stressing the subjective qualities of culture and the latter highlighting the objective. Ideational conceptions of culture therefore emphasize the subjectively experienced qualities of culture, whereas materialistic approaches highlight the objective and quantifiable elements of organizations such as differences in pay, conditions and role. Purely ideational cultural definitions focus on the subjectively experienced perception of a social world without contextualizing it in terms of differential material conditions. Materialistic approaches, however, are considered important by some, as they enable us to understand the material conditions under which subjective cognitions arise and, therefore, allow us to explore intergroup conflict within organizational cultures and structures. Materialist definitions can broadly be separated into two key categories of those who see material conditions as integral to the culture and those who see them as essentially separate from the culture, although helpful as a means of understanding it. To proponents of the latter, therefore:

> the materialist base consists of attributes such as job descriptions, reporting relationships, pay practices, and formally mandated policies and procedures, which are not part of the cultural superstructure. Culture, then, consists of the ideational elements, such as beliefs and values, that emerge to explain and reinforce a materialist base.
>
> (Martin, 2002, p. 59)

We can thus identify a potential relationship between the structural factors of, for example, the workplace and the cultural values of the organization. However, the strength of the relationship (how closely the two are related) and the direction of the relationship (the extent to which materialist factors influence the ideational, or vice versa) remain largely unarticulated. To provide an appropriate explanatory context for the study of the occupational culture of the police, the following distinctions also need to be made: the distinction between organizational and occupational culture and the distinction between public and private sector organizational cultures.

Organizational and occupational cultures

The chapter has so far looked at the concept of organizational culture, a means of describing the ways that groups of people experience, perceive and act within an organizational environment. This approach implicitly assumes that all employees of the organization belong to a corresponding cultural group, and this might be considered problematic in a number of respects. Changes to the structure of organizations over recent decades (both at national and international levels), owing to industrial expansion and contraction, the type of employment offered and the advent of flexible working enabled by technological developments, mean that cultures and organizations no longer share the same borders. The relationship between culture and organization, which is so often portrayed in unproblematic terms, is likely to be subject to over-reach and indicates that, in reality, cultural dynamics might be more closely aligned to occupations than organizations.

Gregory (1983), in a piece of research that explores the impact of culture upon those employed by computer companies in California's 'Silicon Valley', highlights well this apparent disjunction between organizational and occupational culture. To many of the workers that she studied the primary factor that dictated their values and outlook was the role they undertook, not the organization that employed them. Distinctions were made not in terms of which company people worked for but with regard to whether they were, for example, hardware or software engineers. This crosscutting of organizations by occupational cultures leads to some interesting examples of conflicting cultural values between groups. For example, Gregory's work showed the ways in which different occupational groups within an organization, whilst wanting to work on projects based on innovative and new technologies, had very different motivations for doing so. Engineers' interests in such technologies were based on getting products into the marketplace, whereas scientists' were motivated more by the developmental aspects of the work. Crucially, Gregory suggests that these different cultural orientations within particular organizations are due to occupational cultures that are sustained between organizations, rather than being mere subcultures governed by a unique and contained organizational culture. Paoline (2003) develops this point, with reference to the work of Schein (1992) and Van Maanen and Barley (1985), by suggesting that a fundamental difference between organizational and occupational cultures are that the former are top-down and driven by management whereas the latter are bottom-up and driven by core practitioners.

Public and private sector cultures

Using cultural approaches to understand the ways that people act within organizational settings demands an appreciation of the fact that organizations themselves are subject to differentiation based on factors such as size, core business and, of course, the individuals and agencies with which they interact. One of the most pronounced distinctions in this respect pertains to the differences between public and private sector organizations. Schraeder, Tears and Jordan (2005) draw on Denison (1990) to suggest that the main reason for the growth of interest in organizational research is the acknowledgement that organizational culture is fundamentally connected to organizational effectiveness. Recent decades, therefore, have seen an emerging body of work that uses cultural frames of analysis to explain how people work within organizational contexts. Although the primary driver for such work has been a focus on the efficiency of organizations operating within the private sector, increasingly we have witnessed a sustained pressure for government agencies to be run in ways that reflect prevailing fashions in the private sector, a process that may involve both operational and cultural change.

To begin with, however, it might be helpful to distinguish between public and private sector organizations. Schraeder, Tears and Jordan (2005) show how these two broad categories of organizations operate in very different ways. Profound differences occur in respect of decision-making, general policies, means of communication, personnel management, materials procurement, financial management and marketing. At a broader level, Cockcroft and Beattie (2009) draw on the work of Jackson (1993) and Wisniewski and Olaffson (2004) to highlight not only the tendency of public sector agencies to have wider and more complex organizational objectives than private sector organizations, but also that such objectives are often less achievable given the financial restrictions on such organizations. Perhaps the most striking distinction between public and private sector organizations is presented by Williams (1985), who views the evolution of the public sector as a response to the failure of the private sector to provide for all the needs of the communities which they serve.

The work of Parker and Bradley (2000) shows how the 1980s saw the emergence of widespread managerial reforms founded upon new public management ideals of improved cost efficiency, financial accountability and customer focus. This move towards a managerialist orientation has generally been accompanied by organizational change directed at securing the progression of post-bureaucratic organizational forms and, whilst widespread transformation has been championed, according to Sinclair (1991), these changes have been implemented with insufficient knowledge of public sector organizational cultures. This has led to challenging implications at both management and policy levels. One such implication is that the techniques of new public management will not assimilate easily, according to some commentators, within the cultures of public sector organizations and, for Parker and Bradley (2000), the success or otherwise of these reforms can be understood only in terms of these factors.

The impact of these new forms of management are inconclusive, with some suggesting that they have led to improved performance and accountability (Domberger and Hall, 1996) and others suggesting that they have led to increases in stress and decreases in job satisfaction (Bogg and Cooper, 1995). Parker and Bradley (2000) go on to suggest that it is important that we understand public sector organizational culture when exploring options for public sector reform given that we need to assess the potential for synchronization between reform strategies and objectives and the culture of the working cultures that they will be directed at.

Organizational culture and transition

Traditional public sector organizations are subject to different forms of external controls than private sector organizations (Dahl and Lindblom, 1953). Private organizations are effectively constrained by market controls, whereas those of the public sector are increasingly subjected to control by political authority. Furthermore, their objectives and the structures that evolve through which to achieve these are keenly controlled through legislation. Thus political and legal, as opposed to financial, considerations have been the major forces acting upon the public sector, leading to a gradual obfuscation of clear objectives. Traditionally, research suggests that public sector organizations have adopted a structured and hierarchical culture because of both their basic structural stability and their emphasis on procedural regularity. This is in contrast to the developmental cultures which are traditionally found in private sector organizations and which focus on responsiveness to changing external environments, risk-taking and efficiency. Increasingly, according to Parker and Bradley (2000), the new public management signals a change in focus with less prominence accorded to procedural regularity and administration and a greater emphasis upon 'entrepreneurial management strategies, mission statements, performance management, and performance-based rewards' (p. 131). In effect, therefore, we have witnessed a change in what we consider the ideal model for governing public sector organizations with a subsequent underplaying of formal hierarchy and a greater role for financial controls, competition and performance measurement models.

Parker and Bradley's research explored the experiences of staff within six organizations in the Queensland public sector. Its aim was to assess the success with which they had adopted flexible and entrepreneurial values associated with private sector organizations and shed the traditional bureaucratic values associated with the public sector. Despite sustained support for the adoption of the new set of organizational values at management level the authors found that, overall, the majority of staff in these organizations still subscribed to the conventional values associated with the public sector. When assessing the reasons for this apparent failure to succeed in instigating cultural change, the authors put forward a number of potential factors. These included the difficulties with imposing cultural change from above, the fundamental and seemingly intractable differences between public and private sector organizations, and the wide variety of goals and resources (see also Wisniewski and Olaffson, 2004). Furthermore, Parker and Bradley suggested that public sector organizations are inevitably bound up in government strategies and therefore directed not so much by market forces but by political ideologies that push both social and economic agendas. Finally, the authors conclude by suggesting, quite simply, that those who work in the public sector may have different values to those who work in the private sector and draw upon research which suggests that public sector workers tend to be more socially aware and more focused on the public interest than those in the private sector.

Conclusion

The literature of organizational and occupational culture has become integral to our understanding of how employment structures (and the sectors and markets within which they operate) have come to shape the ways in which people make sense of their working world and their place within it. Its real value lies in the extent to which it has posed some quite critical and conceptual questions regarding the natures of occupational and organizational cultures. For example, the literature describes the different levels at which cultural meaning can be identified and, by doing so, the ways in which some cultural meaning becomes much harder to discern or identify. It has also prompted us to question the criteria by which we consider one category, and not another, as a meaningful means of understanding culture. Yet another layer of intricacy is added when we consider the degree to which we can take knowledge gained from one cultural environment and use it to make sense of another. Even if such factors could conveniently be placed to one side, we would still be confronted by questions over the potential for tensions between the organizational and the occupational culture and the distorting lens provided by the wider external market within which that organization operates. All these factors can be considered pertinent to our understanding of the occupational culture of the police.

2 Occupational culture and policing

Introduction

When we direct our attention away from public sector occupational cultures per se and towards police occupational cultures, perhaps one of the first facts that needs to be acknowledged is the level of interest that they continue to generate. The subject area has attracted substantial academic attention over a relatively sustained amount of time and, as Westmarland (2008) notes, has achieved the somewhat distinguished position of being one of the few terms in police studies used by academics and lay audiences alike. Amongst academics, suggest O'Neill and Singh (2007, p. 1), it has become 'an inescapable, controversial, surprisingly stubborn and recurring theme'. That police occupational or organizational culture (the two terms can be used interchangeably in most respects), seemingly above all other such cultures, still generates new literature, debate and disagreement indicates that police behaviour and values, and the drivers behind these, remain contested and of significant social interest. This chapter will highlight the social and political undercurrents that have informed much work into police culture before identifying three key eras of police culture research. For each of these eras of research a small number of key works will be discussed and the main themes outlined. Whilst the chapter presents some definitions of police culture, a selection of works will be drawn on to highlight the difficulties associated with defining this complex area.

The shifting social and political context of policing

To fully recognize the powerful draw that police culture exerts, it is important to understand the ways in which policing impacts on a number of different areas of academic, practitioner and public interest. Changes within and beyond the policing institution have, especially in recent decades, compelled us to reassess what we mean by the term. Likewise, policing has become increasingly sensitive to the vagaries of competing and conflicting political agendas since the mid- to late 1960s, and this has impacted on what the police do, how they do it and, increasingly, how they present both themselves and the information that they generate. Policing continues, at a symbolic level, to articulate the relationship between state and individual particularly in regard to provision of security. At a more practical level, since the inception of the 'new' police, their enforcement of the law has been grounded not only in mandated intervention but in the application of subjective discretion, a theme that has been fundamental to our understanding of police decision-making and its consequences. Furthermore, recent years have seen the police subjected to ever greater degrees of scrutiny by government, media and academics alike, and this has continued to fuel our interest in the police institution, its role, its relation with the public and the behaviour of its officers.

One important factor, therefore, that may explain the enduring interest in the police as a cultural location is the politicization of crime and crime control, which has seen policing and penal policies vie as equals with the more traditional policy issues such as education, health and housing during recent years. Morgan and Newburn (1997) see this emergence of policing as a political issue as a relatively recent phenomenon, with President Richard Nixon articulating popular and growing concerns regarding social issues in the United States during the mid- to late 1960s. Similarly, according to Garland (2001), the election successes of Margaret Thatcher in the United Kingdom and Ronald Reagan in the United States could be attributed less to the resonance of their economic policies than to their ability to provide a voice for broad popular discontent with the post-war social democratic consensus that was increasingly being seen as a cause of, rather than a cure for, a multitude of social problems. Increasingly, therefore, the police became accountable in a political sense for what became known as 'the crime problem'. This notion that the politicization of policing is a 'new' occurrence that has emerged over the last 40 or 50 years does come with a minor caveat, namely, that policing has, at some levels, always been political. For example, to Brogden (1982, p. 1), the police institution is inextricably connected to the political world when he states that 'Nowhere, however, is the confusion over the deposition of the police institution more opaque than in its political relation.' Policing, therefore, becomes political at two different levels. The process to which Morgan and Newburn refer is the politicization of policing at a popular level and focused upon the demands of the electorate, whilst Brogden refers to the political dimensions of accountability within the policing context.

Increased popular concern surrounding crime and order issues, the politicization of policing at the public level and the contemporary tendency towards heightened awareness of risk provide an amalgamated discontent for which the public seek intervention. Interestingly, as Walklate and Mythen (2008, p. 213) highlight, we find it increasingly difficult to separate fear of crime from the broader 'tapestry' of contemporary (and non-crime) insecurities that impact upon our lives. Therefore, changes to the ways in which we frame or perceive our security needs and our increased propensity to seek additional or alternative remedies to these feelings of insecurity provide one explanation of the public's continuing fascination with order, security and the work of the police. These processes have coincided, in some areas, with a marked shift in the public's positioning of their security needs in respect to the ability of the state to provide for them. Mike Davis, in *City of Quartz*, his thought-provoking assessment of the social history of Los Angeles, states:

In the once wide-open tractlands of the San Fernando Valley, where there were virtually no walled-off communities a decade ago, the 'trend' has assumed the frenzied dimensions of a residential arms race as ordinary suburbanites demand the kind of social insulation once enjoyed only by the rich.

(1992, p. 246)

The increasingly contested view of security as either a right to be fulfilled by the state or a commodity to be bought in as a service according to one's own needs provides some explanation of the increasing pluralized terms in which we view policing. Furthermore, it suggests some potentially interesting exploratory avenues regarding comparisons between public and private police cultures, a subject that will be addressed in a later chapter of this book.

Westmarland (2008) describes a number of factors that may explain some of our sustained interest in the culture of policing, and discretion can be seen as central to these. It is considered important for two key reasons. First, the amount of discretion bestowed upon police officers (particularly those of relatively low status) exceeds that enjoyed by those of similar rank in other occupations and, second, the discretion of police officers can have far-reaching consequences. Brogden, Jefferson and Walklate (1988, p. 95) allude to this when they note that the discretion granted requires police officers, on occasion, to make 'subjective judgements' regarding whether or not a crime has occurred or whether there is a substantial likelihood that one might occur. Furthermore, they continue by suggesting that the discretionary nature of much police work allows for an undermining of the equalitarian principles espoused within legal rhetoric through the facilitation of discriminatory practices, for example within the context of stop and search. Similarly, discretion in the policing context is seen by Black (1980, p. 58) as of great importance, as 'Discriminatory decision making by citizens to a degree cancels itself out in the citizen mass, while discriminatory behaviour by legal officials mirrors their own biases, and these are apt to flow in only one direction.' Police discretion therefore represents the measure by which we differentiate between the law as it stands in theory and the law as it is applied by police officers, and the idea that police discretionary powers should lead to biases in the application of the law has long been a topic of debate for police scholars. In his book exploring police accountability, *The Police: Autonomy and Consent*, Brogden (1982) suggests that the police institution has successfully undermined the practical application of judicial practice in three particular ways through the exercising of quasi-judicial functions by officers. First, the decision regarding the application or non-application of a particular law is effectively a judicial decision. Second, legislation such as that pertaining to stop and search (and repealed UK legislation such as section 4 of the Vagrancy Act 1824) negates the legal principle that assumes the innocence of the accused individual. Finally, Brogden highlights how, historically, the police have successfully applied pressure to the judiciary through a variety of means.

The importance of the symbolic interactionist tradition to early work in the area of police culture, asserts Westmarland (2008), is also worthy of note and, in part, this can be attributed to the influence of Becker's (1963) seminal work *Outsiders*.

This sociological orientation, when focused upon the arena of crime and criminal justice, views crime and disorder as being socially constructed, with 'crimes' being the outcome of interactions between members of the public and agents of social control (Noaks and Wincup, 2004). To commentators such as Tierney (2006, p. 131) the impact of these ideas was to break criminology away from its traditional 'absolutist' moorings and to reinvent crime within a 'relativist' context. This 'relativism' introduced a number of complexities to our understanding of crime and institutional reactions to it. For example, Sumner (1994) surmises that the previously accepted relationship between 'norms' and 'deviance' had been cast into doubt, with a growing willingness to accept that the latter was more likely, in practice, to be defined not so much by societal norms but by the occupational norms of those tasked with the police role. Sumner illustrates this point in terms of police practices as follows:

> crime is more of a verb than a noun. In some British police forces, that is actually the nature of the usage. Officers decide whether to 'crime' a case or 'cuff' it (cuff, as in the old bobby's cuff round the ear, rather than formal sanctions). Working police officers recognize that to make something into a crime requires work.
>
> (1994, p. 218)

The shift away from traditional approaches of framing crime and crime control and towards those that stress the socially constructed nature of order was articulated, in the UK, through the National Deviancy Conference, which provided a focal point for radical criminologists. The importance of this 'relativist' paradigm was not lost on those scholars seeking to explore the reality of what Manning and Van Maanen (1978b, p. 215) refer to as 'interaction episodes' between police and policed, given that it lent itself perfectly to the use of ethnographic approaches to generating and understanding data. Interestingly, and despite Noaks and Wincup's (2004) suggestion that British radical criminologists had failed to convert their championing of the ethnographic method into a sustained body of ethnographic work, the methodology has proved integral to research into police culture across the world. Whilst existing police ethnographies continue to stimulate debate and sustain interest in the cultural world of policing, it has to be noted that the tradition of the classic police ethnography largely belongs to a long gone era (Westmarland, 2008).

As radical sociologists began a concerted critique of the nature, and distribution, of power within society their gaze unsurprisingly fell, during the 1960s, upon a British police institution whose status and authority, as Holdaway (1983) notes, were perceived as beginning to weaken. The same decade saw the inappropriate behaviour of some quarters of the Metropolitan Police Force come to light through the infamous Challenor case, where Detective Sergeant Harry Challenor was brought to trial on corruption charges in 1964. According to an obituary in the *Telegraph* newspaper (15 September 2008), Challenor's behaviour had become increasingly 'violent and unorthodox', with one arrested Barbadian purportedly being punched repeatedly by Challenor as he sang 'Bongo, bongo, bongo, I don't want to leave the Congo'. The late 1960s also saw conflict between public and police flaring up during demonstrations such as the Grosvenor Square 'riot' of March 1968, which resulted in 90 police officers being injured and over 300 members of the public being arrested, signalling a very evident watershed in British police–public relations. This is not to suggest that the 1960s saw any demonstrable worsening of the behaviour of either individual officers or police forces. For example, Emsley's (2005) analysis of the 1929 conviction of Sergeant George Goddard explains police corruption not in terms of factors endemic to any particular historical era but as a result of the criminalizing characteristics associated with particular London areas. Ultimately, the 1960s provided a protracted turning point, if not in police behaviour, then in the scrutiny of police behaviour by academic and media commentators. In terms of the latter, Chibnall (1979) provides an enlightening overview of the relationship between the Metropolitan Police and the print media during the 1960s which depicts the *Dixon of Dock Green* iconography of the police as rapidly appearing out of touch with the irreverent mood of the time. In an apparently simultaneous (and ironic) twist, Chibnall (1979, p. 137) describes the way in which, in the aftermath of publicized scandals, policing per se became a fair target for 'critical scrutiny' by newspaper journalists. When such scrutiny transformed into newspaper exposés of police scandal by the *People* and the *Times*, the Metropolitan Police responded in a robust manner. In terms of the former, the article was met with a libel writ and, in terms of the latter, the journalists responsible were subjected to interrogation, trailing and threatening phone calls.

Police culture remains a subject area of interest for a number of reasons which relate to the state and its shifting position and agendas, public perceptions of police function and efficiency, the powers needed to execute the role of the police and the paradigms which academics invoke to make sense of the world around them. The politicized nature of formal social control impacts upon police numbers, roles and responsibilities. Public fear of crime and concerns over personal and community security impact upon their behaviours and their expectations of, and relation to, the state. The discretion that provides the lubrication for the police machinery provides a delicate balance for officers to engage in common sense or compassionate policing or, alternatively, to engage in behaviours that undermine the legitimacy of their work. The emergent model of symbolic interactionism therefore provided academics with the theoretical tools required to explore police decision-making and its role as the negotiable buffer between the letter of the law and the need to resolve human conflict.

In a reflective account about his own motivations to undertake a piece of research on police occupational culture, John Van Maanen (1978c) provides a description that might strike a chord with many who have conducted their own research in this field by presenting an overview of the motivations for academics to carry out such work. He noted that, despite the array of ethnographic work in the field of policing, none of these pieces of work managed to fully debunk the mystique of police work. He comments:

It is as if the field worker, as he is presented in the published works, simply vanished for a period of time into an obscure and often-unnamed police world; became involved in the activities that took place there; attained something akin to a state of grace with the observed; and, then, presto, emerged with the data in hand. Clearly, important contacts were initiated, roles were carved out, and certain kinds of events were (and were not) observed while the researcher was out of view, but we know not how such things were accomplished.

(1978c, p. 310)

One suspects that the rich tradition of research into police culture continues to engage and inspire researchers to fill in the gaps that they perceive in the descriptions of others' fieldwork experiences. Van Maanen continues by suggesting that the language of academia is used as a 'doctrinal or ideological canopy' (1978c, p. 311) that conceals the true motives explaining why police research is undertaken and, to him, the ideological canopies erected by researchers fail to contextualize the position (or, it might be implied, the particular importance) of police research within the social sciences. Furthermore, he suggests that much police research fails either to appreciate or to account for the individual biography of the researcher and its impact on the ethnographic experience. In short, Van Maanen exhorts us to answer the potentially troubling question of why some individuals choose to research the police and suggests that generally most are perceived as being motivated by either an ingrained affinity with or distrust of the subject matter of their research. By doing so, he reminds us that police research, like policing itself, is subject to politicized agendas.

What is police culture?

In the introduction to O'Neill, Marks and Singh's (2007) collection of work in the area of police occupational culture, two of the editors wisely choose to refrain from attempting a definition of police occupational culture beyond that of:

> police occupational culture can best be considered as 'the way things are done around here' for the officers, not always 'by the book', but not always without it either. Police, both public and private sector, have socially constructed ways of viewing the world, their place in it, and the appropriate action to take in their jobs.
>
> (O'Neill and Singh, 2007, p. 2)

There is, of course, a very good reason to exercise caution when attempting to define police occupational culture. For a start, police culture goes by a number of aliases including, according to Westmarland (2008), canteen culture, patrol culture, street culture and police subculture. Furthermore, recent developments in the area have made it increasingly common practice to refer to 'police cultures' as opposed to 'police culture', and it has become difficult in recent years to provide a straightforward definition of police occupational culture that suitably encapsulates all the key concepts and themes that have been identified by authors in the field. This is, perhaps, for one key reason. Quite simply, like many concepts within the social sciences, the concept of police culture has developed over time and mutated to cover new ways of thinking about police culture and, crucially, the changing police world. Waddington, who has robustly critiqued the ways in which we conceptualize police culture, most notably in an article entitled 'Police (canteen) sub-culture: an appreciation' (1999a), has provided the following workable general definition:

> Police culture (or subculture) refers to the mix of informal prejudices, values, attitudes and working practices commonly found among the lower ranks of the police that influences the exercise of discretion. It also refers to the police's solidarity, which may tolerate corruption and resist reform.
>
> (Waddington, 2008, p. 203)

Such a succinct definition is helpful as a means of introducing one to the general themes of police culture, but cannot describe the evolution of police cultural studies over the previous half-century nor alert the reader to the contested nature of many of its core terms of reference. In terms of explaining the gradual progression of work in this area, it is helpful to draw on Westmarland (2008), who has identified three main periods in its development, which might be classed as the early/classic, middle and late. Before identifying and exploring in more depth the themes and concepts of occupational culture, it might be appropriate to address, briefly, some examples of the ways in which police cultural research has developed throughout each of these stages.

Early/classic period work

Part of the confusion surrounding the definition of police culture comes from the fact that much of the classic early work in the field, which laid the foundations and provided the reference points for future work, did not use the term 'police culture'. Probably the first piece of published academic work to explicitly engage with one of the more popular issues to later become associated with police culture was Westley (1953), in a short paper entitled 'Violence and the police', which presented research that would later form the basis of his 1970 book *Violence and the Police: A Sociological Study of Law, Custom, and Morality*. Westley, in the following passage, outlines the key thrust of his research:

> The social definition of the occupation invests its members with a common prestige position. Thus, a man's occupation is a major determining factor of his conduct and social identity. This being so, it involves more than man's work, and one must go beyond the technical in the explanation of work behaviour. One must discover the occupationally derived definitions of self and conduct which arise in the involvements of technical demands, social relationships between colleagues and with the public, status and self-conception.

To understand these definitions, one must track them back to the occupational problems in which they have their genesis.

(1953, p. 34)

To Westley, therefore, an individual's occupational relationships and roles had a substantial impact on the person's sense of self. The hostility with which officers were treated by members of the public, in turn, led officers to adopt essentially negative responses such as overt secrecy, the belief that public respect can be gained through intimidation and the belief that almost any means of securing an arrest is legitimate. Greene (2010), in a profile of Westley's life and work, suggests that the most vital impact of Westley's research into policing was to transform the study of police work from mere descriptive studies of the police role to sociological analyses of the police identity.

The work of Michael Banton provides a fitting contextual comparison to the work of Westley in that, primarily, it presents a comparison between the administration of policing and the work of officers within Scottish and North American contexts. Banton's work interestingly not only charted the differences in policing between these jurisdictions (for example, in terms of the ideological distance between the police and the public, the formality of police officers' manner in encounters with the public and the formal differentiation between rank) but also, unusually for a sociological text on the work of the police officer, saw the police as an effectively functioning institution.

Perhaps the greatest contribution of Banton's work to the theoretical development of the area of police culture was to highlight some areas of convergence in occupational experience and outlook between officers in these different environments, most significantly in respect of their use of discretion. To Banton (1964) police on either side of the Atlantic adopted the role of 'peace officer' and, in a legal sense, pursued a general policy of 'under-enforcement'. This observation converged neatly with the work of Wayne LaFave, a legal scholar whose work found favour with a number of early police cultural theorists like Jerome Skolnick in the United States and Maureen Cain in the United Kingdom. LaFave (1962a, 1962b), in two separate papers for the *Wisconsin Law Review*, pioneered scholarly investigation into the appropriateness of discretionary law enforcement by police officers and concluded by advocating that it was critically important for the police to continue to use discretion in the enforcement and non-enforcement of the law, but that the latter should be subjected to the same level of legal control as the former. The discretionary nature of law enforcement, according to Banton, was further rooted in factors pertaining to the local administration of the police resource, the police relationship with the public and the moral context of police work. The balance between law and morality in the interactions between police and public was considered incredibly delicate given that officers in both the United States and Scotland spoke to Banton of their reluctance to initiate the ultimate sanction of depriving members of the public of their liberty. Banton went on to show how it was police policy in one American city which he visited, when using speed limiting equipment in a 35 mph zone, to cite only motorists driving in excess of 44 mph. Conversely, Banton learnt that, in one Scottish force, any police officer unfortunate enough to be witnessed by a superior officer failing to help an elderly female requiring assistance crossing roads would automatically be reprimanded. Banton's work is of interest, therefore, not just as a comparative piece of police research, nor just for its focus on the use of discretion, but in its ability to highlight the moral, as opposed to legal, basis of much police work. Overall, despite Banton concluding the book with a note of caution regarding what he saw as future changes to both wider society and the role of policing within it (one might interpret his conclusion as anticipating the advent of late modernity, the growing specialization of the police and the increased reliance on community-generated intelligence), his work remained optimistic and upbeat about the legitimacy of the police and their work. This, in itself, represents something of a unique approach within the canon of police cultural literature, and paints a very different view of both police practice and the police occupational culture from Westley's work. To Westley, the discretion of the police led to brutal behaviour as a means of satisfying legal and occupational needs, the former through what he calls the 'pursuit of duty' (1953, p. 41) and the latter as a means of defending the values of the police identity against an untrusting and unsympathetic public. Banton, however, perceived the discretion of the police world as allowing officers the opportunity to engage in moral as opposed to legal policing, a factor that he attributed to the police officer retaining his or her status as a member of the community.

Jerome Skolnick's *Justice without Trial*, originally published in 1966, was a broadly comparative piece of research into the policing of two American cities. His work has proven to be of sustained interest to police cultural theorists, not least for his depiction of the police officer's 'working personality' (1994, p. 41), which can be conceived as an occupationally derived framework through which police understand and engage with the environs and their inhabitants. Integral to Skolnick's work was the idea that police officers' perceptions of their occupational world were the product of three unique and converging factors that represented key aspects of their role – danger, authority and efficiency. Skolnick did recommend, however, that these explanatory factors of the police 'working personality' should not be considered as tantamount to a universal police culture. Instead, he contended that individual and group differences will emerge between police officers, units and forces but that overall these three factors will coalesce to form 'distinctive cognitive and behavioral responses in police' (Skolnick, 1994, p. 41). Like most pieces of early research into what would later become known as police occupational culture, Skolnick's work focused on the specific police role of beat policing as the prime source of cultural knowledge regarding police work given that it represented the primary role of the police and provided, whatever their later specialisms, a grounded set of common experiences for all officers.

Skolnick underlined the core factors of danger, authority and efficiency to explain the ways in which police officers become socialized into the cultural world of policing. Danger and authority were considered as the two main sources of momentum behind the cultural identity of the police, and these occurred against a backdrop of institutional pressure for efficiency. Danger (potential or realized) was crucial to the working world of the police officer, as the resultant suspicion provided a 'perceptual shorthand' to categorize certain members of the public as 'symbolic assailants' (1994, p. 44). 'Symbolic assailants' are, quite simply, members of the public whose appearance or language prompts police officers to expect violence, and these 'aggressors' are perceived, not in terms of their actual propensity for violence or past history, but solely in superficial terms of appearance.

Under Skolnick's model, danger combines with authority to create a pronounced segregation of the police from the public and potentially encourages illegitimate police behaviour. Authority, in particular, serves to separate the police from the policed, causing social isolation that can lead to the resultant cultural response of police solidarity. Simultaneously, the danger inherent to police work serves as a unifying force within the police whilst exacerbating the cultural gulf between them and the public. Skolnick draws a comparative point regarding police working personalities in the United States and the United Kingdom by suggesting that, assuming that police in the latter face a lesser degree of danger in their working lives, there will be less propensity for their authority to be undermined.

Following the comparative approach used by Banton (1964) in *The Policeman in the Community*, Maureen Cain in 1973 published *Society and the Policeman's Role*, which drew on her earlier research comparing the work of police officers in rural and urban areas. Cain's stated aim was to explore the organization and behaviour of the police and to explain the latter in relation to the definition of the police role and the pressures associated with it. In an interesting departure from other early works in this area, Cain's theoretical framework owed more to the traditions of role theory than the more fashionable interactionist theories of the time and employed a variety of research methods including participant observation, interviews with police officers and questionnaires conducted with officers' wives. One significant feature to Cain's work was her introduction of the concept of 'easing' behaviour. This term refers to parts of police life that facilitate officers' lives such as, in rural areas, the accepting of gifts of refreshments and foodstuffs from members of the public. In the urban context, Cain described one eight-hour patrol where only one formal piece of police business needed to be undertaken, with the rest of the time spent indulging in 'easing behaviours', whether trips to police stations or cafés for cups of tea or stopping at pubs to enjoy a drink with plain-clothes colleagues. These behaviours were similar to perks but, apart from providing some benefit to officers, they represented a way for them to become accepted by the community as well as offering opportunities to share or pass on information. The significance of these 'easing behaviours' lies in what they tell us about the ways in which acceptable work practices are transmitted through subcultural norms (Brogden, Jefferson and Walklate, 1988).

Also of interest in Cain's work are the different styles and features of police work that could be distinguished between rural and urban settings. In the rural settings there was an altogether closer relationship between the police and the public not least because of the reliance on the public, rather than informers, for information. Despite this, however, rural officers remained somewhat insulated from the public (with whom officers would be friendly but not friends as such) and, during working hours, from their colleagues. City officers, on the whole, dealt with a more fragmented public and encountered fewer opportunities to develop shared values within their communities because they were less dependent on them. Similarly, their work was more likely to be considered 'both unpleasant and monotonous' (1973, p. 229), because urban officers had a less varied role than their rural counterparts and were less likely to become involved in criminal investigations. Despite this more limited role, their work environment did offer some opportunities for 'easing', including the apparently arbitrary arrest of vulnerable members of the community for public order offences, a practice which provided a means of enhancing officers' status as thief-takers. Another means of relieving the mundanity of much day-to-day work was to 'work up' (p. 229) a beat by developing relationships with people who lived there. This strategy, however, would be more successful as a means of accruing status in rural locations where peace-keeping rather than thief-taking was more central to the police role. Finally, officers in urban settings could resort to 'official' means of job easing by using centrally provided resources for leisure pursuits. Probably the most important way, however, in which the styles of rural and urban officers differed from each other was in the '*much narrower definition of "work"*' (1973, p. 230, italics in original) of the latter.

The above sketches present nowhere near an exhaustive view of sociological research undertaken during the 1950s and 1960s into police work. However, what I have sought to do is to give a brief overview of some of the key works conducted at this time by police scholars. Cain (1973) provides a welcome and concise summary of early work in this area and sees its focus of attention as threefold. First, it tends to highlight the rights of citizens in respect of how the police operate and how they utilize discretion. Second, it concerns the reasons why police officers tend to act in certain predictable ways. Third, and finally, the work focuses on the effects of police actions.

Despite the term 'police culture' having not, at this stage, become a part of the academic language of police studies, undoubtedly the themes being addressed by these writers were concurrent with what would now be taken as key themes within police occupational culture. Westley's primary aim was not just to describe police use of violence but to explore the ways in which such behaviour was legitimated by the role of the police and their relationship with the public. Banton took probably the most positive view of policing and provided an interesting, semi-comparative approach which highlights the importance of discretion, and the balance between legal and moral considerations, to police work. Skolnick probably comes closer than the other writers whose work has been briefly explored in this section to describing police culture when he proposed the idea of the police officer's 'working personality', which suggests that police officers share a common outlook and that these inclinations are the result of the unique combination of three factors of the police world – danger, authority and efficiency. Cain (1973), by contrasting the work roles and relations of officers working in urban and rural locations, highlighted the impact of different environments on the methods and styles of policing used there. Similarly, she underlined the importance of those facets of the police world that bring small but welcome improvements to the officer's working day ('easing' behaviours) and their importance in facilitating our understanding of those norms that underlie police work. Fundamental to all of these four accounts, however, is the idea of 'discretion', which will be more fully addressed later in this book.

Middle period work

If police use of discretion was the core feature of police work that was commonly explored by those writers addressing police culture in the early period, the issue of cultural variation was probably the central theme to much work in the middle period. Whilst earlier works had tended to acknowledge that variations occurred between groups of officers, the main thrust of the work had been on emphasizing core similarities in police work. To middle period writers, policing was more likely to be approached in terms that explicitly acknowledged not only the idea of culture and its use as an analytical concept, but also that cultural variation was a notable element of the social world of the police.

In a book chapter entitled 'Street cops and management cops: the two cultures of policing', Elizabeth Reuss-Ianni and Francis Ianni (1983) provide one of the clearest declarations that, rather than sharing a homogeneous occupational culture, specific and different police cultures could be identified within the police world. They began by drawing upon organizational research to suggest that the 'informal social and behavioural systems' (p. 251) of immediate circles of colleagues have a greater impact upon behaviour than the wider organization. This presents a particular problem for the administration of police agencies where resolution of employee demands is increasingly finely balanced with the organization's need for efficiency and citizen focus. Utilizing a mixed methodology consisting of participant observation and event and network analyses they found that, within their research environment of New York City, they could discern two opposing and incompatible police occupational cultures. The first, characterized as a 'street cop culture' (p. 253), was based on ideologically driven ideas of a police world where officers of all ranks could be trusted, the public supported the police and local politicians left officers to their own devices. In many respects, this highly idealized cultural view of police work represents an amalgamation of a nostalgia-driven view of 'good old days' policing (1983, p. 253) with strongly and commonly held beliefs regarding the ways in which it should be performed and coordinated. Street officers that Reuss-Ianni and Ianni interviewed and observed subscribed to the prevalent view that 'social and political forces have weakened the character, performance, and effectiveness of police work and that as a result the policing function is under strong attack' (1983, p. 254). These officers highlighted the lack of respect from the public, combined with a growing restriction and control from police managers and local politicians, which made the police job more complex, more perilous and less efficient. The 'management cop culture' was seen as generating bureaucratic responses that were then superimposed upon the 'street police culture', increasingly causing conflict, stress and inappropriate police behaviour, and which subsequently fortified the importance of the precinct culture to the officers. Reuss-Ianni and Ianni then explored the reasons for this apparent bifurcation of police cultures within the New York City police. Previously, the 'street cop culture' had provided a coherent and consistent set of values that drew together and unified all levels of the department. Reuss-Ianni and Ianni described the benefits and drawbacks of this cultural homogeneity, where 'The mutual dependence provided a level of morale and esprit de corps; this same mutuality and the secrecy it produced contributed to the institutionalization of widespread organized graft and corruption in the department' (1983, p. 256). They also drew attention to the factors (internal and external to the police) that they saw as causing the apparent fragmentation of the police culture. These included the Knapp Commission (based to some extent on the revelations regarding corruption within the force made by Frank Serpico and others), a growing interest in the rights of marginalized and disenfranchised groups, a decline in the amount of leisure time socializing undertaken by officers (enforced partly by wage increases leading to police officers living outside the city), calls for greater minority representation within the force and a growth in the numbers of officers who had completed programmes of higher education.

Ultimately, Reuss-Ianni and Ianni viewed both cultures as sharing the same broad goals of providing safety and security to the city's inhabitants but, significantly, noted a variation in their definition of these concepts and the strategies by which these may be realized. The 'street cop culture', for example, highlighted the notion of the 'professional' cop using his or her discretion as the basis for making decisions at the local level. On the other hand, the 'management cop culture' took a broader geographical remit and concentrated on its key role of prioritization of limited resources within a complex array of external financial, political and social constraints. The authors concluded by stating that the bifurcation of cultures detailed above is not unusual in any organization that has experienced pressure to change the way in which it coordinates and executes its work. As a response to these new demands, two cultures emerged. One remained loyal to the traditional way of doing the job and the other focused less upon the practical and symbolic world of the front-line practitioner but was more sensitive to local political contexts and media interest. The symbolic icon and language of the 'officer' found itself increasingly lost amongst new management discourses that prioritized 'organization', and these 'incongruent values systems' (p. 272) led subsequently to disaffection and stress. Interestingly, Reuss-Ianni and Ianni saw the decline of a unifying singular police culture as a major cause of stress within policing, suggesting, as other organizational scholars have previously, that occupational cultures do have notable positive impacts.

Another key publication associated with this middle period is Malcolm Young's (1991) *An Inside Job*, written by a police officer turned academic who provides an engaging account of police work in the UK between the 1950s and 1970s. In many respects, the true fascination of this book is the author's reflection on his own transformation of occupational identity as he moved between law enforcement and academic cultures. Simultaneously, however, Young used an anthropological approach to make sense of the 'nuances and specificities of police reality' (1991, p. 63) as he progressed within the police institution. As a new police officer within one of the three divisions of the Newcastle upon Tyne city police, he described the process of becoming aware of the cultural world of the city police officer and the distinctions between 'thief-takers' and 'uniform carriers', 'polis' and 'civvies'. The cultural divisions that separated those officers in the North Shields and South Shields Divisions reinforced the idea of a physical and social environment where boundaries were clearly marked. Minor differences in uniform, accommodation policy and height regulations between neighbouring forces reflected 'alien' and despised styles of policing. As Young progressed to being an aide to the Criminal Investigation Department (CID) and subsequently a detective constable, he charts how he had effectively crossed a boundary from his previous cultural position. To his former uniformed colleagues, his new position was disparaged for its freedom of movement, its apparent lack of control and the failure of most detectives to detect crime. Interestingly, Young's move to CID marks his introduction to what he terms 'the primacy of the statistical world' (p. 82) and a departure from the world of the uniformed officer where an arrest was seen as an end in itself. To Young:

> The detective has therefore moved from the centrally important activity of seizing the villains into a manipulated world where the paper exercise of statistical detections is used to assuage politicians, the media, and a public obsessed with the moral panic of increasing crime rates.
>
> (1991, p. 83)

Whilst, to the uniformed officers of Young's recollection at least, officers working for CID were seen as falling prey, sartorially, to individuality, Young shows how even detectives were still constrained, in some respects, by social conventions regarding appearance:

> To walk into a pub function room as I have often done during the ten years I was collecting fieldnotes and see two or three hundred detectives in their 'uniform' of modern suit and tie, neat haircut, and the fashionable moustache of the times, is to be visibly reminded that there is a narrow symbolic range of bodily correctness within which all policemen can properly operate.
>
> (1991, p. 83)

Young's next move within the institution was one that took him yet further from what he had been socialized into seeing as 'proper' police work and into more remote areas of police operations. As one of only two full-time members of a squad tasked with dealing with a new focus for the police, namely drug users, Young found himself in a position where the austere and prescriptive social conventions of the police world failed to hold either authority or relevance. In his 'marginal universe' (p. 89), he enforced new offences, dressed differently, and lost respect for previously revered systems of the police hierarchy.

Dick Hobbs' *Doing the Business* provides a fascinating ethnographic account of the cultural distinctiveness of the East End of London and its impact on crime and law enforcement. In it he forwards the argument that the form of entrepreneurialism endemic to this specific area represented 'a specific economic and cultural order' (1988, p. 197). To Hobbs, the East End of London and the CID of the Metropolitan Police represented distinct and different environmental and cultural phenomena yet shared key characteristics. Indeed, Hobbs's work draws attention to the role of CID officers and makes a strong case to distinguish them culturally from their uniformed colleagues. In an engaging overview of the history of the CID he details the impact of Sir Robert Mark (former commissioner of the Metropolitan Police), whose unveiled animosity towards CID was a manifestation of his personal characteristics that embraced both conservatism and militarism. Hobbs concluded that the detective role is essentially 'entrepreneurial' rather than 'militarist' and that this distinction placed the two forms of police work in ideological and symbolic conflict.

The entrepreneurial basis of the local environs, coupled with the similarly enterprising nature of detective work, ensured that the local geographic and social culture provided shared symbolic meanings for both officers and villains. The primacy of market forces in the area also meant that relationships between police and local criminals were dictated, not by the formality of police bureaucracy, but through informal interactions based on the trading of different forms of commodity. Hobbs describes one such interaction:

> Consulting a CID officer was the legal equivalent of a 'cash only' deal – no VAT, no due process. However, unless the East-Ender had something to trade no deal was forthcoming. When one man's younger brother was arrested in connection with a robbery he consulted a detective, a drinking-partner of several years' acquaintance: 'What have they got? Nothing solid have they? He never did it. He's not at the heavy; shooters not his thing. What have they got?' When this potential 'client' was asked to 'put up' names, he declined and the transaction was aborted.
>
> (1988, p. 198)

To Hobbs, the relationship between the police and their public was based on their mutual understanding of the rules that typified police CID relations with local criminals. Turn-taking was one rhetorical device used by CID officers to manage, articulate and sustain the CID mythology in ways which belied the departments' relationship to the wider police organization. In such a way, investigations were portrayed in terms that emphasize their similarity to a game where both police and criminal took turns and were either successful or unsuccessful owing to the intervention, or non-intervention, of luck. In this way, the CID officer was recast as 'an autonomous entrepreneur of law and order' (p. 205) rather than a state-sanctioned law enforcement officer, an important distinction for those whose livelihoods relied on their ability to 'fit in' with the local community.

More serious types of crime, such as murder, required a shift from working-class local rhetoric back to the formal and unambiguous police codes of language where officers were quick to straightforwardly identify both themselves and their aims. Murder was conceived by detectives as a 'real' crime and therefore one that could, unlike most incidents, be dealt with in a manner detached from the symbolic and cultural dynamics of the East End. Such a division of presentational codes should not be taken as evidence that formal and informal codes of policing never actually converged, and Hobbs described how CID officers used both verbal and non-verbal working-class styles of communication to become more effective officers. The rhetoric of the CID therefore served as a means of transmitting knowledge regarding the rules of the game that both sides played, thus highlighting the 'symbiotic' relationship between the public and the police force in the area. The entrepreneurial basis for the East End culture was seen as pervading the occupational personalities of both the police officers and the 'villains', and both were seen as players in a game based upon 'the trading of moral identities' (Hobbs, 1989, p. 179), which tended to confuse the distinction between 'cop' and 'criminal'.

These three pieces of research from middle period studies of police occupational culture provide an altogether different take on police culture from that which emerged through early work in the area in that they describe the emergence of significantly different and separate cultures within specific police organizations. For the first time, research in this area was going beyond solely acknowledging variations in police values and behaviours as writers like Skolnick (1994) and Westley (1953) did. Where early writers did acknowledge such variations they were portrayed as aberrations of the dominant cultural themes that the literature described. The work of Reuss-Ianni and Ianni and Young describes the coexistence of cultures that appear to conflict with each other (in the case of Reuss-Ianni and Ianni), cultures that appear, in some cases, to be variations on a similar theme (Young's distinction between uniformed and CID cultures) and, in the case of Young's experiences working for a drug squad, an example of police officers operating under no discernible police culture. To Young, he and his colleagues had become 'aberrant policemen' (1991, p. 90) exposed to new ways of viewing the world and, as a result, they began to drift away from the police institution's sphere of influence. Hobbs also succeeded in drawing out the cultural differences between CID and uniform work by highlighting the different occupational priorities, such as high-quality paperwork (which casts the reality of detective work in a more occupationally appropriate light) and performance in court (which Hobbs lightly refers to as 'repertory justice').

Of considerable interest here, however, is the way in which the middle period of police culture writing brought about not only an awareness of different cultures existing simultaneously within particular occupations but also, in Hobbs's case, an awareness of the relationship between geography and occupational culture. Most significantly, the main difference between uniform and CID officers is that the latter are 'doing the business' (1988, p. 196) in an environment founded on entrepreneurialism and within a framework of relationships that echo those of the trading heritage of the East End whilst the former are more tightly constrained by the culture of the police institution. The occupational culture of the police that

Hobbs described competed with the indigenous cultural framework of the East End to provide a detective culture that succeeded in drawing substantially on the latter's unique geographical milieu. Hobbs describes the East End as a unique environment that can be viewed as a 'cultural community' in the fullest sense of the phrase, owing in part to its heritage of Huguenot, Irish and Jewish immigration. The Irish and Jewish communities left the most lasting impression on the area, with the former contributing to the pre-industrial culture of the area, and the latter providing its entrepreneurial character. Working-class culture, according to Hobbs, represents a reaction to particular social and economic conditions and will vary between regions. Malcolm Young pursues a similar vein when he explores differences in policing styles between the city centre of Newcastle upon Tyne and the outlying divisions, but does so without really exploring the fundamental uniqueness of his chosen geographical area. To Young, the differences between areas were as much a reflection of police perceptions of differences between policing styles as a commentary upon social and cultural differences pertinent to the lives of all denizens.

Evident in the research of this era was an acknowledgement of the growing importance of managerialism to the administration of the police function and its inevitable impact upon the cultural world of the police. Although this phenomenon is more explicitly addressed in Reuss-Ianni and Ianni's work, it is also highlighted within Young's depiction of the pressures that were brought to bear on new CID officers. He outlines the 'tremendous semantic significance' (1991, p. 82) to officers of a 'quality' arrest, within a system that cares only for 'numbers' of detections. Likewise, Hobbs (1988) shows how one of the ways in which the entrepreneurial nature of CID is evidenced is by the way that they respond to the pressure for results that they face. The entrepreneurial CID officer does not just solve a crime; he or she turns small offences into big offences (by generating evidence for more serious charges) or turns a single offence into a number of charges.

Late period work

In this section, an overview of a limited number of later examples of police culture literature will be presented. These are not intended to present a definitive overview of the contemporary literature of this area, but merely to demonstrate the increasingly diverse and complex ideas that have become evident within recent work. For example, later work has tended to critique the relevance of earlier writings especially in respect of the substantial changes that both police institutions and 'policing' as a concept have undergone in recent years.

In *Changing Police Culture: Policing in a Multicultural Society*, Chan (1997) proposed a new approach with which to analyse police culture, prompted by her belief that the majority of research undertaken in the area was limited owing to the use of an outdated conceptual framework. Her research, based on questionnaires, semi-structured interviews and a content analysis of documents, led her to forward four general criticisms of literature in the area. Her first criticism is that most research presents cop culture as too deterministic and inflexible a concept, a theme initially developed by middle period writers such as Reuss-Ianni and Ianni (1983). This is shown by the failure of most accounts to explain internal differentiation between groups of officers who hold different police functions and led Chan (1997) to suggest that cop culture was a more 'fluid' concept than previously acknowledged. Furthermore, any account of police culture should, she suggested, be flexible enough to describe differences within and between police forces.

Chan's second criticism refers to the process whereby police officers become socialized into the occupational culture. To Chan, existing accounts have failed to address the issue in sufficient depth and, accordingly, have painted the individual officer as a passive bystander in what she terms the 'acculturation process' (1997, p. 66). Whilst acknowledging the undoubted potency of occupational cultures, Chan proposed that police cultures should not be seen as inevitably overriding the will of the individual. By way of contrast, she suggested that any theory of police culture should acknowledge the active role played by individual officers in comprehending their institution and the cultural landscape within which that institution existed. Accordingly, Chan placed great emphasis on the importance of understanding the interaction between the occupational culture and individuals' existing attitudes.

Chan's third criticism of existing literature is that police occupational cultures are portrayed as operating in a vacuum that exists independently of external (non-police) contexts. Thus, the fact that political change, the emergence of new social challenges and the impact of new legislation can have a profound effect on the culture of the police needs to be recognized by theories that purport to explain police culture. Under such a model, the culture within a particular station can be particularly affected by an external inquiry, a change in organization or a new piece of legislation. Chan's fourth and final criticism encapsulates her previous points and is that, to a large extent, the dialectic between social environment and policing has been ignored, making it impossible for existing theoretical frameworks to account for changes to, or variations within, cop culture. Only when such a relationship is established will we be able to examine the phenomenon with any sense of objectivity.

Chan, in the light of these issues, proposes a re-conceptualization of police culture within three converging themes. The first is that of recognizing the active cultural role played by individual members of the police force. Secondly, she claims that there is a need to be aware of the fact that multiple cultures may exist within a single organization. Thirdly, she states that there is a need to situate culture within the ever-changing social and cultural contexts of police work. As a means of overcoming these weaknesses, she developed a framework which drew upon cognitive models and Bourdieu's concepts of 'field' and 'habitus'. Traditional models of police culture assume, suggests Chan (1997, p. 73), that a linear relationship exists between 'field' ('the structural conditions of police work'), 'habitus' ('cultural knowledge') and 'police practice'. Such a formulation assumes that a deterministic and causal process exists whereby police work is solely responsible for the generation of cultural knowledge which, in turn, informs police practice. Chan (1997) criticizes this simplistic framework on two main grounds. First, it fails to articulate the extent to which individuals can actively contribute to cultural knowledge and, second, it suggests that the application of changes to the structural conditions of police work would de facto lead to changes in cultural knowledge and, therefore, police behaviour. In its place Chan proposes a model that acknowledges the potential for individual police actors to become the connecting factor between 'field', 'habitus' and police practice. Under this model, there would be no causal assumption that culture was solely informed by the structural conditions of police work and that all police practice was dictated by cultural knowledge. To Chan, therefore, a structural change need not necessarily lead to changes in culture and practice, being dependent instead on the extent to which officers feel equipped to modify their practice to accommodate the change.

Waddington (1999a), in 'Police (canteen) sub-culture: an appreciation', provided us with an equally thought-provoking critique of the literature of police culture in which he forwarded an 'appreciative' as opposed to 'condemnatory' reading of police culture, and this represented a means of restoring balance in an area where, traditionally, police culture had been viewed as being an essentially negative phenomenon. Waddington wisely noted the reluctance of criminologists to 'appreciate' police culture despite the discipline's history of uncritical appraisals of 'criminal' or 'deviant' groups. Furthermore, the normative approach that we have traditionally adopted to understand police culture, he maintained, has had limited success in explaining the cultural aspects of police work. His work provides a thought-provoking critique of approaches to understanding police culture and raises several key themes. The first to be presented in this brief overview is his suggestion that police officers belong to, and contribute to, two police cultures. In this way, he draws our attention to a possible distinction between canteen and operational police cultures, a point of crucial importance to those studying, or researching, police work. His analysis suggests that the methodologies associated with police culture research (generally qualitative interview and ethnographic approaches) have dictated that much of the body of literature in this area reflects oral culture (that is, an analysis of police narrative) rather than physical culture (that is, an analysis of police behaviour). If Waddington's notion of a bifurcated police culture is correct, then an increasingly complex set of questions arise around the relationship between language and behaviour and, subsequently, around the relationship between operational and canteen culture. Perhaps one of the more crucial challenges in this respect concerns the extent to which the informal narrative of the canteen informs the operational culture of the street or merely reflects it.

In short, therefore, Waddington's point is an important one, as it calls into question the relationship between what police officers do on the street and how they later recount such behaviour. This potential differentiation between the 'actuality' and the culturally appropriate 'presentation' of a given event is one that has received insufficient attention to date. However, Waddington's work is of significance in that it invites us to speculate upon not only the existence of seemingly coexistent yet distinct cultures (which pertain to acted and narrated behaviour) but also the essentially palliative rather than instructive qualities of police 'canteen' culture. Waddington (1999a, p. 295) likens the police canteen to the 'repair shop' where the police go to make sense of their working lives in front of an understanding audience. To understand this fully one needs to realize that despite its image the police is a fragile institution. Police officers, like others in marginal (or marginalized) occupations, use the oral tradition of the canteen as a means of imbuing status into their work and skills, whilst simultaneously celebrating their core distinguishing factor – that of their legitimate claim to violence. To Waddington, the palliative as opposed to prescriptive nature of this canteen culture can be evidenced by the nuanced and intricate practices that police engage in that are rarely represented within the banter of the canteen. Assessing the true nature of the relationship between these two cultures (and the extent to which one informs the other) is of central importance therefore to our understanding of the complex cultural dynamics of police work.

Another substantial issue that Waddington develops during the course of the article concerns what he terms the 'interpretative over-reach' (1999a, p. 291) of more linear accounts of police culture. Waddington suggested that, in part, this problem is a consequence of the sociological use of the term 'culture' as a means of distilling meaningful knowledge from a diverse array of values and behaviours. The study of 'police culture' is predicated upon a range of generalizations about the cultural origins of police behaviour. These include, at a fundamental level, an assumption that a substantial cultural 'distance' exists between the police and the public and that this parallels a pronounced division between 'wider' culture and the occupational culture of the police. Waddington unpicks this issue further by claiming that our normative approach to understanding police culture relies on a degree of comparison with other cultural benchmarks. In the example of racism, an appropriate or inappropriate level of racism within a culture would be evidenced through comparison with either an ideal, if not realistic, level of zero racism or an occupational culture more familiar to the researcher. In the case of the latter, suggests Waddington, it is likely that the literature of police culture, as generated by academics, is as likely to help us understand the occupational culture of academia as it is that of the police. In short, in the absence of an appropriate benchmark beside which to assess the intensity of certain cultural dynamics, we assume that whatever it is that we are observing is a manifestation of the occupational culture that we are studying, rather than a product of wider societal forces. Waddington illustrates this point more fully with reference to explanations of police brutality as a cultural norm amongst South African police officers, which, research suggests, can be traced back not to the culture of the police but to the wider culture of apartheid South Africa.

The work of both Chan and Waddington provides extremely useful angles from which to revisit our understanding of police culture. Both are critical of approaches that portray police culture (or cultures) in a linear and deterministic manner, but appear to disagree over the extent to which research should have a normative agenda. To Waddington, Chan's work is condemnatory rather than explanatory. Furthermore, Chan's description of police culture highlights its fluid nature and its chameleon-like tendency to adapt to its surroundings, whereas

Waddington's work suggests that many cultural reference points are remarkably consistent between and within jurisdictions. Moreover, whilst Chan supports the existence of different discernible cultures, Waddington is opposed to what he sees as the 'intellectual fashion that seeks to erode and relativize police sub-cultures' (1999a, p. 295). Overall, the value of these two accounts lies in the way in which they redirect attention towards the relationship between police culture and wider societal culture.

Barriers to the successful definition of police culture

Cockcroft (2007) provides an overview of some of the issues that arise when defining police occupational culture. For example, whilst Waddington's (2008) definition of police culture is entirely appropriate, we find that different police scholars tend to highlight different themes within their definitions. The following descriptions of police culture have been presented by Peter Manning, Robert Reiner and Janet Chan, respectively:

- 'accepted practices, rules, and principles of conduct that are situationally applied, and generalized rationales and beliefs' (Manning, 1989, p. 360);
- 'a patterned set of understandings which help to cope with and adjust to the pressures and tensions which confront the police' (Reiner, 1992, p. 109);
- 'a layer of informal occupational norms and values operating under the apparently rigid hierarchical structure of police organisations' (Chan, 1997, p. 43).

(cited in Cockcroft, 2007, p. 87)

These three interpretations provide us with a diverse selection of themes that identify, respectively, the importance of culture in promoting accepted ways of 'doing policing', a framework of meaning that helps officers to make sense of work-based issues and, finally, a means of resolving the tension between formality and informality within formal institutional structures. All three of these help broaden our understanding of the cultural world of the police officer but are less successful in a definitional sense, owing to the fact that they are, by necessity, very broad and do not articulate the breadth and depth of the subject area.

That such definitions can be regarded as insufficiently specific to really convey our understanding of police culture is a result of a number of factors that are outlined by Cockcroft (2007). The first issue is that of the broad-based role of the police. Like many public sector institutions, policing encompasses a wide range of skills, locations, technologies and roles, and police scholars as far back as Vollmer (1936) have suggested that the police undertake a much wider range of functions than their official obligations would suggest. Similarly, Goldstein (1979) makes the distinction between that which the public believe the police do, enforce the law, and what it is that they actually do, solve problems. Furthermore, as Brogden (1991) reminds us, the role of the police varies between social environments and is contingent upon embedded patterns of industry, employment and the economy within a particular area.

A second factor that tends to inhibit the clarity of definitions of police culture relates to the sociological orthodoxy of viewing it as a fundamentally negative phenomenon. The majority of sociological work into policing has been either 'reformist' (Narayanan, 2005) or 'condemnatory' (Waddington, 1999a) and reflects social sciences' concerns with distribution of power within society. In contrast, scholarly work undertaken into occupational culture from an organizational perspective tends to highlight the more positive aspects to occupational culture, for example in relation to stress reduction (MacAlister, 2004). One somewhat surprising champion for the values of police culture, the chaplain to an Australian police force, published a brief article entitled 'Thank God for police culture' (Beal, 2001) in which he suggested that the sense of community enjoyed by police officers was something to be welcomed in a world characterized by individualism. He concludes the piece by writing:

> The quality of community life one finds within the police culture should be valued and preserved. It mirrors much of what the Christian Church has been trying to establish for 2000 years: a supportive, honest and real community of people who are there for each other through thick and thin. I say, thank God for police culture.

> (2001, no page)

Her Majesty's Inspectorate of Constabulary (HMIC), a body responsible for the oversight of policing in England, Wales and Northern Ireland, in a 1999 report, were equally sceptical of the suggestion that police culture led to inappropriate behaviours at the expense of appropriate ones. They wrote:

> The journalistic shorthand that summarises the thinking of operational police officers as being explained by 'a canteen culture' is as misleading as it is mischievous. It is acknowledged that the location reference is merely evocative of what is seen as a collective attitude. These very canteens witness the conversations of officers who still see service to all members of the public as an intrinsic part of their vocation. The number of officers who are nominated each year for community awards are part of this same culture.

> (1999b, p. 29)

Similarly, it should be noted that Paoline (2003), in his review of police culture literature, cites published work (generally from North America) that underlines a number of potential benefits to the police institution of its organizational culture. It is seen as providing a measure of emotional comfort to officers engaged in taxing roles, enabling new officers to learn the practical skills needed to undertake their role effectively, a potential facilitator of police reform and a means of preventing poor police practice. A third factor that has led to increasing difficulties in developing comprehensive definitions of police culture is associated not so much with new ways of thinking about culture but with recent years having witnessed tremendous societal change, not least in respect of the criminal justice system (Garland, 2001). Factors such as the increasingly pluralized orientation of security provision (Garland, 2001) and the normalization of crime (Matravers and Maruna, 2005) are leading, it can be argued, to a reduction in the potency of the police as an institution and a reassessment of appropriate levels of responsibility and effectiveness. As Loader and Sparks make clear, we have witnessed the emergence of a set of new philosophies regarding crime and its control that draw on 'a diverse, contradictory array of situational technologies, policing styles, preventative strategies' (2005, p. 14). Control of crime and the provision of security has become an increasingly intricate array of relationships that take place against a backdrop of changing criminological knowledge and competing political agendas. In short, policing has changed greatly since the time of the early period writers in this area, and both 'policing' and 'culture' appear, as concepts, to have escalated in complexity over recent years.

To these challenges we might add another and one that highlights the conceptual rift between those who prioritize the understanding of police culture and those who focus predominantly on its effects. In practice, the study of police culture engages with a number of separate but intertwined issues. It touches upon particular behaviours, the social forces that motivate individuals to display those patterns of behaviour and the ways in which police use cognitive and communicative frameworks to understand or express those behaviours (Cockcroft, 2007). So far, we have explored some of the fundamental themes associated with police culture and provided a brief overview of some of its inherent complexities. It should be noted, however, that our interest in police culture is concerned not just with the cultural dimensions of the police world, but with the impact of those factors on the practice of policing. In reality, the primary concern of a great deal of the literature of police culture appears to have been not so much an understanding of the culture of the police but an analysis of those aspects of police behaviour which might be considered inappropriate or illegal, and which are generally attributed to a specific police culture. Such behaviours include heightened sensitivities to gender and race, camaraderie, social solidarity, suspicion, noble cause corruption, cynicism, machismo and a sense of mission, and it is these issues that have tended to become associated with the issue of police culture (in the minds of many academics and members of the public alike). Cop culture has traditionally been conceptualized as a universal phenomenon by virtue of the fact that police officers throughout the world have a large amount of occupational discretion at their disposal to be utilized on a common set of problematical situations. Thus, it could be argued that police officers working in such diverse cultures as the UK, the USA, Asia and Africa all face similar issues regarding public order, crime detection and crime management and that this has prompted a willingness to perceive a comparatively cohesive culture within the occupation. Furthermore, if one takes Skolnick's (1994) concept of the 'working personality' as a cultural template for police organizations, the key factors of danger, authority and efficiency would be present, in some form, in the majority of public police organizations. Increasingly, therefore, police culture has been portrayed as a universal phenomenon with far-reaching consequences, which accordingly demands a set of responses with which to combat it. To all intents and purposes, therefore, criminologists, sociologists and police scholars alike have never satisfactorily explained how, why and where we should differentiate between, and I borrow heavily from Downes and Rock (2003, p. 316) here, police culture as a sociological problem and police culture as a social problem.

The complexity of police cultures

Traditional early accounts of police culture present a standardized description of police institutions, with research conducted by Westley and Skolnick during the 1950s and 1960s acknowledging cultural variation between officers but failing to engage, at a sufficiently explanatory level, with these differences. This presentation of the police institution in such homogeneous terms represented, in part, a somewhat skewed account of police work, concentrating as these researchers did on the work of lower-rank beat officers in predominantly urban areas. Whilst the following chapters of this book will deal in greater depth with the impact of changes to the police institution and its culture, attention will now be turned to some of those specific issues that have at times been ignored in those accounts of policing which highlight the uniformity of the police role and its associated cultural responses. There is no wish to pre-empt here some of the themes that will emerge later in the book, but what follows will help to introduce some of the broad conceptual points that will emphasize and reinforce just some of the reasons why police culture is such a difficult area to define effectively.

Paoline (2003), in the introduction to an article in which he advocates a synthesis of existing knowledge of police culture, suggests ironically that, despite the consensus regarding the importance of culture to the policing world, there is no real unanimity regarding an accepted definition of its nature. In part, this might be attributed to the persistence of a quite narrow set of terms of reference regarding the police role that has become increasingly irrelevant as new policing ideas take hold and as police employees are recruited from increasingly diverse backgrounds. This clear-cut rendition of the police institution, the individuals who work within it and the roles they carry out has met with some criticism, especially in recent years. To Nigel Fielding the problem is straightforward, and he criticizes what he views as simplistic interpretations of police culture for their unimaginative 'cultural universals' (1988, p. 185), which have become embedded through our failure to develop an analytic framework that acknowledges difference as well as similarity in the behaviour of police officers.

Paoline continues by considering these issues at some length and suggests that there is no conceptual structure in place that adequately helps us to explain the source of police culture, the solutions it presents for practitioners and what the consequences of such solutions are. These he considers crucial questions, and he goes on to explain why these are of such importance with reference to environment, the coping mechanisms that the culture prescribes to practitioners and the impact of these on the wider community. Paoline suggests that fundamental to our understanding are the environments within which the police operate, and he makes the case that not only do police officers require cultural prescriptions to allow them to deal with the stresses of dealing with the public, but also that the imprecise nature of the police role, coupled with inconsistent approaches to supervision and discipline, leads to insecurity and stress. Police officers, therefore, find themselves navigating two distinct environments, both of which present pitfalls and hazards, as 'organizational uncertainty is the counterpart to the perceived physical danger within an officer's occupational environment' (2003, p. 201). In turn, the threats posed by these are met with a number of informal cultural solutions, including suspiciousness, 'ass-covering', and a crime-fighter orientation. Through the adoption of these responses, two 'defining outcomes' (2003, p. 203) of the culture emerge, specifically social isolation and group loyalty, which have a further impact on police interactions with members of the public.

Importantly, Paoline stresses the importance of allowing for cultural variation between and within police institutions and identifies the three main axes along which these occur – 'organization', 'rank' and 'officer style'. Organizational factors are significant, as the organizational environment of police work may vary between institutions given a particular location's law enforcement needs. Paoline recognizes that some geographical areas have more pressing law enforcement requirements than others and that, accordingly, police departments will vary in respect of their law enforcement and service provision roles. In turn, these different organizational requirements will lead to different needs amongst officers and, presumably, differences in the form and/or intensity of cultural solutions. Of particular interest here is the work of Wilson (1968), which proposed more of a top-down model of police occupational culture. Styles of policing, for Wilson, varied between different locations, but for reasons associated with the desires of police managers and administrators rather than the particular requirements of a given environment. Despite lower-level officers being 'directed' by the strategies of their managers, Wilson is quick to add the caveat that their effect is 'gross, imprecise, and hard to predict – they shape the over-all style or strategy of the police but they cannot direct or guide police behaviour in the concrete case' (Wilson, 1968, p. 279). Control in such cases is reduced to the application of negative policies with which to inform officers of behaviours that they should not engage in. This failure to apply control through informing officers of what constitutes appropriate behaviour has disadvantages for officers. Telling officers what not to do merely highlights the lack of direction regarding what should be done and therefore is unlikely to be seen as beneficial.

The second factor that Paoline draws upon to explain cultural variation is that of rank. Drawing heavily on those middle stage pieces of work that identified cultural variation between ranks, such as Reuss-Ianni and Ianni (1983), he makes the point that the various ranked levels of the police organization, predictably, have different priorities and ideals and engage in diverse practices. In contrast to accounts that portray a single all-encompassing police culture, Paoline presents a view of police culture where each rank is effectively isolated, culturally, from the others and this fragmentation mirrors the concerns of that particular level of the hierarchy. The culture of lower-level officers focuses predominantly on the immediate and practical concerns of managing their working environments with the least level of harm or risk to the self. For middle-ranking officers, a management ethos is the main cultural driver given their need to liaise effectively with both the more senior ranks and lower-ranking officers. For those officers at the top of the command chain, different concerns lead to an altogether different cultural set based upon the politics of the police organization, issues of accountability and concerns over the perceptions of the institution held by external audiences.

The third factor that Paoline used to explore the issue of variation in police culture is that of officer style. One of the potential disadvantages of traditional conceptions of police culture is that they tend to conflate or confuse the distinction between the organizational culture and the individual's behaviours that arise as a result of it. In short, there was an assumption that individuals would react uniformly to the culture, and this prompted Fielding to suggest that 'one cannot read the recruit as a cipher for the occupational culture. The occupational culture has to make its pitch for support. . . . Increasing experience lays open increasing grounds of contradiction' (1988, p. 135). This acknowledgement of the agency of the individual in relation to the policing institution does pose problems for earlier theories of police culture given that we then, by necessity, have to balance the idea of autonomous individuals encountering a dogmatic occupational culture. Over time, police literature has come to reflect a somewhat uneasy existence of these two conflicting concepts under the assumption that the discretionary basis of much police work means that the culture of the police facilitates independent decision-making or, as Paoline suggests, 'there are some shared attitudes, values, and norms amongst police officers as well as tolerated differences' (2003, p. 206).

This tension in the individual officers' orientation to the police culture is also highlighted through the use, by some authors, of officer typologies which provide different types of category of police officer that coexist yet represent different orientations to certain core characteristics of the police role. Such typologies, according to Paoline, should be seen as subcultures that appear to be relatively consistent between police forces and eras. Reiner (2010), for example, provides an overview of the typologies provided by the likes of Broderick (1973), Walsh (1977), Shearing (1981) and Brown (1981) and proposes, despite the fact that these typologies differ in both purpose and focus, that they all suggest police officers can be divided into one of four categories, which reflect 'an alienated cynic, a managerial professional, a peacekeeper and a law-enforcer' (2010, p. 134). Unsurprisingly, these typologies closely reflect basic differences between lower-rank officers and managers and between detectives and uniformed officers, as well as accounting for personalized or individualized responses to the job and its career opportunities. Such typologies, to Fielding (1988), signal a discrepancy with the occupational culture, obviously providing different prescribed behaviours and values to different individuals. He goes on to question the extent to which the culture is universally endorsed by all members of the occupation and, crucially, whether the sole requirement for cultural membership is to work for the organization. We are therefore left to question whether or not the adoption of typologies of different officer styles allows for a more comprehensive understanding of the cultural world of the police or merely serves to undermine the notion of a single comprehensive culture.

In addition to Paoline's three factors of 'organization', 'rank' and 'officer style' it might be possible to suggest that other factors also have a role to play in explaining variations in organizational culture. For example, Paoline's analysis of the occupational and organizational environments that shape the cultural requirements of police officers fails to highlight the impact that environments have upon the police world in a more fundamental sense. The work of Mike Brogden, especially *The Police: Autonomy and Consent* (1982) and *On the Mersey Beat: An Oral History of Policing Liverpool between the Wars* (1991), shows the importance of probing beyond basic distinctions between 'rural' and 'urban' when assessing the impact of specific geographic locations on policing cultures. Brogden does this by focusing on the city of Liverpool in the North-West of England and charting the lasting influence of its historical development upon the class composition of the police, their work and their relationship with the public.

Brogden's work is significant in that it draws out the unique economic and social characteristics of Liverpool, which, for part of its history at least, was Western Europe's largest seaport. The city's resultant economic infrastructure, which was composed, in part, of 12 miles of docks, led to a central reliance on casual employment practices amongst the poorest sector of the working class, with over 50 per cent of the working population working in shipping and its related industries. The chaotic nature of their working lives contrasted sharply with the rigidly supervised work of police officers, meaning that 'Time, like control, had a different meaning for police and policed' (Brogden, 1991, p. 2). Other factors also contributed to the distinctive social environment, which, ultimately, came to be reflected in styles of policing in the city. Brogden describes how, for a long time, the Liverpool police force was the most heavily resourced (in terms of both personnel and funding) outside the capital, and played a part in many of the new developments in policing. Likewise, Liverpool's economic history persisted in shaping class relations within the city. In spite of its distinguished history and contribution to the maintenance of the British Empire, the city was, by the early 1930s, a city in decline and one whose police officers were marginalized through 'draconian discipline and appalling work conditions' (Brogden, 1991, p. 1). That police identities merged with class politics is perhaps inevitable in such a city, and Brogden (1982) describes a police force divided by stratifications of social class, with officers from the middle classes being overtly antagonistic to unions and their members. Despite this division within the police force, Liverpool was the only force outside of London to witness significant police involvement in the 1919 police strikes that ultimately proved abortive in the face of a failure to organize local and national union support. Of significance here though is the mobilization of the lower classes against, and the support of the merchant classes for, those officers who chose not to strike. Simultaneously, the numbers of members of the middle class who signed up to join the Specials during the strike served to provoke dissent against the lower classes, who viewed this as an 'outright embodiment of class interest' (1982, p. 184). To the Liverpool of the first half of the twentieth century, class relations were 'messy, [and] confused' (Brogden, 1991, p. 2), and some officers appeared to straddle the two conflicting worlds of unionism and policing, with one of Brogden's sources describing his work policing industrial unrest during the 1926 General Strike whilst at the same time sending money back home to support striking family members.

Integral to Liverpool's police–public relations have been pronounced sectarian and racial divides that, of course, mirror wider societal tensions in the area. In terms of the former, Emsley (1996) suggests that there is evidence to support allegations that Liverpool police had, during some sectarian incidents (of which there had been several during the early 1900s), displayed bias towards Protestants and against Irish Catholics. Similarly, the Toxteth riots of July 1981 took place in the geographic and symbolic borderlands between the merchant classes and the secondary economy (Brogden, 1982) and were comparable in many respects to the race riots that had occurred, resulting in the death of one protestor, in 1919. An interesting tangent documented by Brogden (1982) emerges regarding senior police officer attitudes to the causes of racial tension in the city, with reports from both 1919 and 1978 suggesting that problems stemmed, respectively, from relationships between black males and white females and the offspring of such liaisons.

What we get from Brogden's work is an engrossing portrayal of a city whose police seem to defy convenient classification into a linear distinction between police and policed and whose social tensions appear intimately woven into the historical fabric of the environment. Historically, hostilities flared up sporadically in the city, bringing the police into conflict with communities that were keen to air grievances based on religion (for example, the sectarian violence of the early 1900s), class (for example, the bread riot of 1855) or race (for example, the race riots of 1919 and 1981). Above all, the importance of crime and its control was underplayed, with Brogden suggesting that, historically, Liverpool's police were 'uniformed garbage-men' (1991, p. 1) who favoured informal rather than formal means of maintaining the status quo. The laissez-faire approach to crime control in Liverpool is further evidenced by Emsley (1996), who describes the warnings of the Head Constable, Captain William Nott-Bower, in 1890 when asked by his Watch Committee to proceed with police action against brothels in the city. He reasoned that brothels were to be expected within a seaport and, second, that police intervention would displace prostitution to more respectable areas and impact on local businesses. His wish for non-intervention was eventually granted, when members of the local business community complained, adequately illustrating that police use of discretion could also benefit members of the local mercantile class.

The impact of local cultures upon police behaviour is also evidenced by the work of Emsley (2005), who focuses on the case of Sergeant George Goddard, an officer in the Metropolitan Police who was sentenced to 18 months' hard labour in January 1929. Emsley's work provides a timely contribution to debates regarding the ways in which police histories traditionally view police corruption in individual (the 'rotten apple' metaphor) rather than systemic (the 'diseased orchard') terms. By focusing on a particular case, Emsley succeeds in describing how police corruption could be influenced by the nuances of the particular environments in which they worked. Goddard was stationed in the Metropolitan Police's 'C' Division, which dealt with the district around Soho associated with much of the capital's vice industry, and his responsibilities included the regulation of the area's nightclubs and brothels. Whilst the latter were considered illegal and subject to stringent police control, the regulation of nightclubs was generally restricted to alcohol sales outside of permitted licensed hours. This role, however, put Goddard in a unique position. Effectively he controlled which information was passed to magistrates for applications for entry warrants, making him a highly influential player within the lucrative, if legally ambiguous, businesses located in and around Soho. By the time he was arrested in autumn 1928 he had, according to Emsley (2005), personal possessions worth in excess of £17,000, including £12,000 in cash. As a case was built against Goddard, evidence began to surface suggesting that Goddard had tipped off those establishments at risk from police raids, enjoyed the hospitality of hoteliers (whose businesses often relied on prostitution) and failed to act on anonymous information regarding 'disorderly houses', licensing offences and drug dealing. In regard to prostitution, Emsley draws on police memoirs to provide evidence that prostitutes on the Division routinely paid money to Goddard to be eligible for arrest by appointment, a system whereby women would be arrested on rotation at a pre-arranged time, allowing them to concentrate on the work of securing custom unhindered by police attention.

Allegations of police corruption appeared to blight 'C' Division, and Emsley notes how in 1931 one inspector and 26 police constables, stationed at Great Marlborough Street, were discharged for accepting illegal payments. That 'C' Division suffered the most high-profile and perturbing examples of police corruption during the inter-war years appears to highlight the enabling features of that particular environment. The apparently illicit nature of much of the business activity in the area, the fact that it generated considerable wealth and the fact that legislation relating to licensing, prostitution and drugs was unlikely to eradicate these behaviours meant that laws, in this context, were used as tools to manage rather than fight crime. Similarly, in her oral history of British policing, Weinberger (1995, p. 166) notes that exchanges between the police and marginalized groups became 'formalized relationship and ritual' through means of strategies such as the accepting of bribes in return for 'turning a blind eye'. It is this ritualism which partially facilitated at least some of the 'corruption' that emerged around police control of morally ambiguous behaviours.

Brogden's depiction of the importance of Liverpool's historical heritage on the city's style of policing echoes Paoline's ideas of cultural variation, as does Emsley's coverage of the Goddard case, but extends them by acknowledging that police relations with the public are complex, entrenched and rooted in specific localized factors and features. Of importance, therefore, is that these local qualities will influence police opportunities and choices regarding use of discretion, their choice of tactics for maintaining order, the expectations of the public and, of course, the police–public relationship.

Conclusion

The suggestion that police culture is not monolithic (Reiner, 2010) lays the foundations for the successful definition of police culture, whilst simultaneously drawing us towards some incredibly challenging conceptual and practical barriers. Indeed, the concept of 'culture' suggests an implicit uniformity of value and behaviour which, whilst making for a considerably more straightforward analytic model, arguably has little if any relevance to our understanding of policing in contemporary society. When one veers away from the more linear and monolithic depictions of police culture characterized by homogenized actions, thought and expectation, we are effectively opting to choose a model of culture that is characterized by variation, exception and caveat. The inherent complexities of these approaches tend to encourage altogether different views of police culture. No longer does police culture represent merely the informal 'trade' rules that enable police officers to maintain order without falling foul of the laws, institutional procedures or even resource shortfalls that hinder their role. Instead, non-monolithic accounts encourage us to view culture as an altogether more sophisticated concept and, similarly, provoke debate regarding what culture is, the extent of its influence, the effect of different environments upon its potency and focus, its relation to wider societal culture and the extent to which it directs thought and behaviour.

3 Police culture
Traditional approaches

Introduction

As has been described in the previous chapter, our knowledge of police culture has emerged through a number of stages following the initial surge of early research by pioneers such as Westley, Skolnick and Banton. As Westmarland (2008) points out, however, even the earlier depictions of police culture, which tended to highlight the existence of a single culture supported by a linear socialization process, have succeeded in raising, upon later reflection, a substantial number of unresolved issues. These points of continuing disagreement tend to revolve around issues of variation in both the police culture and individual orientations towards it. To writers like Peter Manning (2007), early period work in the area of police culture has provided us with a range of classic but obsolete studies that have been selectively drawn upon to present lifeless caricatures of the police world. However, it is still important to note that any contemporary assessment of police culture must explore the core elements of these early texts. Many authors highlight the tremendous contribution that these classic works have made to our understanding of policing with later accounts also acknowledging that this literature reflects a culture that, as time has passed, has diminished in relevance as a means of explaining contemporary police work (Loftus, 2010).

In this chapter I will draw out some of the key 'products' or manifestations of police culture, that is, the essentially negative issues that are associated with it. First, however, it is probably wise to address the issue of discretion in some depth, as it represents a seemingly constant thread within the sociology of policing. Not least, it signifies the element of freedom that allows some police values or opinions to become physically realized. Similarly, discretion has a deeply symbolic relevance, not just to sociologists studying police action, but to police officers themselves, who have traditionally valued discretion as an emblem of their professionalism. From the earliest pieces of research into police culture, discretion has emerged as an integral element of our understanding of police work. For example, Westley notes that:

> the amount of violence which is used and the frequency with which it is employed will vary among policemen according to their individual propensities . . . the collective sanction for the use of violence permits those men who are inclined to its use to employ it without fear.

(1953, pp. 39–40)

Whilst cultural values regarding, for example, police violence may become more condemnatory, tolerant or nuanced over time and between communities, what remains important is the extent to which discretion allows for such cultural values to become appropriated as tolerated police practice.

Discretion

Klockars (1985) provides an illuminating introduction to the issue of police discretion (or selective enforcement, as he often refers to it) and begins by outlining the definition (adapted from Davis, 1969) that 'A police officer or police agency may be said to exercise discretion whenever effective limits on his, her, or its power leave the officer or agency free to make choices among possible courses of action or inaction' (Klockars, 1985, p. 93).

Three key elements of Davis's definition are highlighted by Klockars. The first element is that discretion is something that is integral to the work both of patrol officers and of police administrators. This point is significant given that traditional conceptions of police culture have tended to highlight the importance of discretion at the lower end of the police ranks (not least through the work of Wilson, 1968, who famously remarked that discretion increases as one's position in the police hierarchy decreases). Similarly, Brogden, Jefferson and Walklate (1988), amongst others, have been effective in stressing the importance of discretion at different levels of the police organization, from senior officers' decisions to pursue or abandon particular policies to the decisions of patrol officers to deal with offences formally or informally. Whilst it should be noted that discretion is applied differently between patrol officers and managers (for example, with the former applying it at interpersonal as opposed to strategic levels), the wide disparity of status within the police hierarchy ensures that discretion has a different form and nature for different ranks, with a greater visibility accorded to those decisions taken at the more senior levels. The second element of Klockars's definition is that, despite the potential for external influence, the power to make a particular decision rests with police officers and agencies. (This idea of external influence can be considered of some importance, especially in the light of discussions regarding the relationship between the police and local political elites described by Punch, 2009.) Klockars does note, however, an alternative definition by Reiss (1974) that proposes that 'discretion' pertains not only to an individual or agency holding the power to make a decision but also to the fact that that decision is not subject to review. The final factor highlighted by Klockars is the issue of action or inaction. In this respect, the application of discretion at street level is characterized by a decision either to act or not to act, and these differently framed discretionary decisions allow for a variety of types of scrutiny or oversight to be applied. As Klockars notes, the decision to arrest is usually accompanied by some form of inspection of the circumstances of that decision, whereas decisions *not* to arrest rarely meet with further consideration.

Skolnick's (1994) *Justice without Trial* provides one of the first sociological appraisals of the importance of discretion to the police officer, drawing on the work of legal scholars in the area such as LaFave (1962b) who supported the application of legal controls to those discretionary decisions not to enforce the law. Central to Skolnick's understanding of discretion was the balancing of the concepts of order and legality. The prioritization of either of these concepts, he observed, necessitates a reduction or expansion of the 'decisional latitude' (1994, p. 69) available to officers, and it is this elusive balance between the two that provides the basis of many of the debates regarding police discretion. Too much latitude arouses suspicions regarding unaccountable use of police power, whilst too little leads to accusations of overt bureaucracy and a dearth of 'common-sense' policing.

Skolnick (1994) goes on to identify two types of discretion exercised by the police, delegated discretion and unauthorized discretion. Delegated discretion referred to that discretion which was conceived as an inevitable part of the police officer's job (and therefore viewed as authorized), whereas unauthorized discretion referred to that discretion which was influenced by the individual officer's personal views. Unauthorized discretion was seen to arise from the fact that 'policemen are rarely supervised, that supervisory (Sergeant to patrolmen) ratios are very high, and that training in most cases is minimal, "internal" control over police conduct is weak' (Manning, 1977, p. 364). Within a UK context, discretion is conceived as fundamental to police work, and the work of Steer (1970) summarizes the accepted position that the police have a considerable amount of discretionary power invested within them and that, inevitably, not all breaches of the criminal law that are witnessed by the police will result in police action. The Association of Chief Police Officers, whilst claiming that officers might be able to use their discretionary powers 'more wisely and more uniformly' (Royal Commission on the Police, 1961, p. 16), appeared to be of the view that the public generally favoured the unbiased and often compassionate way in which such powers were exercised.

Police discretion, according to Jones (2008), has largely appeared incongruent with the public perception of police institutions as hierarchical and disciplined bureaucracies tasked with imposing the rule of law, and he identifies three issues that have led to discretion assuming such importance. First, the disparity between the resources available to the police and the limitless scope for the use of the criminal law leads to the police having to decide which laws are to be prioritized for enforcement and under which conditions. Second, the criminal law represents a set of tools to be used, not as a means of ensuring full enforcement, but as part of a range of options for dealing with particular situations. Officers require a substantial amount of discretion to match the most appropriate law for the position that they find themselves in. Discretion in this sense represents a degree of freedom in the face of the complex and fluid situations and environments that constitute the social world of policing. Officers may also use discretion to decide that, despite grounds for enforcing the law being present, it would be more appropriate for non-enforcement or alternative non-legal interventions to be used. Finally, many police interactions with the public focus on those who are marginalized, less visible and less likely to formally articulate grievances against the police, especially grievances that rest on perceptions of unfair application of discretionary powers.

The work of Klockars (1985) provides us with five further explanations of why discretion appears of such central importance to police work: the 'over-reach of the law'; the 'purpose of the law'; the 'question of priorities'; the 'problem of bad laws'; and the 'power of citizen discretion'. Taking each of these in turn, 'over-reach of the law' suggests that laws are incredibly broad and cover situations and actions for which there are legitimate exemptions. Discretion is necessary to ensure that those people who break the law under circumstances that are exceptional and subject to exemption are not arrested. The 'purpose of the law' is to punish those individuals who ignore its authority, and discretion is required to ensure that those for whom punishment might be unwarranted do not suffer the inconvenience of police action. The 'question of priorities' arises when an officer witnesses a behaviour that is technically illegal but which has not been prioritized, for example by local policing arrangements or by that officer's specific role. Discretion in such cases allows for officers to concentrate on particular crimes, whereas a policy of full enforcement would not. The 'problem of bad laws' refers to the fact that some laws fail to serve a coherent purpose, for example because they were introduced for political reasons or because, over time, they failed to remain relevant to the lives of those living under them. Klockars wisely acknowledges that the police will be unlikely to impose laws that are viewed as irrelevant and that such legislation will be left to 'die a slow and quiet police discretionary death' (1985, p. 101). The 'power of citizen discretion' acknowledges that police discretion, in a great many circumstances, relies on citizen discretion. Citizens use their discretion to choose whether or not to involve the police in a particular situation and, more importantly, may be the deciding influence on any further action that the officer takes. Klockars draws on the work of Black (1971) to present what appears to be an extraordinary finding, that arrests occurred in only 10 per cent of cases where the officer could legally make an arrest but in which the accuser did not want an arrest to be made.

Discretion is often a difficult concept to unthread, not least because of the fact that it concerns the application of abstract legal concepts to the vagaries of human life against a backdrop of resource and priority considerations. Neyroud and Beckley (2001) draw on the work of Kleinig (1996) to identify four different ways in which discretion can be exercised by police officers: 'scope decisions'; 'interpretive decisions'; 'decisions about priority'; and 'tactical decisions'. 'Scope decisions' reflect the ambiguities that are often associated with the breadth of the police role and whether or not the police are the most appropriate agency to deal with a particular matter. 'Interpretive decisions', in many respects, accord with the five points put forward by Klockars mentioned above in that they refer to those situations where an officer is required to decide whether or not formal application of the law is appropriate. In some cases, the officer might decide that, although the law has technically been broken, the most fitting resolution to the situation is based on negotiation rather than enforcement. 'Decisions about priority' reflect the impracticality of implementing full enforcement policies, so the police prioritize certain offences in line with national and local targets, and this has a strategic impact on the deployment and tasking of officers. 'Tactical decisions', again taken at a strategic level, reflect the difficulties in ensuring that an adequate balance is struck between the rights of individuals and those of the wider community.

From the above it is evident that discretion is a central thread running through all ranks of the police organization and that decisions made on the basis of scope or interpretation are more likely to be made by lower-ranking officers and those regarding priorities and tactics are more likely to be made by officers with more strategic roles. Differences in the characteristics of street-level and strategic discretion are, according to Neyroud and Beckley (2001), commonly to be found in respect of the context within which the decisions are made, the time that is available to make the decision, the intricacy of the situation and the number of interests to be represented. Strategic uses of discretion tend to take place in less tense environments and over longer intervals of time but with added difficulties associated with the consideration of a greater number of individuals and options.

Why is discretion important?

Issues of police discretion have a history of underpinning theories and observations concerning police occupational culture. Discretion, suggest Brogden, Jefferson and Walklate, provides the 'space' (1988, p. 35) within which the occupational culture takes hold, with occupational cultures requiring the lack of restriction that discretion allows to fully impact on officer decision-making. Grimshaw and Jefferson (1987) also show how the 'discretionary framework' (1987, p. 290) of police work is increased in particular circumstances, such as when insufficient guidance is given for officers to make informed decisions regarding potential actions. In these cases, officers tend to rely on 'occupational common sense' (Grimshaw and Jefferson, 1987, p. 291) to select the appropriate police response.

Police use of discretion also allows for an intricate understanding of the police institution and its practitioners. Primarily, and as Chatterton (1979) amongst others has observed, the discretion outlined by authors such as Klockars and Neyroud and Beckley provides a marked contrast to some of the more orthodox accounts of a police institution founded on discipline and hierarchy. For Chatterton, therefore, the importance of discretion to policing appears at odds with the presentation of the police institution as one of 'military-bureaucratic discipline and control' (1979, p. 83). Similarly, orthodox historical accounts of the police organization, according to Emsley (2005), depicted it in terms that underplayed the power of the lower ranks and highlighted the role of 'disciplinarian' police leaders in ensuring that officers were effectively controlled. The exploration of the role that discretion plays within the policing world does encourage a view of the police function that stresses an order maintenance as opposed to law enforcement agenda (Klockars, 1985) and, according to Crank (1998), it is precisely these areas of order which lead to a reliance on subjective decision-making. What is notable in respect of this type of decision-making is that it is influenced not just by principles of impartiality but also by organizational requirements and considerations (Fielding, 1988, p. 154).

The issue of police discretion has, of course, ramifications at a more interpersonal level. The subjectivity that informs the ways in which discretion is utilized means that increased attention is paid to stereotypical ideas regarding 'suspicious' or 'normal' behaviours (Chan, 1997, p. 44) in the face of limited guidance as to the application of particular laws. This issue has raised comment amongst several authors, with Brogden (1982) stating that police discretion undermines judicial function and Klockars (1985) proposing that police discretion can be seen as tantamount to allowing police officers to devise their own laws. Central to these arguments surrounding the appropriateness of discretion to the role of the individual officer are concerns regarding whether or not policing is to be considered as an occupation or a profession. Rawlings (2002), assessing the historical context of policing in England and Wales, suggested that beat policing traditionally was viewed as 'low-skilled work' (p. 181; see also Emsley, 1996). Furthermore, despite the increased use of the rhetoric of professionalization over recent years, Neyroud (2003) draws on Friedson (1983) to portray policing as an occupation that fails to readily satisfy the definitions of either 'profession' or 'public service'. Similarly, Bayley (1979) suggests that different countries adopt very different philosophies regarding the extent to which policing is professionalized, with countries like the UK and the USA choosing to impose explicit limitations on the powers of officers. In countries such as Japan, Bayley views the control of police discretion as being achieved through individual self-regulation rather than through limitation of power.

Making sense of police discretion

Neyroud and Beckley (2001) forward four disparate and competing means of analyzing police discretion and its properties. These represent different analytic approaches that can be broadly categorized as 'legal', 'social contract', 'discriminatory' and 'professionalization'. The 'legal' perspective represents the views of academics such as Davis (1975) and LaFave (1962b) who assert that judicial powers have been undermined by the policing institution through the 'mandatory discretion' (Brogden, 1982, p. 24) that is integral to police practice. This position calls for a more robust approach to controlling police discretion and for the increased use of accountability mechanisms. One suggestion in respect of this has been for the imposition of greater control over police decisions not to enforce the law (LaFave, 1962b). The 'social contract' perspective, associated with writers such as Bayley (1994), proposes a more optimistic account of police discretion. Police discretion, from this perspective, is seen as an important means of bridging the gap between the law as it stands at an abstract level and its fair and equitable application in the real world where the rights of individuals and groups have to be considered. The police are accorded a certain level of discretion and are trusted to use it for the good of society. Should police actions be seen as inappropriate, citizens are allowed to confront the police regarding their concerns. Those accounts of police use of discretion that are aligned with the 'discriminatory model' tend to focus less on the legal processes and philosophies that allow for the use of discretion than on the outcomes of its use. The work of writers such as Rowe (2004) and Quinton, Bland and Miller (2000) illustrate persistent concerns that police discretion leads to discriminatory practice by police officers, particularly in respect of the use of stop and search powers against members of ethnic minorities. Traditionally, police literature associated with this model has tended to identify police occupational culture as one of the key drivers of these types of discriminatory practice. Those who adhere to the 'professionalization' model (for example, Davis, 1991) suggest that inappropriate use of discretion can be addressed by organizing the structure of police work along the lines of the professions. To proponents of this model, the solution lies in granting more personal autonomy to police officers rather than less. Top-down regulation, notes Davis (1991), does little to impact on police behaviour and removes officers from the process of developing a framework of occupational ethics. Furthermore, Davis advocates a position whereby the police combine the structured and hierarchical institutional traditions of their occupation with the decentralized control enjoyed by other professional groups. This latter factor of decentralized control, he states, is crucial in defining the difference between professions and occupations, yet Van Maanen (1978a) adds further fuel to the debate when he considers the question of whether we require professionalized police forces *or* accountable ones. The extent to which professionalism and accountability can be considered synonymous, or even as related concepts, is likely to remain an area of disagreement.

Key manifestations of police culture

Traditional research, and many later works, have all highlighted certain residual cultural manifestations that are seen as potentially problematic at a practical level. These manifestations are also generally taken as de facto evidence of a specific and seemingly universal police culture and tend to present, and reinforce, somewhat deterministic accounts of the relationship between culture and behaviour. A number of these key manifestations will be explored in turn in the following sections. The issue of police corruption, whilst considered by many to be a key manifestation, will be addressed separately in Chapter 6.

Sense of mission/way of life

> In the heart of every cop is a sense of morality, strong in some and weak in others, but always present. . . . Cop culture works in large part because cops start out with a common residue of moral values associated with the traditional, small-town that symbolizes mainstream America. . . . Police culture transforms and unifies cops with a shared perception of social justice.
>
> (Crank, 1998, p. 43)

Central to traditional thinking about police culture is the idea that policing represents a way of life, different to those associated with other occupational groupings. The uniqueness of the cultural orientation of the police may in part be due to what

Skolnick (1994) viewed as the convergence of the factors of danger, authority and efficiency. However, literature in the area points to something more emotively driven and value led than Skolnick's explanatory factors might fully suggest. In other words, policing represents a set of values that are viewed, at least by officers, as inherently righteous. This 'sense of mission' (Reiner, 2010, p. 119) comes, therefore, from a perception that policing is not just a 'worthwhile' occupation but an 'essential' one and established upon easily identified and enforceable ideas of right and wrong. This cognitive framing is encouraged from what Brogden, Jefferson and Walklate (1988, p. 32) see as the 'embryonic' images of the occupation that probationers or rookie officers are subjected to during training and which promote a heightened awareness of the importance of the job of the police officer, the commitment required to be a police officer and the thin blue line that separates law and order from chaotic societal influences. The sense of mission becomes more heightened when officers make the transition from probationer to police officer and manifests itself in a number of ways. Not least, Cain (1973) shows how many officers seek to work a 'good pitch' (p. 65), where officers would be more likely to encounter public order issues that allowed officers the greatest possible discretion with regard to choice of action. Similarly, Van Maanen (1978a) shows how the 'moral superiority' (p. 222) of the police is intrinsically linked to their role within the 'moral mandate' (p. 227), and it is this moral superiority, according to Skolnick and Fyfe (1993), that reinforces the views of a politically conservative overclass.

However, and as Reiner (2010) notes, the framework of moral values that is used to bring meaning to policing is somewhat flawed in practical terms. Quite simply, police work fails, in many instances, to reflect the ideological resonance that the sense of mission hints at. When Cain (1973) highlights the importance of 'events' (for example, witnessing a theft being committed or an act of public disorder taking place), the occurrence has symbolic meaning far beyond the immediate police actions that it might provoke. Such 'events', suggests Cain, 'told them [officers] who they were. They became their justification and *raison d'être*' (1973, p. 65). Van Maanen (1978a) provides further evidence for the tension between 'real' police work and the more service-oriented tasks that officers perform when he shows that, even within a busy urban environment, only between 10 and 15 per cent of a patrol officer's time would be spent undertaking types of work that equate with this idealized view of their role. Wilson (1968) shows how, over 40 years ago, police departments that valued crime prevention over law enforcement were earning the label 'progressive', perhaps signifying a decline in the value of the iconography of lower-rank policing in practical, if not allegorical, terms.

The tension between law enforcement and service provision as the defining roles of the occupation are highlighted when young officers, steeped in the 'war stories' (Van Maanen, 1978b, p. 298) of their more experienced colleagues, realize that for much of their time at work they will be the 'proverbial clerk in a patrol car' (Van Maanen, 1978b, p. 304). These tensions, however, are somewhat resolved through 'police mythology' (Innes, 2003, p. 21), which tends to present the crime-fighting role as the key focus of police work and which is, in part, perpetuated by the 'sacred canopy' (Manning, 1977, p. 5) that obscures the reality of policing from the wider public. Amongst the police, storytelling and police rhetoric promote this idealized vision of their work (Shearing and Ericson, 1991; Waddington, 1999a), and the 'common experience of secret knowledge' (Fielding, 1988, p. 185) provides individuals with a collective language and folklore. The 'sense of mission' does however have broader and more fundamental foundations beyond those represented by occupationally located characteristics such as moral superiority and a shared mythology. At the heart of the police sense of mission is their institutional relationship with the state. To Manning (1977), in a reference to the work of the social contract theorist Thomas Hobbes, the police were 'Leviathan enacted', the street-level implementation of the state's traditions, values and morality.

Cynicism/pessimism

> The police officer is frequently a critic of society; through what he sees in the courts, as well as on the beat, he is in an unparalleled position to observe the machinery of society in operation.
>
> (Banton, 1964, p. 144)

To Reiner, police cynicism is the 'Janus face of commitment' (2010, p. 120) and is caused by the discord between police officers' sense of mission and their experiences of the 'reality' of their occupational world. In some cases, this is caused by the sometimes excessively idealistic attitudes held by officers when they join the police force. In research carried out by Chan (2003), of officers who had recently completed their training, 60 per cent were more negative about the police role than previously and only 6 per cent were more positive. Similarly, Walsh (1977) speculated that police cynicism was experienced more acutely by officers from middle-class backgrounds who found their career aspirations limited, and it appears fitting, as Reuss-Ianni and Ianni (1983) propose, that cynicism might not therefore be a cultural attribute solely associated with the police role. With this in mind, however, police cynicism can be seen as having an altogether deeper connotation than those forms experienced by members of other occupations. For example, scholarly explorations of the symbolism to be found in police funerals (see Manning, 1977, and Crank, 1998) serve to underline the moral superiority of the police institution, the power of the state and the righteousness of the police officer. When police officers see the world through a negative prism the effect is to paint an altogether more apocalyptic vision of humankind, which is amply illustrated by Niederhoffer, who asserts that:

> Cynicism is an ideological plank deeply entrenched in the ethos of the police world. . . . When they succumb, they lose faith in people, society, and eventually in themselves. In their Hobbesian view, the world becomes a jungle in which crime, corruption and brutality are normal features of the terrain.
>
> (1969, p. 9)

Police cynicism leads to negative feelings towards, amongst others, the wider public (MacAlister, 2004), minority groups (Chan, 2003), police management (Chan, 2003), new policing styles (Crank, 1998), the judicial system (Skolnick, 1994), detectives who conjure arrests out of nowhere (James, 1979) and even politically motivated increases of police resources (Wilson, 1968). All these heighten police antipathy towards every aspect of the world they inhabit with the exception of, according to Chan (2003), the mythologized and idealized vocation of policing itself. The result of this process is that the moral foundations of the police mandate are soon swept away, leaving a police culture whose 'sense of mission', according to Skolnick and Fyfe (1993), promotes values demanding of lip service but little more. This sentiment is keenly demonstrated by Manning when he describes a police cynicism that sees humankind as 'stupid, fallible, greedy, lustful, immoral, and hypocritical. . . . Man is seen as a translucent Machiavelli, easily uncovered by insightful probing or police action' (1978b, p. 83).

Examples of police cynicism are easily located throughout the literature of police occupational culture. Westley (1970), for example, shows how the police view the 'public as enemy'. Punch (1979) describes senior police officers expressing their disappointment at specialists who hinder police attempts to prosecute young offenders. In his description of the bargaining process that occurs between judges and defence lawyers in prostitution cases, Skolnick (1994) describes a police culture that appears to harbour more resentment towards the intricacies of criminal justice procedure than to individuals who commit victimless crimes. Perhaps one area where the cynicism of the police is most pronounced is in the area of police paperwork. The detectives studied by Dick Hobbs (1988) in his account of detective work in the East End of London, although quick to pronounce the triviality of paperwork to their role, found that paperwork had a transformative quality in that it allowed for the veiled actions of the detective to be articulated in a way that accorded it with a semblance of legal probity. In other words, administrative skills allowed for dubious police work to be transformed into formal accounts where every procedural requirement had been fully satisfied. Other accounts of police work, however, portray paperwork as something to be avoided or, at least suggests Reiner (2010), kept to a minimum. Some police scholars have chosen to frame police enmity to it in ideological rather than pragmatic terms, with Fielding hypothesizing that paperwork functions as a 'metaphor for the bureaucratic model of organization', which contrasts markedly with the orientation of police work depicted in the 'sense of mission' (1988, p. 116). The bureaucratic elements of police work not only undermine the notion of the autonomous law enforcer and reassert the supervisory hierarchy of the institution, but also, notes Fielding (1988), provide a means of challenging officers' ability and professionalism. Understandably, the cynicism of the police finds itself reflected in both the behaviour of the police (for example, in respect to paperwork) and the vernacular of the culture (Crank, 1998).

Suspicion

> This use of quick and incisive classification as a method of imposing control
> is a police art, for classification is the basis of all legal systems.
>
> (Young, 1991, p. 108)

Much of the existing literature in the area of cop culture (for example, Banton, 1964; Manning, 1977; Reiner, 1978; Smith and Gray, 1983; Skolnick, 1994; Crank, 1998) has suggested that police officers tend to be suspicious of behaviours that do not readily accord with their idealized description of a particular social world. This suspicion appears to be a crucial facet of what Skolnick (1994) termed the police 'working personality', and is, according to Crank (1998), a central feature of both the physical and cultural worlds of the police. Fundamental to police suspicion is the notion of 'incongruity' (Manning, 1977; Sacks, 1978; Mooney and Young, 2000), and this can relate to people looking 'out of place' or displaying 'odd' behaviour or indeed any activity or occurrence that offends the officers' 'conception of order' (Skolnick, 1994, p. 46). Where this subjective benchmark represented by the 'conception of order' causes difficulties is in the inevitable over-reach with which it is applied. That is to say, police suspicion will lead to people being stopped by the police who are not engaging in illicit behaviour but whose location, demeanour or behaviour would suggest otherwise (Skolnick and Fyfe, 1993). That police officers themselves are often unashamedly aware of this cognitive orientation is evidenced by one officer, interviewed by Banton, who stated that 'The police mind means that you suspect your grandmother and that's about the strength of it' (1964, p. 207).

There is some evidence to suggest that police suspicion has been reinforced not just by the role that they undertake, but by legislative provisions to support their work. That the police should be afforded the legal power to subjectively define what constitutes suspicious behaviour was enshrined within sections 4 and 6 of the Vagrancy Act 1824 (also known as the 'sus' laws), which empowered officers in England and Wales to arrest individuals in public spaces who they suspected had intent to commit a criminal offence. The 'selective enforcement' (Brogden, 1982, p. 244) of these largely unregulated powers over time became a part of routine police work, although recent decades have seen attempts to introduce more objective regulation of these powers. Most notably this is evidenced through the introduction of the concept of 'reasonable suspicion' (see, for example, *Terry* v. *Ohio* in the United States, *R.* v. *Simpson* in Canada and the Police and Criminal Evidence Act in England and Wales). Crank (1998), however, highlights an inconsistency in the relationship between the legal appropriation of suspicion and its utility as a cultural 'craft'. His criticism rests upon the idea that any attempt to objectively articulate suspicion, at a cultural level, is liable to present itself as a clumsy technical arrangement that fails to adequately portray the intangible and intuitive consciousness that the police experience when reading the social world around them.

Skolnick (1994) claims that the suspiciousness of the police can be traced back to the element of danger associated with police work. Many occupations may make claims to the inherent danger that their practitioners face, yet policing is different in that the sources of danger are the same public whom they are charged with serving, thus blurring the distinction between 'public' and 'enemy'. Furthermore, Wilson (1968) makes an additional distinction by stating that order maintenance policing (as opposed to crime and traffic work), despite statistically presenting a lesser risk, creates greater anxiety for officers owing to its greater propensity for unpredictable behaviours. The centrality of the 'threat–danger–hero' concept to the police mythology (Manning, 1977, p. 302) draws together a variety of aspects of police institutional life from promotions and recommendations to the respect of their colleagues. That the notion of danger remains so embedded within the collective psyche of the police rests to an extent both on organizational traditions and on practical considerations. With regard to the former, most police forces adhere to a tradition that all police officers, regardless of rank, have at some point undergone the cultural baptism of patrol work, meaning that, despite divergent career trajectories, all police officers have a common knowledge of the core location, value and lore of police work. Danger impacts at a more immediate level in the shape of Skolnick's concept of the 'symbolic assailant' (1994, p. 44), and police officers are, from their introduction to the force, made aware of the part that danger will play in their occupational lives. One of the purposes of police training, therefore, is to develop the 'craft' of suspicion. Furthermore, with their introduction to the streets, officers develop a 'perceptual shorthand' (Skolnick, 1994, p. 44) through which they can cognitively filter and assess the extent to which individuals' behaviour or language represents a potential physical threat. Police suspicion is supported by both the institutional moulding of the officer through training and the practical strategies that police develop for dealing with the unpredictable potential dangers that their work subjects them to. The extent to which police training or the experience of police work acts as the primary driver for police suspicion is naturally hard to assess, although much research evidence suggests that official police training insufficiently prepares recruits for the reality of police work (see Harris, 1978; Bittner, 1983). Some literature also suggests that police attitudes are more likely to be 'caught' rather than 'taught' (Police Training Council, cited in Fielding, 1988, p. 91).

Isolation/solidarity

> Relationships among officers are structured in such a way that they are mutually supportive, and their common interests bind them into a cohesive brotherhood that personalizes task performance as well as social relationships.
>
> (Reuss-Ianni and Ianni, 1983, p. 258)

Two interrelated factors which also contribute to the police officer's 'working personality' and therefore to police culture are police solidarity and social isolation (see Skolnick, 1994, and Reiner, 2010). Under normal circumstances, suggests Skolnick (1994), police officers encounter great difficulty in forging (and maintaining) relationships with those who belong to different occupations from themselves, even when factors such as age, race, class and religion have been accounted for. This social isolation is inextricably entwined with the concept of police solidarity, and both are subject to variations of intensity under certain external conditions. Whitaker (1964), for example, forwards the idea that police solidarity has increased with perceived decreases in police authority. When, therefore, the police feel under increased threat, through legislation, restructuring or increased public hostility, there may be a tendency for the solidarity and camaraderie within the occupation to increase, resulting in a corresponding rise in officers' isolation from the public. That the culture of the police is essentially inward facing is to be expected given the occupation's reliance on 'secret knowledge' (Fielding, 1988, p. 185), 'the need for mutual secrecy and trust' among police officers (Cain, 1973, p. 190) and Skolnick's (1994) claims that the camaraderie of the police as co-workers is reflected outside the workplace in their leisure activities.

The twin factors of isolation and solidarity therefore reflect the tendency of police officers to withdraw emotionally from the cultural world of the wider public and to subsequently invest more into their relationships with colleagues. The importance of solidarity to the occupational culture cannot be overstated. To Punch, secrecy and solidarity represented the 'distinguishing characteristics' of the cultural world of the police officer (1983, p. 224), and they continue to play an integral role in the framework of beliefs that informs their relationships not only with other officers but also with the public. Equally, the work of Wilson showed how police solidarity manifested itself in 'defensiveness, a sense of not being supported by the community, and a distrust of outsiders' (1968, pp. 48–49). Over 40 years later, Reiner (2010) describes how police officers continue to experience difficulties in successfully shifting between the cultural world of the police and that of civilians.

Police solidarity is made possible by a number of factors common to the police world. Reiner (2010), for example, notes the detrimental impact of public antagonism, occupational stress and shift work and how these cause a withdrawal from meaningful interaction with non-police officers, a process that facilitates the '"them" and "us" outlook' that permeates the culture of the police (p. 122). A similar theme is developed by Van Maanen (1978a), who, in his depiction of the cultural grouping of the 'asshole', underlines the strict delineation between the police and the public and shows how police officers use the term to portray those who seek to restrict or even scrutinize police action. At the same time, public attitudes towards policing and those who undertake it help to reinforce the camaraderie of the police and to sustain the division between police and public. One pertinent factor here concerns the 'moral division of labor' (Harris, 1978, p. 273), which describes how highly regarded members of particular occupations manage to avoid discrediting themselves through undertaking the less attractive types of work associated with that occupation. Drawing on Carlin's (1966) example of higher-status lawyers who refuse to undertake divorce work, Harris extends the concept of moral division to suggest that there are entire occupations, such as policing, that are considered 'dirty'. The public recognize the value of the police role, but have no desire to associate themselves with either the work of the police or those who undertake it. In other words, 'the respectables hire the police to do their dirty work for them' (Harris, 1978, p. 273), be it 'dirty' in either a physical or a moral sense. Furthermore, the public perception of those who undertake the 'dirty' forms of work associated with the regulation of public morality is that the people who do this kind of work are unlikely to adhere to the 'moral norms' (Skolnick, 1994, p. 55) that they are paid to enforce. Thus, the conflicting occupational needs both to combat danger and to live in accordance with austere principles hint at a potential tension between the norms of the police working personality and the police role in regulating the moral life of the citizenry. At no point, however, should we assume that police solidarity is a simple response to public opinion and that the police do not actively foster and thrive on this *esprit de corps*. The uncertainty that characterizes much police work (especially in regard to police encounters with the public) provides an impetus for the police, wherever possible, to establish elements of certainty in their social world. Hence, Manning (1977, p. 306) draws our attention to the importance of ritual to the police world and, in particular, to police solidarity. The unpredictability of police interactions with the public is matched only by the certainty of the camaraderie of their occupational grouping.

Evidence of the ways in which camaraderie and solidarity influence police officers has been presented by several police scholars. For example, Smith and Gray (1983) found that police solidarity manifested itself in the institutionalized practice of the protection and 'covering up' of colleagues' infringements of procedure. Evidence of this was cited within their research when the authors interviewed the head of a crime squad who claimed that, in the event of one of his men getting into 'trouble', he would 'get all of us together and . . . script him out of it' (1983, p. 72). Punch (2009) explores the same problem within an American context when he writes about the Mollen Commission, which was put together in 1992 in an attempt to investigate anti-corruption procedures and allegations of police corruption within the New York Police Department (NYPD). After a painstaking investigation, the Commission concluded that one reason for continued police corruption within the city was a police culture that 'exalts loyalty over integrity' (Mollen Commission Report, cited in Punch, 2009, p. 69). Punch's work is of particular interest here, as he shows how investigations into the probity of the NYPD through the Lexow, Knapp and Mollen Commissions have achieved little more than to highlight the recurring cycle of corruption, investigation, recommendation and purge that has characterized the force for over a century. The power that camaraderie appears to exert over officers suggests that sanctions exist to use against those officers who do not wish to commit themselves to the norms of the group. One example of this is the case of Serpico, the American officer whose experiences led to the formation of the Knapp Commission in 1972. Frank Serpico was an American of Italian descent who joined the New York Police Department in 1959. Accounts show him to be conscientious, hard-working and staunchly devoted to the force. By the time that he joined a plain-clothes team he had forged a reputation as an outsider who alienated himself through his relatively sophisticated demeanour. As a detective, he found himself confronted by wide-spread corruption that had become far more than a cultural aberration and was 'highly organized, well regulated and almost bureaucratic' (Punch, 2009, p. 59). Serpico's refusal to integrate himself within this system led to him being ostra-cized. In turn, when his superiors failed to respond to his concerns regarding what he saw as the systemic corruption amongst detective colleagues, he made contact with the *New York Times*, a move that 'broke' the story. Serpico continued to work in the NYPD, but was reputedly shunned by colleagues, on one occasion placing his life at risk. For Punch (2009), the Serpico case is important for two fundamental reasons. Not only does it draw attention to the challenges that face those officers who fail to internalize the predominant cultural values of their team, but it also shows some of the potential measures that are brought against whistle-blowing colleagues. Solidarity, therefore, proves of interest to police scholars because of the part it plays in the concealment and justification of illegal, deviant or inappropriate police practice (Chan, 1997).

The vision of police solidarity presented so far does portray the issue in incredibly consistent terms. Police officers are seen as belonging to a rigid and prescriptive culture where camaraderie appears to be assured. Maguire and Norris (1994), however, make the point that much of the evidence for police solidarity emerges from studies of patrol or beat officers rather than detectives and cite the work of Baldwin and Moloney (1992), who found that feelings of solidarity amongst plain-clothes officers was limited to their 'teams'. This sig-nals a divergence of opinion with Skolnick's (1994) hypothesis that portrayed solidarity as uniformly present both within and between ranks. Similarly, both Cain (1973) and Young (1991) outline what the latter refers to as the 'fractured rivalry' (p. 82) between uniformed officers and their detective counterparts. Young (1991) continues by noting how uniformed officers who take up a role on a CID team are seen by their uniformed colleagues as traversing a cultural gulf into a disparate set of police values. Further factors may also account for differentiations in levels of solidarity within the police. The work of both Reuss-Ianni and Ianni (1983) and Wilson (1968) suggests that 'managers' and 'cops' adopt subtly different cultural values and that these will limit the degree of solidarity between, if not within, these particular groups. Similarly, the 'tribalism' with which Young (1991) characterized relationships between offic-ers in different forces finds scant support in Brogden's (1991) historical account of Liverpool policing, which describes the 'occupational isolation' (1992, p. 35) of the average Liverpudlian police officer. Finally, Skolnick (1994) makes a case to suggest that American and British police officers experience social isolation for subtly different reasons, American officers being isolated through the antag-onism of the public and their British counterparts through their self-imposed 'impersonal authority' (Reiner, 2010, p. 122). Social solidarity and social iso-lation therefore can be seen to act as complex and self-reinforcing 'push' and 'pull' factors that help define many aspects of the police–public relationship owing to the ways in which they define 'police', 'public' and, crucially, the dif-ferences between the two.

Police culture and gender

> In effect, there is no real place for a woman in this world, and whenever possible it seeks to exclude this structural intruder by claiming she is a sensual, illogical creature, needing protection from her own aberrant nature and from the violence and malevolence of others.
>
> (Young, 1991, p. 251)

In 1991, Malcolm Young in *An Inside Job* described the police institution as a 'primarily masculine domain' driven by imagery of 'hunting' and 'warfare' (p. 191) and one which is, ideologically at least, a polar opposite to the formulaic qualities that have traditionally been associated with the female gender. Although Heidensohn (1992, p. 77) raises doubts as to the universality or authenticity of rigidly masculine portrayals of police work, an emphasis on stereotypically male attitudes and behaviours has for a long time been regarded as an integral element of cop culture (Reiner, 1992; Maguire and Norris, 1994; Skolnick, 1994). Whilst police literature addressing the gendered nature of policing is not particularly expansive, the idea that the police world is fundamentally based on traditional male values is beyond doubt (Silvestri, 2003). Furthermore, Westmarland (2008, p. 267) suggests that such 'institutional sexism' (transmitted through traditions, institutional arrangements and cultural knowledge) limits the ability of the police to provide appropriate levels of service both to female members of the public and to females employed within policing agencies. To fully appreciate the gendered qualities of police culture, there is a real need to understand the role that 'masculinity' plays in the occupational culture of the police and how this impacts on police conceptions of gender.

Female police officers still experience minority status within police forces throughout the world. In the United States, analysis by the Bureau of Justice Statistics (2010) suggests that female officers number just under 100,000 and represent 15.2 per cent of the total number. In England and Wales, the Home Office (2010) presents data that indicates a considerably higher percentage of females at 25.7 per cent, amounting to 37,066 officers. Police forces throughout Western Europe and North America have experienced substantial increases in numbers of female officers in recent years. In England and Wales, for example, Home Office figures show an 8.7 per cent increase in numbers of female officers between the years 2000 and 2010 (Home Office 2000, 2010). Nevertheless, this marked differentiation in representation of males and females within the police has been an entrenched feature of police forces for many years and has been assumed by some to be a substantial factor explaining the prevalence of an exaggerated masculinity amongst many police officers.

If we look back historically, however, evidence emerges to suggest that the tradition of separating male and female police roles may also play a substantial role in explaining the male orientation of police work. Women have played a part, albeit an irregular one, in the policing of England and Wales since the late nineteenth century. Emsley (1991), for example, describes the Metropolitan Police's employment of female staff to visit women convicts as early as the 1880s and, by

1889, the formal creation of 14 police matron positions. The formalization of the police matron function proved advantageous in that it relieved police wives of some of their unofficial responsibilities, especially those related to both searches and supervision of female and juvenile offenders. The advent of the First World War provided yet further opportunities for female employment in the police, prompting former supporters of the suffragette movement to form the Women Police Service and the National Union of Women Workers to introduce voluntary women patrols. Both organizations, interestingly, engaged themselves in pursuing the moral, rather than legal, protection of female members of the public (Emsley, 1991; Rawlings, 2002), a focus that would prove to be remarkably enduring. Whilst opportunities for female employment did arise throughout the first half of the twentieth century, owing in part to the exigencies of two world wars, it was not until 1947 that the Police Federation formally abandoned its strident opposition to female police officers (Rawlings, 2002). The Police Federation's original position on women police is addressed by Judge (1994), who states that, despite the recommendations of the Report of the 1929 Royal Commission which urged greater female recruitment, its opposition centred on two simple yet fundamental issues: first, that policing was a man's job and, second, that to employ a female constable was to deprive a man of his work and his wage. Judge's account of the meeting of the Police Council, at which consideration of the Royal Commission's recommendations took place, shows that there was almost unanimous rejection of these proposals, and he goes on to show how the Federation's representative, Constable Albert Goodsall, regarded those female officers employed in the Metropolitan Force as displaying 'a tendency to find immorality where it did not exist, and so to get into difficulties from which the men had to extricate them' (Judge, 1994, p. 55).

Owing in part to growing public and political support for the woman police movement and in part to the tenacity of Miss Dorothy Peto, a female officer and campaigner for the cause, it soon became obvious that the Police Federation's position would eventually become untenable, although it would be another 40 years before circumstances presented a substantial opportunity for increasing the number and status of female police officers. The early 1970s were a troubled period for policing in England and Wales, with under-recruiting forces directing their inadequate resources on to law enforcement priorities that did little to bolster the service provision role of the police mandate (Rawlings, 2002). At the same time, the police were seeking to subtly reorient the balance between these two elements of police work through the introduction of specialized service work (especially in the area of juvenile liaison) that prioritized constructive police interaction with the public whilst downplaying the former emphasis on crime work.

This shift towards preventative work with young people was not, however, a wholly new focus for the attentions of the police. The welfare of juvenile populations had been a traditional role within the policing institutions of England and Wales, and Emsley (1991) describes some officers, following the 1870 Education Act, as being tasked with ensuring school attendance amongst local youth populations. To some commentators, however, this progressive form of policing was welfare tempered with control, a set of interventions legitimized by emerging theories regarding the role of the immediate environment as a catalyst for criminality (Brogden, 1982). What it did signal, in terms of the gendered order of police work, was a specifically defined female role within the very male world of the police officer. The partial repositioning of the police role in this way did appear incredibly well timed given that 1975 saw the introduction of the Sex Discrimination Act (SDA), which, whilst paving the way for the modern female police officer, failed to fully impress upon individual forces the requirement of full 'gender-integration' (Silvestri, 2003, p. 47). The immediate response to the introduction of the legislation was a substantial increase in female applications to join the police, but those who were successful in their applications would continue to find that the female officer's role was defined within very narrow parameters. Heidensohn (1992) illustrates this with narratives taken from interviews with two female officers:

- 'from the training school, the atmosphere had been that you were second-class police because you were really just going to sit-around fiddling with children and young people';
- 'we dealt mainly with the aliens, missing persons, truants, child abuse, neglect'.

(Heidensohn, 1992, p. 120)

The separation of male and female officer roles is well documented within police literature (for example, by Smith and Gray, 1983; Brogden, Jefferson and Walklate, 1988; Graef, 1989; and Young, 1991), and this is reflected in a wider distinction between the genders in policing. One potential explanation for this is through the concept of 'hegemonic masculinity', which Fielding (1994, p. 47) draws upon to describe the ways in which masculinity is expressed within policing contexts, especially that of the canteen culture. His analysis suggests that 'hegemonic masculinity' is evidenced through cultural values of 'aggressive, physical action', 'competitiveness and preoccupation with the imagery of conflict', 'exaggerated heterosexual orientation' and 'rigid in-group/out-group distinctions' and that these combine to create a masculine cultural milieu that denigrates values and qualities associated with the female gender. More traditional literature has focused upon related areas such as police drinking and overstated heterosexuality. Research conducted amongst members of the London Metropolitan Police Force in the early 1980s highlighted the importance of alcohol to officers, noting that, for CID, drinking had become a central aspect of occupational life, whereas for the uniformed officers it was an integral part of their social lives (Smith and Gray, 1983). Alcoholism has been considered a persistent problem for police forces (Reiner, 2010) and can be considered a historical legacy from the days when it was accepted custom for publicans and public alike to give beer to their local bobby (Brogden, 1991). That alcohol featured prominently in the working lives of detectives was partly an artefact of the occupational requirement of detectives to become a part of the same world as their quarry. Whilst there remained some truth in the adage 'you don't meet crooks in church' (Punch, 2009, p. 43), alcohol presented a more symbolic purpose to Hobbs's East End detectives, for whom 'A sufficiently high regular intake of alcohol functions as an embalming fluid, preserving a deviant rebellious image of detective work' (1988, p. 196).

The prominence given to displays of overt heterosexualism by male officers within the police occupational culture, likewise, cannot be overstated. Substantial evidence exists to suggest that gendered power differentials are to some extent embedded within police agencies. For example, Smith and Gray (1983) described initiation rituals of 'stamping' female recruits' bare backsides with police station ink stamps, which, the authors suggested, carried three symbolic meanings: the treatment of females as objects; the humiliation of females; and symbolic sexual assault. This gendered duality is not a phenomenon restricted to interpersonal encounters between officers and appears at all levels of the organization. For instance, the denigration of female officers demonstrated by the *Police Review* (a British publication aimed at police officers) organizing a competition to discover 'The Prettiest Policewomen in the Land' (Young, 1991) finds parallels with Brown's (1997) description of her experiences of having to observe the Ms Hungarian Policewoman beauty competition at a conference in the mid-1990s. At a more routine level, Westmarland (2001) describes the sexualized banter that occurs between officers whilst in the detached environment of police vehicles and which, intriguingly, combines a physical appreciation of females with a measure of disdain. The heterosexuality of the police culture ensures that officers will profess to being attracted to female members of the public, but the division between police and public ensures that they will not be considered equals.

More seriously, research suggests that female members of the public may be at risk from the exaggerated heterosexuality of the police. In a widely cited piece of American research into police sexual violence, Kraska and Kappeler (1995) used federal litigation and media data to highlight 124 crimes (including 37 sexual assaults and rapes) committed by on-duty officers against female members of the public over a 14-year period. The authors use the findings of this piece of research to challenge existing discourses that frame police sexual violence within commonly used narratives. One such narrative sees innocent officers being 'corrupted' by females offering sex in exchange for clemency in consideration of minor misdemeanours that they have committed. Instead, Kraska and Kappeler advocate an understanding based on factors such as the structural position of the police, its inherent sexist culture and, perhaps most importantly, the pronounced disparity in power between male officers and female citizens. Some research suggests that these gender differentials also manifest themselves in more sympathetic treatment of females in custody. Women are, such research suggests, treated with more courtesy and are less prone to be physically assaulted than their male counterparts (Holdaway, 1983). For example, Skolnick (1994) explores how the ambiguities thrown up for police officers by the complexities of gender relations create considerable problems for male police officers. Females rarely belong to the cognitive category of 'symbolic assailants' (Skolnick, 1994), as they are unlikely in most cases to represent a threat. Instead, Holdaway (1983) presents women as 'disarmers', a symbolic category defined by their publicly perceived vulnerability and one which is incongruous with the status of offender.

The cognitive dissonance that appears to emerge when male officers encounter female offenders seems to highlight further essentialist stereotyping within the masculinist culture. Women are readily placed into objectified and dichotomized categories such as 'wife/whore' (Heidensohn, 1985; Brogden, Jefferson and Walklate, 1988; Brogden, 1991) and 'rough/respectable' (Cain, 1973), a restricted array of roles that has little relevance to the reality of female experience. Extracts from interviews with female officers evidence the simplistic ways in which they are perceived by their male colleagues:

- 'If you say anything, it's "Oh, how about more Women's Lib?" There is no consistency. One minute you're holding the baby and the next you're a "Women's Libber"' (Graef, 1989, p. 202).
- 'When I joined, you were either a nymphomaniac or a dyke, you couldn't be normal' (Loader and Mulcahy, 2003, p. 215).

The masculine orientation of the police culture, therefore, has far-reaching consequences in terms of how it shapes the ways in which male police officers relate to female members of the public, female colleagues and gendered crimes. At its most extreme, the 'organizational, structural and cultural environment' (Kraska and Kappeler, 1995, p. 97) of the police both legitimizes and facilitates acts of sexual violence against female members of the public. Furthermore, legislation can be viewed as supporting sexist cultural police practices. Skolnick describes how the police officers that he studied operated under a formal order entitled the 'Venereal Disease Quarantine Procedure' that empowered officers to quarantine prostitutes, those associated with brothels and anyone engaging in a 'lewd or lascivious' (1994, p. 105) manner. Furthermore, in the jurisdiction where he undertook his research, the district attorney's office introduced a policy recommending that *every* woman arrested for prostitution offences should undergo medical tests for venereal disease and, consequently, could be quarantined for up to eight days in the local jail. In practice, holding rates varied greatly, with most officers complying with the requirement only in around 25 per cent of cases, although one officer in Skolnick's sample quarantined in 48 per cent of arrests. In England and Wales, similar powers were available under the Contagious Diseases Acts of 1864, 1866 and 1869 (Brogden, Jefferson and Walklate, 1988; Emsley, 1991; Rawlings, 2002) to protect unsuspecting men from contracting sexually transmitted diseases by subjecting women to physical examination by medical staff. Both the legislation and its implementation have been criticized on a number of grounds. First, the legislation can be considered sexist and encouraging of stereotypical views of women (Brogden, Jefferson and Walklate, 1988). Second, the problematic relationship between prostitutes, as low-level but permanent suspects, and the law means that police discretion will lead to differentiations of enforcement and therefore to uneven police intervention (Brogden, Jefferson and Walklate, 1988). Third, the use of these degrading powers against working-class women (many of whom were not prostitutes) was considered an arbitrary application of powers designed to humiliate on the whim of an officer's suspicion (Emsley, 1991). Finally, accusations began to surface that officers were waiving their powers in return for payment from prostitutes.

The historical treatment of female members of the public may be considered to provide a partial explanation of more contemporary expressions of the gendering of the police occupational culture, especially in the case of female victimization. A fundamental stereotypical classification within the police officer's 'working personality' is that of the 'woman as the victim', and this tends to reinforce outdated perceptions of the female gender. Interestingly, MacAlister (2004) draws on research to suggest that the victim status accorded to women is dependent, to a degree, upon the type of crime that they have experienced. In other words, some victims were more likely to be accorded legitimate victim status than others. Whilst elderly female victims of crime would generally be met with unconditional sympathy, younger females of criminal offences would not, especially when the offence was either domestic or sexual in nature. Brogden (1991), in his account of policing Liverpool in the inter-war years, describes how domestic issues were regarded by communities as beyond the scope of the police and that intervention in such cases usually ended in action being taken against officers. The net effect of police non-intervention in such cases was to privilege the male over the female. Similarly, early work in the area of police occupational culture tended to focus on the impact of sexist attitudes upon police responses to allegations of sexual crime. In particular, ideas of victim precipitation and contributory negligence meant that female victims of sexual crime were often treated inappropriately. For example, descriptions presented by Smith and Gray (1983) indicate that some male officers investigating sexual offences with female victims implied that victims provoked or even enjoyed their experiences. These findings appear to have a degree of geographical universality about them, with work by Jordan (2001) in New Zealand and Temkin (1997) in Great Britain highlighting rape victims' negative perception of police responses. In the most extreme cases, Jordan (2001) likens the reporting process to a secondary victimization, intensified by a general reluctance amongst police officers to grant a sympathetic hearing except in cases of stranger rape and where physical injuries were also presented. To Smith and Gray this exposure of police officers to female victims leads to a 'devaluing of qualities associated with women' (1983, p. 91).

Within an organizational context, sexism has also both restricted the entrance of females into the force and had implications for their future careers. Prejudice against female police officers by their male colleagues traditionally centred upon the idea that female officers are of inadequate physical stature for the types of work undertaken by the police. The female officers whom Smith and Gray (1983) interviewed claimed that male officers were prejudiced against them mainly on the grounds of physical strength and their doubts that females were sufficiently physically equipped to undertake police work efficiently. Those female officers who do exhibit physical strength risk contradicting culturally ascribed ideas concerning appropriate female behaviour, and those who do not risk reinforcing those cultural stereotypes (Bryant, Dunkerley and Kelland, 1985). Surrounded by such an omnipresent male culture, female officers often have to struggle to become accepted as 'real' officers, and those who do succeed will do so only partially and at the cost of their femininity (Young, 1991).

Gender differences appear to underscore various facets of the working life of female officers, and many of these relate to an exaggerated concern over sexuality by male officers. Graef's fascinating collection of police narratives provides a rare insight into the experiences of female police officers in which all policewomen are 'plonks' (derogatory British police term for female officers), those who engage in sexual relations with male colleagues are 'relief bicycles' and those who do not are 'lesbos' (Graef, 1989). Herein lies one of the contradictions of police work, that whilst male police officers draw out and reinforce simplistic depictions of human sexual relations through talk with other males, they remain uncomfortable dealing with the reality of gendered crimes (Westmarland, 2001) a factor that has ensured historically that female officers have found it difficult to gain attachments to detective units, where, it is claimed, masculine attitudes are at their most prevalent. The apparently deep-rooted antipathy to female officers within the male culture is a result of the threat that they pose to the informal and male-based working rules of the occupation and therefore to the existing 'police myth' (Hunt, 1984).

The literature of gender and policing outlines common concerns amongst female officers regarding harassment, role differentiation and restricted promotion prospects. In part, it was assumed that the Sex Discrimination Act of 1975 would succeed in ending inequality and promoting less discriminatory attitudes towards female officers, although it had little immediate effect upon the reservations held by police staff associations, the Police Federation and Her Majesty's Inspectorate of Constabulary (Brown, 2000). In terms of exploring the views of female officers following the introduction of the Sexual Discrimination Act, the work of Holdaway and Parker (1998) is important, as it explores female experiences of police work in an era when discrimination on grounds of gender had been made illegal. Crucially, their research depicts a correlation between the rigid gender expectations held of female officers and their subsequent experiences within the police organization and, in doing so, highlights gender-based marginalization. One of the primary findings of this piece of work was an apparent division of police labour drawn on grounds of gender. Female officers who took part in the research were less likely than their male colleagues to state that they were working in their preferred role. Furthermore, many reported feelings of frustration at the narrow range of crime work that they were assigned, focusing as it did on victim work (predominantly with victims of sexual and/or violent crime), non-adults and domestic disputes. Fundamental to these perceived issues is the role of supervising officers who assign tasks to specific officers and whose decisions led to female officers taking on different roles, experiencing excessive constraints on their work and being allocated to less hazardous beats. Nonetheless, it appears that one area of policing where female officers experienced less restriction was in attending training courses, with 48 per cent of female respondents attending equal opportunities training in comparison to only 17 per cent of males. This apparently rigid division of occupational opportunity represents to Holdaway and Parker the active prevention of female officers from accessing, and taking part in, the dominant culture of their workplace.

In no part of the police force were these divisions so pronounced as amongst detectives in the CID. Holdaway and Parker (1998) found that female officers represented only 7.5 per cent of CID staff despite more female than male officers expressing an interest in transferring to a post there. One reason given for the restricted female representation in detective work was that their previous experiences of police work would have not contained sufficient crime work. One area where criminal investigation work was undertaken by females was within sexual offence and child abuse units, although these units remained separate from CID, their staff were not accorded detective status and their work was not formally recognized as appropriate experience for a future CID role. For those females who did transfer to CID, the unit represented a very different cultural experience from that of their uniformed work and one that was not wholly appreciated by all male or female officers. The detective culture appeared more prone to gender-based cultural division than the uniform culture, and women in CID reported that they were less likely to feel accepted by their colleagues, less likely to be fairly appraised by their supervisors and more likely to witness sexual harassment. The fairness of selection procedures for CID roles was also questioned by officers of both sexes, although significantly more so by females.

The marginal position of female officers in the police institution meant that they felt less able to question their work assignments, experienced pressure to perform their work to a higher standard than their male colleagues and received less encouragement from line managers, prompting the researchers to note the vastly diverse occupational worlds of male and female police officers. One partial explanation for the division of the police world in such ways was the perceived influence of external factors (for example, domestic responsibilities) that was seen to impact on female officers' commitment to the institution and, simultaneously, to reinforce male attitudes regarding essentially 'female' qualities. The experience of gender also appeared to play a significant role on female officers' perceptions of the promotion process. Female officers' understandable concerns regarding combining their police role with other roles (most notably as mothers) were reflected in male prejudices, leading to substantially more female than male officers suggesting that there existed potential for conflict between their work and home lives, despite the fact that a greater proportion of the male sample were parents than the female. A significant finding of the research was that the fundamental and gender-driven divisions within the police force being investigated were largely caused by widespread beliefs that female police careers were different to male police careers. Underpinning this was the widely held assumption, identified by Holdaway and Parker (1998), that female officers would eventually leave the force to marry and start a family, making the organization more likely to choose to invest in a male officer's career than a female's.

Brown (1997), in her comparative review of policewomen in Europe, notes that a number of common stages of female integration can be identified between national jurisdictions. The introduction of female officers to police forces is often realized after much pressure and only then in respect to staffing shortfalls caused by state crisis or catastrophe. Opposition from male officers continues even in the face of legislative developments introduced to facilitate female integration and is supported by discourses that play on a perceived mismatch between the masculine values of policing and the physical and dispositional characteristics of females. Having gained integration, female officers will commonly undertake 'housekeeping' roles (Brown, 1997, p. 13) such as administrative support or, when used operationally, work with females and juveniles. One area of difference, however, between jurisdictions has been the rate at which female police work develops from an administrative to an operational role, with Brown noting a more restricted administrative role in French and some Eastern European police forces. Despite the progression of females within police forces that has been realized over recent decades, Brown (1997, p. 15) concludes that they still represent a 'marginalized minority', an assertion that echoes Heidensohn's (1992) view that full cultural membership of the police is denied to females.

Police culture and race

> Bobby Hall apparently was considered a somewhat 'uppity' Negro. Evidence produced at the trial indicated that the tire theft charge was a sham for, as suggested in the Willingham testimony, Hall's major crime was to challenge the power of the sheriff to confiscate his pistol.
>
> (United States Commission on Civil Rights, 1961, p. 8)

Discrimination against members of ethnic minority groups has become a recurrent theme within the literature of police culture. Police research has consistently found evidence of police discrimination against ethnic minorities (Smith and Gray, 1983; Skolnick, 1994) and for it to be remarkably consistent over time in both the United States and the United Kingdom (Brogden, Jefferson and Walklate, 1988). Like discrimination on the grounds of gender, racial discrimination impacts on both the external and internal relations of police forces in that it is seen as a driver for discriminatory behaviour against both members of the public and those members of ethnic minorities who join the institution. Traditionally, police racial discrimination against ethnic minority communities has focused on two primary questions. First, do members of ethnic minorities receive the same quality of police service as other sections of the public? Second, do the police actively target certain ethnic groups whilst undertaking operational police work (a process that earned the politicized epithet of 'nigger hunting' in the work of Joe Hunte, 1966)?

Before exploring the intricate issues that surround these two factors, it is necessary to explore the historical precedents of police relations with minority groups. Whilst Loader and Mulcahy (2003) are correct to assert that the orientation of the police to issues of ethnicity only came to the fore in the 1960s, it would be unwise to assume that prior to this period the police had not differentiated between national and ethnic groups. For example, Emsley (1996) describes how the Victorian era saw a recasting of the Irish as criminal in view of what was seen as their propensity for use of violence amongst themselves and against police officers (see also Cain, 1973, and Brogden, 1982). Similarly, police oral histories also present evidence of tension between the police and members of London's Irish communities. One officer, serving during the 1950s, claimed:

> We had Cricklewood with a large Irish population as part of our territory so we used to have regular fights over there. There used to be a pub on Cricklewood Broadway . . . I think it was the Crown . . . and they actually had a police box at the end of their forecourt and the favourite game on a Friday and Saturday for the Irish guys was to pick up the phone in the police box and say they were just being assaulted by 20 people and could we come and help. Basically, when we got there in the cars and the van and whatever we'd find them all out on the forecourt applauding . . . so we could never give that a miss so we'd get out of the van and give 'em a thump anyway. So, I mean we had that kind of fun.
>
> (Cockcroft, 2001, p. 121)

Similarly, Jewish communities, whilst shedding a 'criminal' reputation applied during Georgian times, still represented a culturally alien environment to most police officers, prompting them to distrust those who lived in such communities (Emsley, 1996). To the Liverpool police of the 1920s the black population and their mixed-race children were seen as particular problems (Brogden, 1982). These examples provide some evidence to suggest that police racial discrimination has been, if not a historical constant, then a recurrent issue within the history of policing in England and Wales. The work of Banton (1964) highlights, within the southern United States, a tendency for police officers to fail to emotionally engage with the lives of African-Americans, showing, for example, how white officers may fail to express the same compassion to African-American victims of domestic violence as to white victims. A similar reluctance has been highlighted by research into British police officers (Smith and Gray, 1983), many of whom were reluctant to investigate incidents involving Asian members of the public or which were thought to be racially motivated. Similarly, Cain (1973) shows how police officers were more likely to give freely of their time to higher-status members of the public by contrasting the assistance given to an American Air Force officer in locating a party venue whilst failing to advise a homeless ethnic minority male on the availability of accommodation.

Foster (1989) identifies two separate types of police racism, one in which officer prejudices do not impact on the way they relate to colleagues and citizens from ethnic minority backgrounds, and the other in which they do. Indeed, she shows how officers who privately recognize their own racial prejudices will often deal with members of ethnic minority groups in an appropriate and professional manner. This particular form of racism has not always been viewed as constituting a significant operational issue in that it will not impact on police interactions with members of ethnic minority populations, although may be likely to impact on relationships with colleagues from ethnic minority backgrounds. Furthermore, Skolnick (1994) notes that officers in the United States became gradually aware of the political power of ethnic minority groups in the wake of the civil rights movement and accordingly became less inclined to act inappropriately against members of minority groups. The second type of racism that Foster's work identified (where officers' practice is influenced by their prejudiced views) has been seen as a culturally embedded problem within police forces on either side of the Atlantic for several decades.

Much research has consequently highlighted an essentially negative set of police assumptions about ethnic minority groups, in the United Kingdom in regard to individuals of West Indian descent and, in the United States, towards African-Americans. This is not to suggest that members of these groups are the only ones to perceive police biases against them, but that the majority of research has focused on the experiences of these two main groups. One of the first pieces of police research to address this phenomenon was Westley's paper 'Violence and the police'. In it, he describes how police officers assume that African-Americans and those who live in low-rent neighbourhoods do not respond to civilized treatment and quotes an officer who states that:

> The colored people understand one thing. The policeman is the law, and he is going to treat you rough and that's the way you have to treat them. Personally, I don't think the colored are trying to help themselves one bit. If you don't treat them rough, they will sit right on top of your head.
>
> (1953, p. 40)

Similar examples of police racism were presented in the Justice Report of the United States Commission on Civil Rights (1961). It found that African-Americans were more likely than any other group in American society to experience police brutality. In the two-and-a-half-year period leading up to June 1960, 35 per cent of allegations of police violence were made by African-Americans, who, as a group, represented only 10 per cent of the population. Moreover, two-thirds of allegations originated in the southern states and the District of Columbia. This publication presents an uncomfortable account of both the intensity and the extent of police brutality in the United States during the twentieth century, detailing as it does cases involving the deaths of civilians and even serious assaults upon black police officers by white colleagues.

In the United Kingdom, similar evidence emerged throughout the latter part of the twentieth century, although Whitfield (2004) notes how, originally, police responses to large-scale immigration centred on issues not of crime but of morality. Interracial sexual relationships were viewed by the public at large (and the police) as a threat to traditional ways of life and were connected to fears over the exploitation of white women by immigrant males. Such perceptions have been commonly held since the 1950s and further reinforced by public comments made by senior officers within the larger city forces, such as those made by Superintendent John Ellis in 1987, inferring widespread West Indian involvement in drugs and prostitution in the Chapeltown area of Leeds (Farrell, 1993). Popular fears of links between West Indian communities and vice appear to have been overplayed, however, with Metropolitan Police figures appearing to show that, in London, West Indians were one of several racial groups involved in such crimes and that their involvement varied considerably (Whitfield, 2004).

Over time, police relations with the West Indian communities in the United Kingdom appeared to deteriorate and, by the 1970s and 1980s, young black males were seen as violent, lazy, difficult and anti-police (Smith and Gray, 1983; Graef, 1989). Routine tension between police and young black males was punctuated by tragedies such as the death of David Oluwale, a homeless Nigerian man, in Leeds in 1971. Oluwale, after being beaten by and then urinated upon by two police officers, was chased into a river, where he drowned, the officers being subsequently convicted of assault rather than the manslaughter with which they were originally charged. Likewise, the Institute of Race Relations (cited in Bowling and Phillips, 2003) revealed that 16 black people had died in the United Kingdom over the 22-year period to 1991 through police use of force or inadequate care. Such events took place against a cultural backdrop in which racial prejudice and discriminatory language were apparently seen by many in the police as acceptable. In the aftermath of the Deptford fire that killed 13 young black people in London, a researcher working on the Policy Studies Institute study into police and public relations was asked by a police officer, 'How many of these niggers actually fried in this barbecue at Deptford, then?' (Smith and Gray, 1983, p. 116). Similarly, even those officers tasked with liaising with West Indian communities did not always opt to use appropriate language, as was shown at the Police Federation Conference of 1984 when Inspector Peter Johnson, who had previously served on the National Police Training Council and the Home Office Working Party on Race Relations, referred to 'our coloured brethren or nig nogs' (Brogden, Jefferson and Walklate, 1988, p. 126; Farrell, 1993, p. 114).

Racial prejudices held by police officers are mirrored, to some extent, by negative perceptions of the police amongst members of ethnic minority communities, and Crank (1998) suggests that the mutual distrust between the two groups can partly be explained through routine police work representing a self-fulfilling prophecy for police biases. Research from both the UK and the USA does show that negativity towards the police is experienced differentially within and between ethnic minority groups (Smith and Gray, 1983; Reiner, 1985). For example, distrust of the police is greatest amongst marginalized young black males and occurs to a lesser extent amongst Asians (Smith and Gray, 1983). What was less clear during the 1970s and 1980s in the UK was the extent to which this distrust was shaped by interaction with the police or by ideological opposition to the police at a more symbolic level.

Evidence from both sides of the Atlantic does appear to suggest that the differential application of police powers to individuals of different racial groups has traditionally played a large part in explaining resentment of the police amongst ethnic minorities. Racial profiling has been a constant theme in police literature for almost 50 years and continues to be presented as evidence of prejudicial police behaviour. A somewhat ironic example, presented by Reiner (2010), describes how Professor Henry Louis Gates of Harvard University, and credited with being the first to identify the unwritten law of 'D.W.B. Driving While Black', was arrested in 2009 for breaking and entering his own house. Generally, however, American and British research appears to indicate that young marginalized ethnic minority males are stopped more frequently than other racial groups (Smith and Gray, 1983; Reiner, 1985). There is much evidence to support the view that police officers stop a disproportionate amount of young and male Afro-Caribbeans. Smith and Gray interviewed one Metropolitan Police constable who, when asked what criteria he used to make a stop, replied, 'How does an experienced policeman decide who to stop? Well, the one that you stop is often wearing a wooly [*sic*] hat . . . is dark in complexion . . . has thick lips he usually has dark, fuzzy, hair.' Another police constable is quoted as saying, 'If I saw a black man walking through Wimbledon High Street I would definitely stop him' (Smith and Gray, 1983, pp. 129–130).

Racially disproportionate stop and search statistics may be explained, in part, in terms of the presumed criminality of ethnic minorities. Ethnic minorities were 'by definition' considered suspicious (Cain, 1973, p. 118), a point which Crank (1998, p. 206) expanded upon by suggesting that police held 'cognitive predispositions' that equate particular crimes with particular ethnic groups. These differences may also be explained more subtly in the way that they reflect the different orientations of particular police departments. For example, Wilson (1968), in his study of differing organizational styles of policing in the United States, found that police departments run in a legalistic style, with law enforcement as a priority, tended to arrest significantly fewer members of ethnic minority groups for disorder offences than those operating under watchman styles where order maintenance took precedence. Interestingly, officers operating under the latter style considered African-Americans as lacking sufficient family and community controls and therefore used legislation intended to counter intoxication or disorderly conduct to control these sections of the community.

In the United Kingdom, probably the most visual manifestations of the problematic relations between the police and ethnic minority populations have been the widespread civil disturbances witnessed in towns and cities throughout 1980 and 1981, in Birmingham and Tottenham in 1985, in Bradford in 1995 and throughout northern towns in 2001. Those that occurred within the 1980s have attracted significant academic analysis and a government inquiry led by Lord Scarman. The catalyst for the Brixton riots of April 1981 was the Metropolitan Police's 'Operation Swamp 81', a saturation policing exercise that saw 120 officers (both uniform and plain-clothes) tasked with using 'sus' laws to stop and question 'suspicious'-looking members of the public. Of 943 people stopped during the four days that the operation ran, 118 were arrested and 75 charged. Over half of those stopped were black (Bowling and Phillips, 2003). Research continues to suggest that there is scant evidence that stop and search has had a substantial impact on criminal behaviour, and it is seen as leading to reduced confidence in the police, especially when used disproportionately amongst minority groups (Quinton,

Bland and Miller, 2000). Whilst Scarman's report into the Brixton riots suggested that the implementation of 'Operation Swamp 81' led to a 'crisis of confidence' (Scarman, 1982, p. 196) between the police and members of the local West Indian community, the ongoing symbolic policing presence in black people's lives also played a considerable role (Reiner, 1985).

Many within English police forces had been reluctant to accept the charges of racial prejudice aimed at both the police as an institution and the individuals who worked for it, and this was reflected in the mood of the Police Federation. The chairman of the Metropolitan Federation at that time, John Newman, reputedly told the then Home Secretary, Willie Whitelaw, in response to comments regarding the need for the police to respond to the needs of ethnic minority communities, that 'The police officer sheltering behind a riot shield from a barrage of petrol bombs cannot be expected to exude love and harmony towards the ethnic minorities, if it is they who are throwing the bombs' (Judge, 1994, p. 378). Following the publication of the Scarman Report, the Police Federation formally welcomed the recommendation that the police should draw more officers from ethnic minority backgrounds (Judge, 1994). This suggests a change in direction from that reported by a former Home Office minister (cited in Loader and Mulcahy, 2003), who recalled a speech made by a former Home Secretary, Roy Jenkins, to a conference of the Metropolitan Police Federation. Within the speech, the suggestion that the police should be covered by the anti-discriminatory measures of race relations legislation was met with derision, prompting some members of the audience to walk out.

The years 1966 and 1967 saw the introduction of, respectively, the first Asian and the first black police officers in England, a progression that, whilst 'inimical to dominant conceptions of the "English Bobby"' (Loader and Mulcahy, 2003, p. 218), was seen as a welcome step in improving relations between the police and ethnic minority groups (Rowe, 2004). One of the challenges regarding the timing of this move towards integration, according to a Police Federation representative quoted in Loader and Mulcahy (2003, p. 219), was not whether ethnic minority officers would be accepted at that time by liberal white communities, but whether they would be accepted on a Saturday night in Camden Town outside the Mother Redcap pub. The implication here is that ethnic minority police officers should be employed only when they can work in the same challenging environments as their white colleagues, and this, in many respects, echoes the problems faced by black police officers in the southern United States, who in some cases, traditionally, were not allowed to arrest white members of the public (Banton, 1964).

Policing literature from both the USA and the UK tends to acknowledge the political dimensions surrounding integration of ethnic minorities into police forces (Banton, 1964; Rowe, 2004), and the problems that this causes in respect of racial conflict within the institution (Crank, 1998). Indeed, one might argue that the potential benefits that have been experienced as a result of the introduction of ethnic minority officers have been partially negated by discrimination against those same officers. Banton (1964) describes how black officers in the United States were considered lazy, and oral historical evidence from England also tends to echo the experiences of women who joined the police force. For example, 'I had to be twice as good as my peers to be seen as being their equal, yet I had to do half a thing less than them to be sacked' (ethnic minority officer from Manchester, quoted in Loader and Mulcahy, 2003, p. 220). For many Afro-Caribbean or Asian officers, the issue of race appeared to be as divisive within the police station as it was in the communities that they policed and, by 1999, the Metropolitan Police in England were facing 31 unresolved cases of racial discrimination (Rowe, 2004). This issue is further confused, according to Rowe, by responses to remedy the lack of ethnic minorities serving at senior levels within the police service. These have, in the past, worked upon a deficit model that prescribes extra personal leadership training to resolve what are seen as individual as opposed to institutional failings in accounting for the lack of senior officers from ethnic minority backgrounds.

Much has been written about police racism and its possible link to police culture. However, conclusions are hard to draw because of the fact that police racism takes many forms and can be used to describe racist attitudes which are or are not acted upon, the way in which crimes are recorded and police attitudes to officers from ethnic backgrounds. Such a breadth of issues might mean that simple and succinct explanations are unlikely to adequately explain police racism, especially when police officers themselves often deny allegations of racial bias by claiming that they are merely telling the truth about race issues (Graef, 1989; Skolnick, 1994). In particular, there exist tensions between explanations that see police racism as an individual issue, an institutional issue or a societal issue. Individual explanations tend to view discriminatory attitudes amongst police officers as the result of individual predispositions towards prejudice and stereotyping. For those individuals who display attitudes associated with the psychological concept of the 'authoritarian personality', police work may appear an attractive occupational choice (Colman and Gorman, 1982; Skolnick, 1994), and this explanation appeared to find some favour with Lord Scarman in his report into the Brixton riots. For example, the report adopts a focus that emphasizes an individual as opposed to institutional understanding of police racism (Rowe, 2004), referring as it does to the 'ill-considered, immature and racially prejudiced actions' of younger officers (Scarman, 1982, p. 105).

Institutional explanations of police racism became more prevalent following the publication of the Macpherson Report in 1999, in which the Metropolitan Police were branded institutionally racist. Traditionally, however, the concept of institutional racism had lacked clarity, and Macpherson's report, unlike Scarman's, provided a clear and appropriate definition:

> The collective failure of an organisation to provide an appropriate and professional service to people because of their colour, culture, or ethnic origin. It can be seen or detected in processes, attitudes and behaviour which amount to discrimination through unwitting prejudice, ignorance, thoughtlessness and racist stereotyping which disadvantage minority ethnic people.
>
> (1999, p. 634)

This definition is significant for two main reasons in that it represents a shift away from individual explanations of racism and focuses on outcomes more than intent. Despite the concept attracting some criticism (Bowling and Phillips, 2003) for encouraging generalizations that all officers are racist and for failing to hold individuals to account, the labelling of the police as institutionally racist has facilitated a growth in anti-discriminatory policies. Sociological explanations propose that police racial prejudice may have origins in wider societal discrimination and have remained popular with a number of police scholars on both sides of the Atlantic (Reiner, 2010). Crank (1998), for example, draws on the work of Williams and Murphy (1990) to highlight the ways in which discrimination, segregation and slavery have historically exerted a detrimental influence over police relations with ethnic groups. In this respect the police represented 'a social and moral barometer of the society they inhabited' (Crank, 1998, p. 208), a sentiment previously voiced by Sir Robert Mark, the former commissioner of the Metropolitan Police. This point is further explored by Banton (1964) in relation to the experiences of African-Americans in the southern United States, who were expected to exhibit deference to white members of the public in terms of everyday social interaction yet were, theoretically, bound by the same rules as them. For many of the white members of the police and public alike, African-Americans were considered to have insufficient dignity to make arrest a shameful experience, and this might account for differences in levels of arrest between white and black members of the public. Police racism, therefore, mirrored the racism of the working and middle classes from which the police tended to recruit the majority of their officers (Reiner, 2010) and, accordingly, accounted for the relatively low levels of differentiation in levels of racial prejudice between members of the public and the police (Bayley and Mendelsohn, 1969; Skolnick, 1994). Despite this, racial discrimination by police officers has largely become viewed as a problem of police culture as opposed to wider culture.

Conservatism

> The police force is ultra right wing. No doubt about it. If you air a left-wing view you're called a lefty pinko faggot! There are a lot of closet lefties, though. There are also some PCs who are out-and-out Nazis.
>
> (Black London Metropolitan Police constable,
> quoted in Graef, 1989, p. 139)

Another major element of cop culture is that of conservatism (Farrell, 1993; Skolnick, 1994; Reiner, 2010), with Reiner claiming that the majority of police officers are conservative 'both politically and morally' (2010, p. 126). Skolnick (1994) during the course of his research came across only three police officers who considered themselves to be politically liberal, a predictable finding for an organization so deeply directed by '"honor related attitudes" of commitment, moral order and tradition' (Manning, 1977, p. 20).

Furthermore, conservative values based on small-town traditions are replicated within the police owing to the police service being a traditional vehicle through which the working classes can achieve middle-class status (Crank, 1998). The conservatism of the police, therefore, is the conservatism of those groups for whom police work remains an occupational choice, although we should resist the temptation to paint the conservative moral outlook of the police as being entirely unambiguous. Skolnick (2008), for example, suggests that the moral conservatism of the police is not so much founded upon 'apple-pie-and-motherhood values' but upon the subtle differences of 'dead wrong, wrong, but not bad, wrong but everybody does it' (Skolnick, 2008, p. 37).

Police conservatism may be influenced by several factors. Reiner (2010), for example, notes that public order policing has often revolved around labour disputes and union activity and that political policing is central to Brodeur's notion of 'high policing' (1983). Traditionally, police literature has highlighted an ingrained antagonism of police officers to the political left, whilst, in Britain at least, the early 1980s saw a Conservative law and order manifesto lead to the police becoming 'instrumentally and symbolically' (Loader and Mulcahy, 2003, p. 273) embedded in the political terrain. Any pre-existing police sympathy for the Conservative Party was magnified by the full implementation of the Edmund-Davies pay increase that the party had pledged to implement if successful in the 1979 General Election, resulting in police officers enjoying a substantial financial benefit. This, however, did cause problems for the police in subsequent industrial disputes, with the police facing accusations of being 'bought' by the government to break strikes (Judge, 1994).

Although twentieth-century history is littered with instances of the policing of left-wing demonstrations, it would not be prudent to assume that this automatically implies a police bias against the left wing. There were several disturbances caused between 1934 and 1940 when the British Union of Fascists (BUF) clashed with left-wing groups and where the police became involved, and Skidelsky (1975) claims that the police were impartial during such occasions and were supportive of neither the fascists nor the socialists but merely adopted a pragmatic pro-police stance. Contested accounts, however, do emerge, and Temple (1995), for example, argues that collusion between the BUF and the police did occur.

Whilst Reiner (2010) highlights the congruence between the structured and regimented world of police work and conservative values, some evidence suggests that CID work has traditionally been an exception, with Maguire and Norris highlighting the 'autonomy and discretion' (Maguire and Norris, 1994, p. 20) that necessarily characterizes detective work. In a fascinating overview of Sir Robert Mark's attempts to dismantle the CID, Hobbs (1988) shows how it was Mark's conservatism and adherence to tradition that made him so highly value uniform work and the preventative principle and to loathe the autonomy of the CID, which he famously denounced as 'the most routinely corrupt organization in London' (Mark, 1978, p. 138). For most officers, however, the authority upon which their role relies necessitates some wider belief in or attachment to the values underpinning the laws that they enforce. Skolnick (1994), for example, describes from his research the experiences of a young African-American who joined the police for political reasons from a background in civil rights advocacy and who was unable to overcome the disparity that became increasingly evident between his political views and his police role.

In England and Wales, the rigid political conservatism of the police may over recent years have shown signs of decreasing. The advent of the Sheehy Report of 1993, which recommended a major reorganization of police roles and pay, was the Conservative Party's attempt to modernize the police force in the wake of similar restructuring of other public sector professions. Resistance from the Police Federation (Morgan and Newburn, 1997) led to a warm welcome for the new shadow Home Secretary, Tony Blair, at the 1993 Police Federation Conference and was followed by 23,000 officers attending an open meeting at Wembley Arena in London. Whilst Sheehy's recommendations were not all introduced, in retrospect they signalled an end to the special status that the police had previously enjoyed (Loader and Mulcahy, 2003). Similarly, evidence suggests that police officers in England and Wales have, from the mid-1990s onwards, been less likely to support the Conservative Party, owing not only to dissatisfaction with the continued drive towards managerialism but also, in part, to dissatisfaction with right-wing analyses of social problems (Reiner, 2010).

Conclusion

Whenever one presents the manifestations of police culture, especially those as described by traditional or classic writers, one becomes wary of being seen to associate a series of essentially negative attributes with the culture of the police. In part this reflects the 'reformist' sociological orientation of much of the work into police culture, and neglects some of the research undertaken into police culture from those undertaking organizational research. This distinction is an important one in that much of the research undertaken by scholars of organizations (rather than criminologists and sociologists) highlights the positive role played by organizational cultures in sustaining efficiency. At the same time, the fundamentally politicized background that has provided the backdrop to much police culture research has tended to produce accounts of police culture that, whilst developing our understanding of the police, have failed to truly reflect the complexity of policing. To writers of early accounts, little attempt was made to differentiate between the assorted manifestations of police culture that were highlighted. In other words, there remained a blanket assumption that officers were subjected to negative cultural values and would succumb to them. Under such models, one can be forgiven for interpreting culture as a blunt instrument through which attitudinal and behavioural control is implemented uniformly and without exception on those individuals who choose to join the police. More contemporary accounts of police culture have tended to portray culture in more problematic terms, and these criticisms of traditional accounts will be covered in the following chapter.

4 Police culture(s)
Explaining variation

Introduction

As shown in the previous chapter, early research into police occupational culture largely downplayed the scope for variation in police behaviour and orientation at either the individual or the institutional level. Accordingly, police culture was generally taken to refer to a standardized set of cultural values and behaviours, and these were portrayed as being universally internalized by police officers. Despite reassurances from some commentators that police culture should not be viewed as 'monolithic, universal, nor unchanging' (Reiner, 2010, p. 132), it is fair to say police culture has been represented in a rather limited and inflexible way, owing to what Sklansky views as 'cognitive burn-in' (2007, p. 20). In other words, just as the culture of the police is seen as encouraging a rigidified and narrow interpretation of the social world within which police officers exist, so our ideas about how this process works are similarly grounded in assumption. A general trend within the police culture literature of recent years has been an acknowledgement of the worth of approaches that highlight greater degrees of cultural variation and is, in part, prompted by the evident limitations of earlier research and the increasing complexity of both policing and the societies within which it takes place. Accordingly, this chapter will highlight recent changes to the context of police work and the impact of these upon the police at a cultural level.

Variation and the world of the police officer

Whilst early research into police culture is often portrayed as misrepresenting the fluidity and variation of both police behaviours and culture, some literature had hinted at a level of complexity yet to be widely recognized. Whilst, in part, this might be a result of society resembling an 'unmanageable social domain' (Manning, 1978a, p. 8), Manning continues by highlighting the importance of organizational factors:

> An individual's 'organizational' behavior varies with what the organization is said to require or permit, with his particular place in the organizational

hierarchy, and with the degree of congruence between the individual's personal definition of the role and the organization's definition of his role.

(1978a, p. 9)

Similarly, Fielding, addressing this issue from a UK perspective, wrote that 'Of course "the" occupational culture is actually many subcultures; nuances and colourations arise from regional differences, differences of ambition, divergent perceptions of the police mission, varying experiences of the organization, and so on' (1988, p. 157). Manning (1978a) continues by postulating that a number of assumptions can be derived from the core values of the police occupational culture and that these relate to a number of issues, including the danger that the public represent, the importance of 'experience' and 'respect' to police officers and the nature of crime and criminals. Importantly, these core assumptions regarding the relationship between police and the wider world apply principally to lower-ranking officers without a college education and exclude ethnic minority officers and those working in rural areas or administrative roles. Further differences regarding the style that officers adopt have been highlighted, amongst others, by Reiner (2010), who shows how academic work has highlighted four distinct officer approaches or orientations to police work (which correspond to Reiner's categories of 'bobby', 'new centurion', 'professional' and 'uniform carrier'). Likewise, distinctions exist between officers in managerial and lower-status roles (see, for example, Reuss-Ianni and Ianni, 1983). These cultural discrepancies are typically exposed when police officers become promoted to the senior ranks and, thereby, are drawn into a more formal ideology of policing more closely equated with the values of society and more removed from the 'dirty work' which, for lower-status officers, represents police work. Moreover, the existence of such cultural factions may undermine the perceived solidarity of the police, which, when subjected to scrutiny, often appears more intense from outside the police force than from within it.

Perhaps the most widely cited piece of traditional or classic literature that highlights the variations endemic to police practice comes from Wilson's (1968) research into the administration of law enforcement in eight American communities. In particular, his work focused upon the ways in which patrol officers exercised their order maintenance and law enforcement functions and the ways in which organizational orientations and legal limitations impacted upon these. His work has undoubtedly provided a foundation for later studies that emphasize variation within policing at a behavioural, if not a cultural, level, and from his research he concluded that three distinct institutional approaches or styles to the administration of the police role could be identified. The first was the 'watchman' style, which was founded above all else on order maintenance. Whilst order maintenance is prioritized in most communities, temporarily, under certain conditions, the 'watchman' type represents a style of policing in which order maintenance has become the core operational value of the department. Under the 'watchman' model, minor violations of the criminal law, such as the 'victimless' crimes of vice and gambling, were generally tolerated, owing to them taking place amongst a diverse population that failed to achieve a consensus view on acceptable standards of public order and moral behaviour. Juveniles were expected to engage in low-level criminal behaviour and so were dealt with informally. Similarly, African-Americans were 'thought to want, and to deserve, less law enforcement' (1968, p. 141). Crime attracted formal intervention only when it reached a particular threshold of seriousness or when behaviour fell beyond the wide-ranging limits of what was considered appropriate or, more importantly, acceptable. In most cases, the criteria for formal intervention were dependent not so much on the legality or otherwise of the displayed behaviour but on the reactions of the particular community that it occurred within and the perceived consequences of the act. This style of policing reflects a traditional American approach that resists a relentless enforcement of the law and was to be found in diverse communities characterized by diverging views of acceptable standards of behaviour. Whilst formal intervention was generally resisted, laws against disorderly conduct and public intoxication were used regularly, as they represented a powerful yet 'low-risk' tool with which to reacquaint the public with the local limits of tolerance. Offenders were unlikely to dispute or resist such charges, as they constituted a low-level punishment with little associated stigmatization and were, unlike most minor offences, unlikely to look bad on a police officer's record.

The 'legalistic' style, however, represented an approach that reduced opportunities for officers to use discretion by advocating a law enforcement focus and was identified in areas characterized by high arrest rates and high ticketing rates for motoring offences. In direct contrast to the 'watchman' style, the 'legalistic' adopts a universally applied threshold for acceptable public standards, and the law is, as far as possible, universally and evenly applied to all. Officers adopt formal and 'institutionalized' approaches in their dealings with members of the public and, whilst specific groups might perceive that they experience inappropriately high levels of police attention, evidence generally suggests that officers in fact act fairly. Where choices arise regarding disposals for certain crimes, officers are actively encouraged to opt for the more formal, and Wilson describes how the police persuaded those retail businesses that apprehended shoplifters to seek prosecution rather than to accept restitution. Whilst Wilson acknowledges that police officers, when uninstructed, appear to veer towards under-enforcement, administrators saw a number of advantages associated with this approach. In a world where 'police chiefs are broken by scandal, not crime' (Wilson, 1968, p. 181), the 'legalistic' approach offers administrators the opportunity to defend themselves from allegations of corrupt behaviour (which are associated with excessively high levels of discretionary police practice) whilst simultaneously evidencing effectiveness in the enforcement aspects of their role.

The final style of policing outlined by Wilson was that of 'service' and incorporated elements of both the 'watchman' and 'legalistic' models by responding to both order maintenance and law enforcement requests. Under the 'service' style, interventions, whilst frequent, were generally informal and were made possible by the values of the community being policed and the orientation of the police administration. The communities where this style of policing tended to become established were middle-class and displayed a consensus on the dimensions that public order should take. Accordingly, the local police administrators did not demand officers to focus exclusively on law enforcement. The lack of division along lines of class and race allowed officers to concentrate on service provision, traffic management and dealing with juveniles and 'outsiders'. For those issues that required a law enforcement response, specialized units were developed, leaving 'regular' police officers free to fulfil the needs of the community by overlooking minor misdemeanours, keeping 'undesirables' at bay and generally maintaining order. In deference to community wishes, almost 40 per cent of police personnel were employed on foot patrol, and rigorously high standards of moral behaviour were expected by police officers whilst on duty and in their private lives. As with the work of Banton (1964), Wilson describes, under the 'service' style, the ways in which police officers fail to rigidly enforce speed limits if they perceive that the public find them 'unreasonable'. For example, following a collision on one stretch of road in the area being researched, Wilson reports that the speed limit was reduced from 50 mph to 35 mph, yet officers intervened only with those driving in excess of 50 mph. The 'service' style, therefore, represents a philosophy of policing based on satisfying the requirements of communities with well-defined notions of acceptable and unacceptable behaviour. The focus on public satisfaction ensures that police departments in these areas employ individuals whom they view as less likely to generate public complaints of 'discourtesy or inattention to duty' (Wilson, 1968, p. 208).

These varying styles of departmental administration are to be considered of some importance to our understanding of police culture, as they highlight the potential for police behaviour to be shaped by the convergence of community values and expectation and police management orientation. To what extent this represents a moulding of the culture, however, is debatable. For example, the strict discipline that is brought to bear on officers operating under a 'service' style does lead to resentment amongst officers. Wilson charts, for example, the perception of severity and unfairness felt by some officers under 'service' models, with one member of his interview sample complaining that he would welcome the same rights as criminals in regard to the departmental discipline which he was subjected to. Whilst officers might toe the line, they might not always agree with it. Perhaps more importantly, however, the different orientations of 'watchman', 'legalistic' and 'service' styles of police departments represent very different styles of political influence. As Wilson (1968, p. 228) shows, in spite of this local politics generally intersect with policing only in a 'particularistic' way. That is, rather than suggest the general direction of police strategy, political influence will be felt in regard to specific issues, most notably gambling, street crime and public complaints. The police, therefore, whilst not universally influenced by community pressures, may feel the impact of some in regard to particular issues. They therefore tend to frame the politicization of local issues as attempts by non-police groups to seize control of the police agenda. In short, therefore, styles of policing emerge as a response to local political structure and orientation. The 'watchman' style tended to occur in those areas characterized by local political arrangements that prioritized a low level of public service, low local taxation and a moderate level of order maintenance. Politics spilled over into law enforcement in several respects. The public were to be policed in a laissez-faire style unless their behaviour impacted on the quality of life of others. Police officers' appointments and promotions were matters for local political elites, and locally owned vice enterprises, for example, were allowed to prosper as long as they remained low-level and unobtrusive to those who might find them distasteful. In part, local police officers were happy to turn a blind eye to certain criminal acts, as crime rates were generally not high and political pressure for low taxes ensured that police officers and police forces alike resisted the lure of 'professionalism'.

Police departments operating under the 'legalistic' style in Wilson's study managed, in many respects, to avoid the problems associated with navigating the external demands brought to bear by politicians, pressure groups and the wider community. This was largely achieved by the adoption of a 'professional' orientation. This professionalism was evident in a law enforcement focus that appeared agreeable to the public, with many applauding the efficient, if slightly rigid, application of the law. However, the focus on professionalism, whilst negating external pressures, could exacerbate internal tensions between administrators and officers through reliance upon overtly bureaucratic systems. These systems tended to alienate police officers through overzealous disciplinary procedures and unfair promotion mechanisms and could result in extremely low morale amongst officers, thus indicating that the removal of political influence comes to some forces at a substantial price.

In the 'service'-styled departments, politics played a much more limited role in comparison to 'watchman'-based areas. Whilst the appointment of police chiefs was inevitably a political intervention, other examples of such interference were largely noticeable by their absence. For these smaller, more affluent and more socially cohesive communities the requirements of the community were substantially less ambiguous than those of other more divided communities. Similarly, the deference that the police showed to the local community led to a proactive style of police work that attempted to foresee and pre-empt potential problems before they became major issues. The hiving off of crime functions to specialized units allowed officers generally to adopt a service role that helped ensure that divisions between police and public did not arise. Interestingly, politics appears not to have played much of an explicit role in police–public relations in 'service'-style departments, for the reason that officers tended to live in the communities and assimilate with the dominant social values. In one of the areas run in the 'service' style studied by Wilson he noted that officers and residents alike shared common political affiliations and that this probably leads to political issues failing to cause substantive problems for the police institution. Integral to this approach is a focus upon 'community relations', but through a lens that places the onus upon the police to evidence their responsiveness to the service rather than crime-related demands of the local population.

By providing an overview of the ways in which local politics and administrative orientations provide a steer on the occupational values and actions of police officers, Wilson's work provided a flexible portrayal of policing that can be considered a precursor of Chan's work. However, whereas Wilson's research portrays police styles as being imposed upon individuals, Chan's places a greater emphasis on the importance of understanding the interaction between the occupational culture and the individuals' existing attitudes. Similarly, whilst Wilson portrays variation at a behavioural level, the extent to which this further impacts at a cultural level remains unaddressed. Nevertheless, his work is important in that it highlights the need to recognize the divergent demands placed upon police forces in different societal contexts and the subsequent ways in which police styles adapt to satisfy these.

Police culture and contemporary contexts

Whilst it is beyond doubt that the works of early writers such as Skolnick and Wilson have immeasurably enhanced our understanding of police work, there is a tendency to overlook the fact that their status as classics of the field often makes us reluctant either to question their relevance to today's policing landscape or, alternatively, to portray them as superfluous at every level. In this section, I wish to highlight some of the changes to the police world that may prompt us to re-evaluate the relevance of some traditional concepts within police culture.

Gender

Changes to the structure of police hierarchies have presented some inherent threats to the masculinist cultural values that have been described within tradi-tional accounts of police occupational culture. For example, Brown (2007) shows how recent trends towards focusing upon intelligence work, crime prevention, community work and reassurance policing, whilst hinting at a less overtly mas-culine policing domain, have largely failed to detract from gendered attitudes to, and styles of, police work. In part, this may be due to new styles of policing ultimately being underpinned by managerialist developments that have become associated with the emergence of a 'smart macho' culture. The new terrain of police work, whilst diverting attention away from traditional law enforcement roles, has become increasingly identifiable as a quality-focused and managerial style of policing, whose participants 'are fierce, tough, forceful, and quick think-ing, displaying ruthlessness, competitiveness, and risk taking' (Silvestri, 2003, p. 15). The net result is that 'filing a routine report of command unit statistical returns is made almost as fraught with competitive masculinity . . . as an opera-tional exercise would be' (Brown, 2007, p. 209). Evidence suggests that the tra-ditional under-representation of women in the police, especially at higher levels, continues to persist, as does sexual harassment (Brown, 2007). Similarly, despite changes to police policy and structures to facilitate greater equality between the genders, discrimination is still present if not as overt or as consistent as previously seen. In many respects, the intransigence of this issue is due in part to the police service externalizing discrimination as a condition that afflicts individuals rather than institutions. By adopting an explicit stance of gendered neutrality, argues Silvestri, policing institutions do not acknowledge the gendered nature of either their structure or their culture and continue in their failure to suitably accommodate the female gender. Those women who succeed in being offered roles within detective units, notes Westmarland (2001), soon become alienated through being assigned repeatedly to sexual investigations. For those who take up senior positions, solidarity with other females is not apparently supported by the culture, a point articulated by one of Silvestri's interviewees, who stated that 'It's like being in the sisterhood with no sisters' (Silvestri, 2003, p. 159). The convergence of police culture and gender throws up other challenging and perhaps unexpected dynamics. Waddington (1999a) notes little differentiation in the values and beliefs of male and female officers in terms of an orientation towards law enforcement, with female officers valuing the same types of 'action-packed' work as their male colleagues. Indeed, he cites research by Bryant, Dunkerley and Kelland (1985) which suggests that female officers object to discrimination that fails to allow them to undertake the same work as male colleagues. Such evidence, however, might require some further analysis. Waddington himself highlights the problematic relationship between what is said, what is experienced and what is done within police contexts (see Chapter 5). These findings may suggest that female officers have become fully assimilated into the masculinist nature of the police culture or, alternatively, that female officers feel pressured into displaying the masculinist values associated with the culture.

Race

Whilst race has been a traditional dimension of research into police culture, there is evidence that over recent years it has been taken increasingly seriously as a cultural issue within police forces. For example, the Macpherson Report (1999) can be considered a central development in any analysis of the relations between police and ethnic minorities, in the UK, although some doubts persist given the failures in implementing the recommendations of the Scarman Report (Rowe, 2004). If nothing else, Macpherson made race a central concern of policing and led to a raft of initiatives to combat the institutional racism which was seen as endemic to the police world. One of the proposals of the report was for the establishment of a black police association in each constabulary. O'Neill and Holdaway (2007), in an assessment of the impact of such associations on police occupational culture, make a number of interesting observations. First, whilst the London Metropolitan Police's black police association had a sufficiently large membership to exert a substantial degree of cultural influence, such authority was not shared by all ethnic minority staff associations (EMSAs), particularly those in rural areas where small numbers of ethnic minority officers provided less opportunity (and less motivation) for membership. At the same time, when EMSAs do exert cultural influence, it will be as 'a *police* occupational culture' (2007, p. 261, italics in original) and will differ from the mainstream occupational culture only in respect of certain topics of race and ethnicity. Second, where cultural change in regard to race and ethnicity does occur, it is difficult to isolate the extent to which one particular factor (in this case, staff associations) can be seen as the cause. Third, there appeared to be some difference of opinion regarding the extent to which EMSAs should aspire to change attitudes, actions or both. These factors are important insomuch as they provide some glimpses into the acute difficulties associated with understanding police occupational culture. For a start, O'Neill and Holdaway show how ethnic minority staff associations hold a subcultural rather than counter-cultural position to the mainstream police culture. In other words, race and ethnicity are the sole dimensions in which ethnic minority police officers' cultural orientation will differ from that of other police officers, providing a subtle variation rather than an opposing cultural stance. The authors' suggestion that explanations of cultural change are hard to attribute to particular sources is also of interest, as it highlights the methodological challenges of exploring cause and effect in a cultural context as well as the politics of an organizational context where senior officers are sometimes happy to take plaudits for change regardless of the substantive cause. Finally, as shall be seen in Chapter 6, the relationship between attitudinal change and behavioural change is of great interest to those exploring occupational culture. If, as O'Neill and Holdaway suggest, the work of EMSAs will have enjoyed more success in changing actions than in changing attitudes, one is again confronted with the difficulties in measuring culture as a tangible phenomenon.

Unionism

Although not a new development, police unions have largely escaped the scrutiny of those writing about the occupational culture of the police. As in the case of EMSAs, police unions present an interesting focus for investigating police culture in that they provide a context for understanding the way in which police cultures can accommodate interest groups that may find themselves focused upon cultural change or, alternatively, resistance to cultural change. Marks (2007) assesses the cultural significance of police unionism, its potential for innovation or resistance in the face of new work practices and the extent to which unions are part of, or opposed to, the wider police culture. These tensions appear to represent, at times, a challenge for ownership of the police agenda between those, on the one hand, advocating a managerialist orientation defined in terms of systems, outputs and efficiency and those, on the other hand, who propose a more traditionalist view of policing based on custom, common sense and, above all, the thin blue line.

It appears that members of police unions primarily identify with the symbolism of their occupation rather than the union movement. Despite this, whilst police unions and management alike share broad agreement regarding the role of the police, differences do occur in how the respective sides portray their vision and the ways in which it is to be delivered. Thus, modern police management is countered by a view presented by police unions that tends to invoke a particularly Keynesian version of police work where the police have a monopoly on the provision of security and changes to this balance are to be resisted. That such symbolism has been maintained is probably testament to the embedded resentment to change in some quarters. The impact of new public management has been particularly marked for some, and the move from a 'hierarchical bureaucracy' to a flatter structure of command, whilst potentially providing challenges of control, has tended to exacerbate the divisions between those in administrative and patrol roles. And whilst it is difficult to chart the extent to which managerialism has impacted on the culture of the police it is possible to see police unions as adopting, in different situations, broad stances of either resistance or support in relation to occupational initiatives. Police unions can be conceived as generally adopting an approach that resists innovation and change to their members' working practices.

O'Malley and Hutchinson (2007) in a similar overview of the role played by unionism in the police understanding of their world note how the increased corporatism under managerialist agendas has led to a reinvigoration of police unionism. In some occupational sectors its impact has seen 'industrial relations' superseded by 'human resources management', a development which encourages greater collaboration between labour and management and therefore one with potentially negative consequences for unionism. On the other hand, however, police corporatism has led to increased division between managers and patrol officers, the latter of whom largely resist new managerialist practices that aim to uncover 'the inscrutable knowledge systems of "closed" institutions and professions' (O'Malley and Hutchinson, 2007, p. 164). They suggest that, overall, the emergence of managerialism has strengthened rather than weakened resistance to changes in police practice and that this has rejuvenated rank-and-file support for the police unionism movement. Further to this, they suggest, two key conclusions can be posited: first, that a surge in support for police unionism amongst lower ranks will hinder the spread of corporatism and, second, that this backing will serve to embed the traditional cultural principle that the values of policing are inescapably informed by street policing. The work of Marks (2007) and that of O'Malley and Hutchinson (2007) are both of interest in that they help us to make better sense of the role that police unionism can play in rearticulating the traditional values of lower-rank police officers during periods of change to policing institutions. Similarly, and as O'Malley and Hutchinson (2007) note, an appreciation of the importance of police unionism allows us another tool with which to investigate the cultural world of the police, especially during a time of convergence between the public and private police sectors.

Education

Throughout recent history we have seen major transformations in Western police institutions in terms of the 'types' of individuals recruited to undertake policing roles. Traditionally, police work was an occupation oriented towards, and attractive to, lower-middle-class and upper-working-class males. In a revealing anecdote from Fielding's research into police training he noted the extra scrutiny given to graduates who applied to join the police. In 1979, over 50 per cent of university-educated applicants to the police force where his research took place were rejected on the grounds of their motivation to join the service, with one member of the recruitment board apparently declaring that 'I wouldn't touch them [graduates] with a disinfected barge pole' (Fielding, 1988, p. 24). Conversely, Fielding notes the lengths towards which the force actively sought to recruit individuals with military backgrounds. In part, this can be attributed to the traditional 'pragmatism' or 'conceptual conservatism' (Reiner, 2010, p. 131) of policing. Young (1991) also charts the resistance traditionally exhibited by rank-and-file officers towards the world of academia when he recounts his own experiences of returning to a uniform position after a sabbatical spent undertaking a degree. Although carrying the status of 'ex-real polis' (a local term for a bona fide police officer) he also arrived with the distrusted label of 'academic'. He recalls how, within his police force, the traditional strategy adopted for dealing with local academics visiting police stations to conduct research was simple. They were placed by officers in a room with 'data', secure in the knowledge that the visitor would learn nothing about the reality of police work and therefore allowing the officers to preserve the 'purity of their adversarial world' (Young, 1991, p. 117), a comment that echoes Hobbs's (1988) reflection on the disparity between paperwork accounts of police work and its 'reality'.

There has been, however, a tentative but noticeable coming together of policing and academic institutions in respect of training, research and other forms of collaboration and, whilst police attitudes maintaining that 'to be educated was to be deviant' (Punch, 2007, p. 110) may not be as embedded as previously was the case, specific tensions do remain. Punch (2007) in an essay highlighting the relationship between policing and academia makes a number of observations. First, since the inception of the 'new' police, he suggests that there has traditionally been an emphasis upon avoiding the elitist taint of the military hierarchy by recruiting from below. Second, this state of affairs persisted until the 1960s, when forces, in the UK, introduced schemes for some officers to attend university. Third, the educational profile of senior police officers in England and Wales has changed greatly of late, and Punch suggests that, effectively, this change in profile has meant that senior officers are now expected to have at least one higher education qualification. Fourth, despite such changes it is often difficult to reconcile the values that underpin universities with those of the police institution. Fifth, the seemingly intractable barriers between the two sets of institutional values have started to erode in recent years, and this perceived 'secularisation' (2007, p. 113) of the police can be attributed to two interrelated issues. Changes to the nature and intensity of the threats that confront communities, the advent of a changed technological landscape and increased public scrutiny of police practice have necessitated a move towards enhanced police professionalism. Simultaneously, one potential benefit of the rise of police managerialism has been the transformation of the police institution from one that is inward-facing to one that is outward-facing and where, in some respects at least, cultural dogma fails to inhibit openness to new ways of thinking and the forging of new and productive inter-institutional relationships.

One pioneering scheme run, in the UK, by the University of Essex and Essex Police, and which saw some officers given the opportunity to study for a full-time social sciences degree, was viewed by Punch as largely successful. Graduates who took part in this scheme were viewed as benefiting in terms both of social capital and of generic skills which enabled them to play innovative roles within the transforming police landscape. Such skills also led to a questioning of force ideology and to tensions arising between graduate and non-graduate officers, with Punch (2007) describing an occasion on which a graduate officer was censured by a senior officer for using the words 'implicit' and 'explicit'. Whilst Punch provides a generally optimistic assessment of contemporary police forces imbued with increasingly tolerant cultures, which he partly attributes to a growing proportion of graduates amongst new police recruits, there are two particular trends which he sees as barriers to effective integration with the higher education sector. The first is that it is often difficult to justify wholesale university education for police officers on the grounds of value for money. Secondly, the importance of professionalization to the new landscape of policing has impacted on the 'types' of higher education made available to police officers.

The 'liberal' educational opportunities offered by Essex Police were echoed by Malcolm Young's experiences during the 1970s of being awarded a Home Office scholarship to read social anthropology at Durham University and reflect a largely bygone era. Nowadays, the convergence of higher education and policing is reflected in a large number of vocational degrees that focus on police matters, rather than allowing individuals to step outside of their work role and to mix with students from different backgrounds. In part, this may reflect wider debates regarding the confusion between police training and police education (see White, 2006, and Wood and Tong, 2009), yet, despite such reservations, Punch views education as a key element in improving police practice and mitigating what he sees as some of the more negative elements of the police culture. However, in terms of the latter, Punch admits that graduates entering the police will not provide a panacea to many of the more negative traditional artefacts associated with the culture of lower-ranking officers.

In a British context, Sir Ronnie Flanagan's review of policing has recommended a shift from police training to education, although it is difficult to tell, at present, whether or not higher education will become the preferred setting for it. Indeed, as White (2006) notes, it appears that police institutions have failed to consider the context within which to situate the educational frameworks that they develop. One result of this is that the unintended consequences of police training (what White refers to as the 'hidden curriculum') undermine the stated values of the organization. As White suggests, 'We seek to engender creative problem solvers, but the hidden curriculum values teach compliance and conformity, and a reliance on experts to do the thinking' (White, 2006, p. 396). The argument being proposed here is that cultural change within the police cannot be achieved by passively 'teaching' appropriate values or cultural knowledge to probationers. Quite simply, the level of engagement required to internalize such values is not encouraged by an approach to education that values passivity. Furthermore, Chan (2003) highlights the challenges of pursuing police educational curricula premised upon professional and reflective practice when occupational experiences tend to reinforce contradictory ways of thought and behaviour. It therefore remains the case that street work often undermines the best intentions of the classroom.

Police culture in changing social environments

One of the most prevalent transformations of policing in recent decades has been the emergence of a type of police work that reflects the loosening of the state's monopoly on the provision of security. The broadening base of security provision is reflected within the literature of policing by a trend towards focusing upon 'policing' rather than the 'police', and it is this acknowledgement of the pluralization of police work that has led, as Newburn (2003) rightly notes, to increased references to 'security networks' and 'commodification' in the context of police provision. The increasingly privatized context of policing represents an incredibly broad area covering the complexities of new communicative technologies and their application in commercial and community settings as well as more traditional surveillance and patrol services.

A brief overview of late modern society

Behind this new and emergent security market can be found a convergence of changing social factors. These lead not only to new forms of individual lived experience amongst members of the public but also to demands being made on the police to respond to new levels and new forms of insecurity. The stability of our home, work, welfare and political infrastructures has been inverted to such an extent that 'social change becomes the central dynamo of existence and where anything might happen' (Young, 2007, p. 59). Likewise, the post-war consensus of values has largely been replaced by the dissonance of individualism, and such fundamental changes resonate throughout all aspects of our existence, not least in increased feelings of vulnerability to threats from within, and from outside, our communities and in growing demands on the state to respond to the perceived sources of these risks.

From the 1970s onwards many advanced industrial societies were transformed, via late modernity, into high-crime societies (Garland, 2001), and it is this shift that is fundamental to explaining heightened awareness of risk and, therefore, heightened fear of crime. In the past there had existed widespread consensus surrounding crime and its control. Crime was unproblematic in that it failed to capture the public consciousness to the extent that it has of late and, generally, the focus was on the pathological rather than the mundane. For everyday crimes with rational decision-making or straightforward opportunity as a key explanatory factor little, if any, concern was generated, and greater energy was spent on those acts that hinted at criminal dispositions. In other words, therefore, the majority of illegal behaviour failed to contravene moral standards and generate real concern amongst the public. Regardless of recurrent concerns regarding crimes such as paedophilia (see Kitzinger, 1999), recent decades have seen trends towards net-widening and the expansion of crime-based interventions (Goldson, 2000). For example, in England and Wales, the introduction of over 3,000 new crimes over a ten-year period (Whitehead, 2008) has contributed, arguably, to a normalization not only of crime but of 'a new level of crime-consciousness, a new depth of emotional investment, and a new salience of crime in our everyday lives' (Garland, 2001, p. 164).

Whilst substantial attention has been paid to the role that media coverage plays in facilitating these processes (see Cohen, 1972, and Hall, Critchley, Jefferson, Clarke and Roberts, 1978), public concern about crime is invariably connected to non-crime issues. Fear of crime becomes intertwined within a wider 'tapestry' of unrelated insecurities (Walklate and Mythen, 2008, p. 213), leading to a process that has tended historically to see fear of crime become synonymous with the symbolic threat posed by the young. As noted above, we have witnessed a growing intensity of concern about what should be loosely referred to as 'criminal' behaviour, a process characterized by Young (2009) as representing a shift from one of moral indignation to one of moral panic. The distinction here is a subtle one, and one that signals a growing recognition not just of a contravention of moral norms but of an accompanying perception of threat. Whilst concerns about the behaviour of young people have been amply charted historically (see Pearson, 1983), recent years have seen a growing tendency to formalize these concerns through intervention rather than solely moral censure.

The causes of such insecurities are undoubtedly many and complex, and it is possible to identify more removed factors that undoubtedly contribute to this phenomenon. Ajzenstadt (2009), in a paper exploring a moral panic in Israel concerning single mothers who claim welfare benefits, provides a thought-provoking appraisal of the role played by political philosophy, most notably neo-liberalism, in stimulating popularly held insecurities around non-criminal behaviour. Similar ideas can be found in the work of David Garland (2001), who shows how the move towards neo-liberalism and neo-conservatism in the later stages of the twentieth century (demonstrated by the policies adopted by the respective administrations of Ronald Reagan in the United States and Margaret Thatcher in the United Kingdom) signalled the emergence of new forms of political rhetoric that encouraged social division. The intervention of the state in the lives of the public was increasingly questioned by those who thought that, 'far from the welfare state ameliorating the problems of a market society, it carried the diseases of "welfarism" and dependency' (Young, 2007, pp. 106–107). To Ajzenstadt (2009) the moral panic represents a 'government technique' (p. 84) encompassing a variety of purposes, including the regulation of individuals who pose a risk to society from their non-adherence to the tenets of neo-liberalism. Similarly, moral panics are used to repress those accounts that situate the cause of social problems in structural inequality and to promote values based on free market ideology to our understanding of society.

Late modernity, globalization and risk

The rise of late modernity has led to fundamental changes in the basic concept of community, specifically in so far as it signals, to paraphrase Young (2007, p. 194), a loosening of the moorings between the community and its specific physical environment, thus leading to a multiplicity of communities. Young's analysis describes a series of pluralistic communities inhabited by different subcultures of varying intensity and, whilst relations, at one level, might appear disjointed between such groups, 'crosscutting alliances' (2007, p. 195) that transcend cultural divisions do emerge. The subcultures that develop are not statically frozen but are reinvented and rewritten over time. Meanwhile, the collision of global and local communities means that, whilst some community subcultures have a specific geographic location, others are 'virtual communities'. Notions of difference appear embedded, yet shifting, within late modern societies and, unlike traditional communities where cultural values were largely underwritten by consensus, within the late modern community values become increasingly more fluid and disputed. At the same time, processes of globalization and the growing integration of localities through global networks have led to substantial social change, which in turn has, Young (2007) suggests, generated extensive uncertainty. Integral to this process are rising inequalities of income, which become manifested at both intra-national (in the case of growing margins of difference between high and low earners) and international levels (in the case of differences between wealthy and poor states). These differences are important in that they lead to relative deprivation and a perceived incoherence between 'universal' benchmarks for opportunity and lifestyle that are betrayed by structural inequalities. Globalized market societies have further physical impacts on the life experiences of individuals through their transformative qualities, which have introduced volatility to workplaces, communities and families and which have resulted in fractured personal histories, at least in respect of the dictates of tradition. The extent to which such changes actively exclude people, in both a material and a political sense, should not be underestimated. In the same way, the dehumanizing aspects of these processes are seen by Young (2007) as being an important factor in explanations of intergroup conflicts, in that they lead to the reconstitution of identity, a process made more difficult with the decreasing power of 'class' as a symbolic cultural reference point. Given the transformative power of globalization at individual, community and national levels it is perhaps natural, as Young proposes, that crime itself has failed to escape its influence, with a subsequent growth in crimes motivated not by simplistic materialistic desires but as a means of expression.

Risk has emerged as a key concept within this new social landscape and refers not so much to an increase in the amount of risk in any quantitative sense but to a change in orientation to chance. At the same time, the scientific and technological advances of recent eras have contributed to new and different threats to our security, which subsequently attract further scientific attention to deal with associated secondary risk (this 'scientization' of risk is explored by Ericson and Haggerty, 1997, p. 113). Developed as a sociological concept by Beck (1992), the notion of 'risk' has been seized upon, in a criminological sense, as a means of understanding the way in which societies and individuals position themselves in respect of the threats posed by crime. Johnston (2000a) explains this transformation in terms of a shift from societies characterized by a resigned acknowledgement that life contains hazards, to those where such hazards are identifiable, quantifiable and, to some extent, avoidable. The growing extent to which perceptions of risk become embedded in our day-to-day lives leads to a substantive change in the focus of our lives from one of positive, 'normative ends such as social equality or social justice' (Johnston, 2000a, p. 70) to straightforward avoidance of personal harm. This transition from social to asocial, characterized by a tendency towards the 'individualized, privatized, and instrumental' (Ericson and Haggerty, 1997, p. 258), paralleled the rise of neo-liberalism witnessed during the same period with two main results, according to Johnston (2000a): first, that the social world had become increasingly fragmented and, second, that the role to be played by the state in respect of crime and order maintenance was to become radically altered.

Late modernity and the reconfiguration of security

Whilst it is incredibly difficult to disentangle the respective parts played by the concepts of globalization, late modernity and the emergence of risk, as a whole they represent a number of challenges for policing, public expectations of the police and the nature, intensity and purpose of police occupational culture. Broadly, the significance of the change is articulated through the shift from traditional communities characterized by consensus and stability to contemporary societies characterized by fragmentation, plurality and risk. Many of the problems subsequently faced by the police can be considered global and have resulted in both new threats and new ways of policing. The heightening of economic and cultural divisions has given rise to new social classes that sit outside traditional class divisions, and family, occupational and leisure patterns have experienced substantial change, leading to new lifestyles. Moreover, individualism has become linked with excessive consumerism, and the relevance of these distinct yet interrelated changes to the core terms of reference of the police culture is multifaceted and will, no doubt, stimulate further debate over coming years. However, it is likely that the fragmentation and fluidity of wider culture will continue to contribute to accounts of police culture that emphasize change as much as continuity.

The move towards globalization has fundamentally blurred the boundaries of the state, the market and wider communities (Johnston, 2000b). Simultaneously, the experience of late modernity has led to growing insecurity, a change in the configuration of space and an increasingly pluralist security framework (Wakefield, 2003). Similarly, these developments have led to new forms of territorial and policing arrangements, with Davis (1992) drawing attention to the growing use of private security within reconstituted and mass privately owned geographical settings. Whilst Davis's observation that, 'In cities like Los Angeles, on the bad edge of postmodernity, one observes an unprecedented tendency to merge urban design, architecture and the police apparatus into a single, comprehensive security effort' (1992, p. 224) might strike some as somewhat dystopian, it is true to say that the provision of security has undergone significant change largely in respect of the growing commodification of security, the advent of new forms of publicly accessible territory and the associated growth of alternative non-state provision.

Central to this is the emergence of a privatized policing industry that, in recent years, has succeeded in breaking the monopolistic hold that the state police previously held over the policing function. Explanations of this phenomenon have tended to focus upon the displacement of Keynesian approaches to policing and the emergence of neo-liberal rationality (see, for example, O'Malley and Palmer, 1996). As Keynesian approaches to governance are superseded, so we witness a reduction in the scope of state provision of services. With this hollowing out of the state comes a drawing in of its boundaries and its responsibilities and the emergence of a gap between the expectations of the public and the state's willingness or ability to provide services. This gap is then filled by private providers, which supply those services previously offered by the state to paying customers. Johnston (2000b, p. 124) highlights three broad types of privatized security provision – 'physical security', 'electronic security' and 'staffed services', which exist in parallel to 'in-house' services for specific institutions or jurisdictions. Whilst it is hard to chart the exact size of the private security sector, what is beyond doubt is that the private sector not only matches, but exceeds, the work undertaken by many public forces (Jones and Newburn, 1998). Jones and Newburn do, however, present two caveats to this finding of their research within a London borough: first, that, whilst private provision en masse meets and exceeds the roles of state provision, provision remains fragmented and specialized and, second, that 'high' policing functions such as those pertaining to security at a national level unsurprisingly fail to be mapped by the private sector. What should be noted is that these processes, especially the privatization of public space, are especially more pronounced within North America than in the United Kingdom (Jones and Newburn, 1998). In North America more individuals are employed in private security than in public police agencies (Johnston, 2000b), and Jones and Newburn (1998) remain sceptical of the extent to which the United Kingdom has experienced a comparable growth in mass private property to the United States.

Despite such differences in experiences of private policing, Singh and Kempa (2007) provide a timely overview of the impact of private policing upon police occupational culture. Whilst the majority of research into private policing to date has focused upon the roles, size and governance of this sector, they explore the parallels between the occupational orientation of officers in private and public policing domains. Whilst the research findings, from fieldwork undertaken in South Africa, might not juxtapose seamlessly with other national contexts they do highlight a growing convergence of the two sectors. In terms of the breadth of the role undertaken by private security personnel, like Jones and Newburn (1998) the authors found that many public police roles were also being undertaken by private sector counterparts, especially following the rapid growth of the South African private security sector during the 1990s. The occupational culture of the private sector also mirrored that of their public police counterparts, with Singh and Kempa noting the emergence of different styles of policing similar to Reiner's typologies of 'bobby', 'new centurion', 'uniform carrier' and 'professional' (2010, p. 133) and cultural variations between those working in contract and in-house security. Interestingly, it appears that private policing, like public policing, is essentially concerned with reactive law enforcement rather than proactive crime prevention, and this may account for an occupational culture that, despite certain geographical inconsistencies, largely parallels the documented public police cultures of the mid-twentieth century. In explaining these similarities, Singh and Kempa suggest a number of factors. Private policing, in a reminder of traditional research into public police culture, tends to attract authoritarian individuals who may harbour long-term ambitions to join the public police. Likewise, management positions within South African private sector companies are often held by those who formally held security positions under the apartheid regime, thus contributing to the continuing paramilitary characteristics of a form of policing where training courses promote strategies based on the concept of force rather than of service. What should be noted, however, is that private security cultures will reflect a very limited type of 'public interest' (2007, p. 315) and, as Singh and Kempa argue, the culture of those private policing employees in their research, whilst reflecting many of the themes of 'classic' police culture, did show some differentiation, for example in respect of management being recruited externally rather than internally. What is important, they conclude, is that police culture literature can aid our understanding of a part of the security sector which is inextricably tied to the market economy that has emerged to satisfy our changing security needs.

Managerialism

Broadly managerialist strategies, associated with the private sector, have had an increasing role to play in the United Kingdom over recent years, with some tracing their foundations to the Planning, Programming and Budgeting System of the early 1970s (Southgate, 1985). However, to many, the key moment indicating the arrival of the managerialist agenda, within a UK context, was Home Office Circular 114/83 (*Manpower, Effectiveness and Efficiency in the Police Service*), circulated in 1983, which stipulated that 'value for money' should be an overarching consideration when resourcing police work. As a memo, the document did not constitute policy, nor was its remit particularly broad. However, at a symbolic level it represented an unequivocal statement of the future direction that senior officers and police authorities would be expected to take in quantifying the level and type of 'quality' that they delivered in return for the funding that they received. Five years later, Home Office Circular 105/88 (*Civilian Staff in the Police Service*) paved the way for further developments regarding the increased civilianization of the police service.

These changes can largely be seen in the context of the collapse of the post-war political consensus regarding cross-party commitment to public services. Under the burgeoning new right of the 1970s, Long (2003) suggests that two criticisms were put forward of public sector policy: first, that the market, not the public sector, was the most efficient means of distributing resources and, second, that an oversized welfare state was incompatible with the return to values stressing individual responsibility. Momentum was sustained, within a policing context, with the publication of the Audit Commission (1990) report *Effective Policing: Performance Review in Police Forces and the Policing Reform White Paper* (Home Office, 1993), although it was the Sheehy Report (1993) that has provided a well-weathered focal point for what became a slow-brewing revolution in police management. Amid a flurry of activity to provide a statutory footing for managerialist and 'best-value' changes

(Police and Magistrates' Courts Act 1994, Police Act 1996, Local Government Act 1999, Police Reform Act 2002 and the Police and Justice Act 2006), annual police performance assessments were used to measure effectiveness in 23 core activities, therefore allowing comparison through a 'league table'. By 2008 the British government's commitment to performance management was articulated by the then Home Secretary, who stated that 'Performance management is central to policing' (Home Office, 2008: i). Police opposition to such reforms, whilst entrenched for many years, has partly eroded more recently and has led, according to Cockcroft and Beattie (2009), to a widening of the division between management and patrol ranks within police organizations. In part, this move towards 'professionalization' in policing, under the auspices of managerialism, has tended to entail decreased discretionary freedom for practitioners on the streets.

In an evaluation of a police performance regime in an English police force, Cockcroft and Beattie (2009) highlight the ways in which prescriptive performance indicators can lead to a number of changes to police practice. Their findings tend to support earlier research by FitzGerald, Hough, Joseph and Qureshi (2002) that found that quantitative targets in respect of policing outcomes led to demotivated staff and a decrease in the powers of middle managers. Both the HMIC report on police integrity (Her Majesty's Inspectorate of Constabulary, 1999a) and Miller (2003) have noted the relationship between performance pressure and poor police practice, not least in respect of the ways in which performance measurement regimes invariably go beyond the measurement of practice and actively aim to modify it (Levi, 2008; Cockcroft and Beattie, 2009). The rise of performance regimes, therefore, has been accompanied by a trend for such measures to be used as a means of reinterpreting the police role as fundamentally narrower than traditionally has been the case. Furthermore, they also fail to represent the true extent of the police role (in particular, those aspects that are service oriented or which do not generate easily understood quantifiable data) and may also generate unhelpful or inaccurate data. Ultimately, however, the importance of these mechanisms can be judged by the fact that they are unable to measure every aspect of the police role (Butler, 2000). This suggests that, under such regimes, police prioritization of the role is reduced to 'what gets measured gets done'.

The rise of performance as a driver for police practice therefore represents a fundamental change to policing, which can be analysed at multiple levels. As evidenced above, the 'professionalization' of policing through the introduction of performance regimes, apart from changing the ways in which officers work, also has much value as a means of explaining how policing is evolving at a more fundamental level. One key aspect of the move towards professionalization has been to place hitherto unrecognized levels of importance on the presentation, if not the reality, of police work, and this has arguably rendered policing 'hyper-real' (see Baudrillard, 1994) through the distortion of the distinction between the two. Increasingly, observe Ericson and Haggerty (1997), police organizations are tasked with generating data for external agencies, and policies are routinely developed regarding which types of knowledge can be conveyed to which sort of agency in which particular format. In turn, these policies provide a framework that informs officers' understanding of the social world that they inhabit. Within this new policing environment, where the police are invested with an authority not only to 'shape the narratives surrounding crime, disorder and risk, but also to circumscribe the parameters of what is acceptable, normal and appropriate' (Cockcroft and Beattie, 2009, p. 534), the epithet of knowledge workers (Ericson and Haggerty, 1997) seems wholly appropriate.

The likelihood of managerialist initiatives, under the banner of new public management, to affect cultural change are presently unclear. Fundamentally, however, it is evident that a number of tensions emerge at a practical level when implementing such initiatives within public sector organizations. Public sector organizations tend to be characterized as having considerably broader aims than those in the private sector (Williams, 1985), and this has considerable implications for the ways in which 'success' is measured. Not least, the strategic domains upon which performance measurement regimes are based need to consider not only the core tasks of the institution and the concerns of the community but also the values and norms of front-line practitioners. The power of Williams's work is in that it succeeds in describing the causes of some of the cultural challenges that might be encountered when trying to 'managerialize' police institutions. Central to his argument is that the public sector arises as a response to the inability of the free market to fulfil all the requirements of the public, that performance measurement schemes tend to be inaccurate as measures of quality outcomes and that they often fail to reflect the knowledge of practitioners. Research has found that, whilst some officers might 'play the game' by conforming to what might be viewed as arbitrarily chosen performance targets, this could not automatically be considered as evidence of cultural change. As with the case of equal opportunities legislation, new policy developments might change behaviour but not, as the work of Loftus (2009) shows, change police values. Similarly, research by Cockcroft and Beattie (2009) suggests that the introduction of performance management initiatives may actively cause conflict with core concepts of the dominant police culture. Officers working under schemes that allocated points for arrests and form-filling complained of competitiveness, overcharging, manipulation and needless arrests. Similarly, core parts of the police role (such as reassurance work and crime prevention work) were not reflected appropriately within the performance mechanism. Officers who had been in post for a short time tended to find the regime more helpful than those with a longer amount of service, with the latter being less likely to use the points system as a guide to action. To some, the scheme appeared as an affront to officers' professionalism, as it tried to direct officers to undertake those particular tasks which could be easily measured and not to engage in those which were altogether less quantifiable. Older officers, especially, were unlikely to react positively to having the definition of policing reinterpreted from above.

Risk aversion

A relatively recent development, at least within UK policing contexts, is that the police have become increasingly subjected to accusations of 'risk aversion'.

This issue was highlighted by Sir Ronnie Flanagan in his review of policing (2008). It is understandable that, given the growing reorientation to risk that has become so prevalent in wider society (see Beck, 1992), it would have some unintended impacts upon policing. Flanagan's report, in particular, highlights the relationship between the decrease in police discretion, the subsequent increases in police bureaucracy and a growing tendency for officers to allow themselves to become overly directed by rules and policies, a process which he claimed had become supported by the occupational culture. Subsequent consultation by the Risk and Regulation Advisory Council (RRAC) led to the publication of a report, in 2009, that concluded that risk aversion within police forces was a reflection of the impact of risk in wider society. Furthermore, the report noted that risk aversion represented a corrosive influence, as it led to officers adopting excessively bureaucratic and rule-based working patterns that were incompatible with latter-day police arrangements. Whilst the report advocated a more 'flexible policing environment' (2009, p. 19) and a move towards repositioning responsibility as an individual rather than governmental issue, it remains to be seen how this agenda will unfold, in policing terms, over the coming years.

In an article that explores the relationship between policing and risk, Heaton (2010) draws attention to some of the factors that have contributed to the risk aversion that is seen as permeating contemporary policing. Primarily, he distinguishes between the status of risk within the private and public sectors, noting that, for many private sector institutions, risk is accompanied by the potential for considerable 'positive' effects. In contrast, for public sector institutions, like the police, risk-taking is less likely to be perceived as leading to benefits substantial enough to be justified. As Berry (2009, cited in Heaton, 2010) suggests, risk is integral to police work, and unnecessary risk-taking jeopardizes not so much the financial stability of the institution but, more importantly, its 'organizational reputation' (Heaton, 2010, p. 76). Furthermore, the RRAC (2009) notes the breadth of factors that have led to the preponderance of risk aversion in the police, drawing specific attention to: individuals who actively prey on public perceptions of risk; a profusion of information; a zero-tolerance approach to failure; calls for immediate government intervention; and disempowered individuals and communities. Whilst these factors can be considered significant hurdles to a more positive risk orientation within the police culture, risk aversion is facilitated further by a failure to satisfactorily articulate the difference between 'blame' and 'accountability'. Furthermore, legislation and agency review are both considered additional external drivers towards risk aversion. One solution that has been proposed to risk aversion is the promotion of 'entrepreneurial policing' (see Smith, 2008), a concept that balances risk-averse policing with more 'creative' entrepreneurial approaches. The culture of the police, suggests Smith, reflects class divisions in wider society, with those of the status of constable and sergeant generally reflecting traditional working-class norms of deference to the middle classes. Whilst Smith makes a case to argue that the rank system stifles entrepreneurialism and privileges 'the politically astute networker' (2008, p. 12), he goes on to suggest that entrepreneurialist cultures can be encouraged by team working, criticality, goal-oriented work, pragmatism and decision-making borne of partnership work.

The issue of risk aversion amongst the police offers some interesting contexts for debate regarding the nature and extent of police occupational culture given that it appears fundamentally at odds with the accepted values identified by early work into police culture. What appear to emerge are two conflicting accounts. The 'risk aversion' model suggests that the growing professionalization of policing has been accompanied by a decrease in the levels of officer discretion and a growing culture of rule following. Police officers are increasingly viewed as less likely to engage in 'innovative' policing and are increasingly 'controlled' in a culture where they feel inadequately supported to make decisions for themselves. Punch (2009), however, takes a somewhat contrary stance by considering the persistence of police corruption in a number of diverse police jurisdictions. For example, in the UK context he shows how the convergence of pressure for 'results', a culture of silence and ineffective independent scrutiny of the police has led to acute challenges to reforming police behaviour. Similarly, within the USA, the development of accountable police forces has proven difficult, with ingrained resistance towards civilian-led complaints mechanisms. Research cited by Punch (2009) describes how police departments in the USA have failed to fully enforce reform measures and, in some instances, actively sought to reduce their effectiveness. He goes on to note that 'there is something about the nature of policing that distorts perceptions and deflects good cops onto deviant paths while encouraging bad cops to become rogue cops . . . police corruption will always be with us' (Punch, 2009, p. 235). It would appear difficult to rationalize these two accounts. One suggests that discretion has been squeezed out of the system to such an extent that officers have become unimaginative automatons who rigidly enforce laws and who are too afraid to 'innovate'. The other, as described by Punch, presents policing as having an inevitable skew or tendency towards corruption, which inevitably indicates a concerted rejection of procedure. Whilst Flanagan's concern over a culture of risk aversion might resonate at some levels, Punch's concerns for police services that veer towards corruption unless resolute leadership is in place do suggest an incomplete picture of cultural drivers and inhibitors of risk-taking behaviour. Amidst these ongoing debates regarding risk aversion within UK police culture, Heaton (2010) suggests that it is difficult to assess the extent to which cultural change will be successful or otherwise in changing police attitudes to, and use of, discretion. In conclusion, he notes that much of the impetus for risk aversion itself stems from the actions of central government, an accusation that appears to carry some weight given the moves, over recent decades, to reduce the freedom with which police exercise their discretionary powers.

Bridging traditional and contemporary depictions of police culture

Above I have presented a number of loosely based themes that might act as conceptual reference points from which to explore police culture through a contemporary lens. By way of reiteration, these suggest that policing is subject to differentiation as a result of wide-ranging social and cultural change, the shifting demands of local populations and the assessment of the relative merits of particular styles of policing in specific communities. The latter appears to be especially true of the localized nature of policing in the United States, although differences have also been observed within the United Kingdom, where, for example, research has addressed differences in policing styles between rural and urban areas (Cain, 1973; Loftus, 2009). Whilst early work into police culture tended to focus upon commonalities between officers, their orientation to the role and their interactions with the public, more recent analyses of police work have tended to address 'difference' in policing, and this has forced a reassessment of the extent to which a specific police culture can support a variety of different policing styles in diverse contexts.

Contemporary analyses have also highlighted not just the explicit differences that exist between styles and attitudes of policing, but also those factors that would initially appear to challenge the primacy of a rigid police occupational culture. Government-led inquiries and increases in representation through recruitment and equality legislation may all be considered as having a part to play in reducing explicit denigration along the lines of, for example, gender and race, yet have still led to concerns regarding discriminatory attitudes being pushed 'underground' and therefore made more powerful. Police unionism, again, might be considered one factor that would mitigate some negative aspects of the occupational culture. However, it appears that police unionism might further embed traditional cultural practices given its conservative character and its embodiment of the 'traditional' crime-fighting image. A fundamental aspect of police unionism is that it is a curiously apolitical unionism that is unashamedly pro-police, and this tends to eclipse its potential for links to the wider trade unionism movement. In a similar way, the much touted potential of education to be a key factor in the transformation of the police force appears, at present, to be limited. Whilst higher education qualifications have become increasingly important for promotion to senior police positions, the role of higher education in lower-level police work, the cultural core of the occupation, remains ambiguous.

Assessing the impact of private policing on police culture remains an interesting issue. Whilst the most likely area of inquiry regarding the relationship of private security to police culture will be the extent to which private police culture reflects the main themes and directions of public police culture, the move towards partnership work has provided areas for future research. For example, Wakefield (2003) and Jones and Newburn (1998) have described the ways in which effective partnerships can emerge between public and private police, with Jones and Newburn finding during the course of their research that almost 90 per cent of private security companies had what they would describe as 'good' or 'very good' relationships with the public police. Given this gradual loosening of the public police's monopolistic hold over the security agenda, there do appear to be opportunities, through partnership work, for a revision of the isolationist worldview held by many to be fundamental to the police culture. Alternatively, however, some also propose, as Singh and Kempa (2007) and Shearing (1997) do, that we are witnessing a process of convergence between the private and public police.

Where these authors differ is in describing the nature of this convergence, with Singh and Kempa noting a growing militarization across both sectors, whereas Shearing suggests that growing similarities between sectors can be explained as a result of the neo-liberal and market-led forces that have transformed the public police, making them increasingly preventative rather than reactive in outlook. One conclusion, which appears beyond contention, is made by Singh and Kempa when they suggest that we need to escape the 'binary depictions' of both sectors and to look at the ways in which they interrelate within a shared security context.

Police institutions have diversified in terms of both the roles that they undertake and the make-up of their workforces and have done so against a backdrop characterized by accelerated social change. Bethan Loftus (2009, 2010) provides a refreshing approach to contemporary police culture that helps us to extend our existing framework of understanding. She suggests that community policing, the advent of new public management, changes to traditional recruitment demographics and the ongoing politicization of the police have made the occupation unrecognizable, in some respects, from that which provided the basis for much of our early knowledge of police culture. Additionally, she draws our attention to the 'new social field of policing' (2009, p. 21), characterized by legal and political changes, the policing of diversity and increasing levels of social exclusion that have further impacted, culturally, upon policing. The most significant of these changes, argues Loftus, has been the impact of 'identity politics' on the cultural realm of the police, leading to a growth in demands for equality along predominant axes of ethnicity, gender and sexuality. This has had two substantial effects on the police: first, it has limited the extent to which the cultural values of many police officers can be explicitly expressed and, second, it has implications for the ways in which the police engage with people from specific social groups.

Arguably, the emergence of 'identity politics' as a threat to traditional police cultures can be traced back to the aftermath of the riots of the early 1980s and the publication of Lord Scarman's report into the Brixton riots. During the intervening years, British society has become increasingly diverse, and the police have strenuously articulated their commitment to diversity in all its forms as a policy priority. What we have witnessed, therefore, is the materialization of a 'new *politics of policing diversity*' (Loftus, 2009, p. 35, italics in original) that plays into direct conflict with the traditional cultural tenets of rank-and-file police officers. The substantial changes to policing during this period corresponded with wider social change associated with the shift from a modern society to a late modern society. One facet of this shift has been, according to Young (1999), a disproportionate exclusion of large sections of the population both from labour markets and from civil society and their drift towards the attentions of the criminal justice system. Similarly, we have also seen a growing tendency to reposition crime and disorder as problems caused by individual rather than structural factors as old ideologies have been replaced by the ascendancy of crime prevention discourses. It is within this context that Loftus (2009) presents a strong argument to suggest that the rise of identity politics has coincided with a gradual decline in the political relevance of both class and poverty. Loftus draws on the work of Zurn (2005) to explore the meeting of the politics of recognition and those of distribution and questions whether acknowledgement of diverse identities can coexist with a commitment to deal with financial marginalization. A possible conclusion, of course, is that it is a more feasible political aim to recognize previously denied social identities than to put an end to structural inequalities. Correspondingly, Loftus draws on the work of Haylett (2001) to describe the ways in which class has become the key differentiating factor that the police can utilize to create 'legitimate' targets. 'Excluded from notions of multiculturalism', writes Loftus, 'poor, young, white men stand forward as the embodiment of disorder and distaste' (2009, p. 45).

The diversity agenda and the rise of identity politics, whilst causing what Loftus terms an 'interruption' to the occupational culture of the police, has failed to represent a shift in traditional cultural values. Indeed, the transformation of policing in this way has encouraged a mood of resistance amongst those officers who resent the implications of these changes. The language of diversity comes to be seen as a tokenistic and politically correct gesture that, whilst impacting on how officers express themselves, does little if anything to alter their opinions and values. Among the more practical consequences of this attempt to reorient police values is that the marginalized white male becomes an 'unproblematic terrain' (2009, p. 160) for the types of discretionary policing previously experienced by ethnic minorities.

Fundamental, however, to Loftus's analysis is not that class has suddenly become a new target of police attention in the wake of the diversity agenda, given of course that class can be mitigated or exacerbated by other distinctions. Instead, Loftus suggests that the importance of class to the work of the police has been unsuccessfully represented within existing police scholarship, given that it largely fails to identify class as a consistent and embedded factor in the police psyche outside of analyses of the introduction of the New Police (see Storch, 1976) or in respect of outbreaks of industrial unrest. What is important here is the impact of identity politics as a factor that actively inhibits the expression of culturally motivated police actions and attitudes. The white urban poor emerge as a contemporary social grouping for whom no specific cultural recognition has been forthcoming in terms of police policy and, as a result, this has led to the persistence of class-discriminatory policing. This might be considered ironic in the light of historical work by authors such as Brogden (1991) for whom class was always the prioritized social domain of police work.

Conclusion

Variation has always been a part of police work, not least because of the fact that particular areas have distinct security and order requirements and these will lead to different forms of police action and priority. However, the importance of works such as those of Wilson (1968) is not to be seen just in terms of the way in which such works chart varieties of police orientation, but in the way that they account for it. The populations of different communities had, noted Wilson, different values, exhibited different behaviours and held different thresholds of tolerance to particular behaviours. Significantly, these came to dictate the type of policing that would occur in different areas, and it becomes evident that, in some areas, the police directed the citizenry and, in others, the power was firmly in the hands of the communities. Furthermore, the impact of local political structures and elites also impacted upon the way in which the relationship between the police and the public would be played out. The world which Wilson describes for us is one in which policing becomes subjected to the intricacies of local social pressures and, whilst not being articulated by Wilson, hints at the idea that police culture is subject to change between locations.

The work of police culture writers over recent years has, in many respects, followed Wilson's lead, although with a greater degree of sophistication. Wilson's focus on behaviour has been supplanted with a tendency for greater attention to be paid to culture (and the ways in which culture and behaviour are related). There has also been a growing acknowledgement of the role of both change and continuity in respect of manifestations of police culture or cultures. Issues such as race and gender continue to be a primary domain for many police culture writers, yet, increasingly, concepts such as unionism, education, managerialism and risk are all being drawn upon as ways of exploring change in the police world. And it is variation that has become the dominant currency, arguably, for writers in this field. The era of simplistic binary depictions of police culture has given way to reference to the fluidity of police cultures and, simultaneously, the search for meaning has become increasingly difficult when the deconstruction of the police world means that little uniformity of behaviour or culture can be identified. Interestingly, however, a synthesis of the two approaches has been hinted at by the work of Loftus (2009), and the class-based nature of police culture has provided a potential anchor for our understanding of police work in a world where constant change has tended to obscure even the most persistent features of the cultural landscape.

5 Researching police culture

Introduction

Whilst a tremendous amount of time and effort has been spent by academics undertaking research into police culture, we rarely reflect on those factors that shape the form and remit of such studies. It is perhaps helpful therefore to acknowledge the ways in which police research has gone through different stages, historically, which reflect different academic and policy considerations and that these have impacted upon our knowledge of police culture. A related issue concerns the purpose of policing research and the extent to which its focus and orientation are to understand policing at a cultural level or to develop ways of dealing with culturally determined police issues. This is a subtle distinction yet one which leads to a diversity of research projects and methodologies which will have widely varying outcomes. Finally, this chapter will highlight some of the definitional, methodological and analytical challenges of police culture research prior to discussing a broader set of orientations within which to conduct research into police culture.

The context of police culture research

Police research, as an identifiable subject within the social sciences, began to emerge during the early 1960s, shortly after the advent of modern criminological research, which took place towards the end of the 1950s (Reiner and Newburn, 2007). Whilst these developments took place simultaneously on both sides of the Atlantic, there existed subtle differences between the two countries. In the United States, the focus appeared to be primarily on the civil rights implications of police work (as evidenced, for example, in the 1961 report of the United States Commission on Civil Rights), especially in regard to the use of discretion, a matter that generated considerable research from legal scholars such as LaFave (see LaFave, 1962b). This trend in early police research was reinforced during the 1960s with the growing influence of labelling theory, which shifted attention away from those who broke the criminal law to those who enforced it, placing police research in the United States at the centre of legal, social and theoretical debates.

As in the United States, policing research in the United Kingdom was the result of developments both in criminal justice and in the social sciences. By the late 1950s, the 'Golden Age' of English policing was coming to an end, with recorded increases in crime rates, a perceived deterioration in relations between the police and ethnic minority groups and a cooling of the mutual respect that had previously been the defining characteristic of the police relationship with the middle classes (Reiner, 2010). The 'celebratory' manner which permeated orthodox accounts of the police (see, for example, Howgrave-Graham, 1947) was increasingly being contradicted by concerns surrounding individual corruption and wider issues of police accountability (Reiner, 1997).

Before long, research on both sides of the Atlantic was beginning to diversify, in the United Kingdom not least because of the growing politicization (Neyroud, 2003) and managerialism of the police, and this resulted in the coexistence of two broad types of police research. One type continued to explore the class-based nature of policing and control (reflecting the sociological orientation of symbolic interactionism through the application of labelling theory), whereas the other was fundamentally rooted in the need for research into specific policy issues and was generally funded by the police and other state agencies and departments. In the United States, the civil rights agenda was beginning to wane as the focal point for police research and came to be replaced by a more organizationally oriented research agenda. A brief resurgence of research that explored concerns of both police efficiency and accountability was made possible during the late 1980s by the advent of community policing (Reiner, 1997), although even policy-oriented research in the United States has, in recent years, become jeopardized through substantial cuts to research budgets. This has occurred despite the assertion, made by Sherman (2004), that between 1980 and 2001 criminology learnt more about crime than it had in the last 200 years, an argument he supported by pointing to the decrease in homicide rates over the corresponding period. Reiner and Newburn's (2007) claim that this reduction of funding for research into policing is due to a distrust of the social sciences by governments tends to reinforce the view that police research is as liable to politicization as policing itself.

Reiner and Newburn describe the ways in which research into policing has passed through a number of stages defined by 'consensus', 'controversy', 'conflict', 'contradiction' and 'crime control'. The consensus agenda resulted from the apparently tranquil and unproblematic policing of the 'austere, socially rigid, monochrome world of the late 1940s and 1950s' (Loader and Mulcahy, 2003, p. 14). This era, whilst representing perhaps the most appropriate matching of police service to society that the United Kingdom had ever experienced, was, unfortunately, about to witness substantial and unprecedented change over a particularly short period of time. By the late 1960s and early 1970s, British policing was finding itself increasingly tarnished through widely reported incidents that heightened concerns over police practice not least in respect to corruption and discrimination. At the same time, British police forces were increasingly tasked with the control of public demonstrations that, whilst not always directed against the police, had the effect of placing the police physically and ideologically against sections of the community with whom they had hitherto enjoyed relatively harmonious relations. Whilst the consensus research agenda is reflected in the publication of Banton's (1964) *The Policeman in the Community* (Reiner and Newburn, 2007), the new wave of British police scholarship largely rejected the consensual focus of old and moved towards a more wholesale adoption of the critical orientations found in sociological theory. These they used to develop accounts of policing which were far removed from the optimistic tone of Banton's work. Whereas Banton had focused on police work as an example of a successfully functioning institution, under the controversy agenda attention was directed to inappropriate police practices facilitated as a result of police discretion. The conflict agenda of police research constituted a progression from the controversy agenda, signalling an approach less informed by labelling theory and more explicitly by Marxist thought. This process was accompanied by a broadening of the focus upon police practice from an individual level to one centred upon larger and more systemic issues such as police accountability. Therefore, whilst labelling theory progressed our understanding of the interpersonal dynamics at play in police–public encounters, these led to broader questions regarding the distribution of power in society, which necessitated a move towards more macro theories.

The penultimate stage outlined by Reiner and Newburn is that of contradiction and was made possible by the emergence of left and right realism, which had developed in response to a growing political consensus between political parties on crime and criminal justice issues. The element of contradiction in this stage comes from the diverse and sometimes contradictory views espoused under criminological realism, which represented an attempt to deal with 'the crisis of etiology and penality' (Young, 1994, p. 80) through a movement towards less explicitly ideologically grounded theories. The realist enterprise therefore represented a rejection of the grand narratives, such as Marxism, which had failed to provide policy-relevant knowledge with which to combat crime. Whilst realist thinking, in the United Kingdom, was largely represented by left realism and in the United States by right realism, this period also gave rise to a new administrative criminology that rejected the abstracted and ideologically tainted paradigms of previous models. Recent years, according to Reiner and Newburn, have seen yet another police research agenda emerge, which focuses purely on 'crime control', a development that reinforces the shift from ideological to pragmatic concerns in our exploration of crime and police work.

Over a relatively short space of time social, intellectual and political change have all impacted on the nature and purpose of police research, with, arguably, the latter as the key driver. Whilst critical research into police work is still undertaken, it is no longer as central to police scholarship as it once was, as opportunities for applied research, driven by concerns of efficiency, effectiveness and economy, have increased. In many respects, this recent history of police research and the different functions that it has served invariably bring us back to broader arguments regarding the purpose of criminology and police scholarship. Whilst traditional work in the field was driven by intellectual curiosity of the roles and practices of societal institutions (especially in connection with questions of accountability and inequality), recent years have seen the social sciences adopt a more support-ive, rather than adversarial, role in the generation of knowledge regarding issues of order and control. This development means that the role of police research has become increasingly contested, and analyses by both Zedner (2003) and Eric-son (2003) have highlighted this. To Zedner, these apparent tensions reflect, first of all, insecurities over criminology's status as either an empirical or a critical discipline, a distinction that she asserts is largely unhelpful. Secondly, criminolo-gists, note Zedner, harbour concerns regarding their influence outside the academy and are easily prone to succumb to the view that policy-led criminology is of greater relevance than academy-led criminology. By way of conclusion, she suggests that both approaches have particular and specific uses and that crimi-nology's real power lies in its ability both to establish 'normative frameworks' and to engage in 'imaginative conjecture' (Zedner, 2003, p. 235). There is a more forceful argument, such as that proposed by Ericson (2003), which downplays Zedner's view of criminology's more speculative or theoretical contribution. Ericson's view is that criminology and associated disciplinary areas such as police studies are intrinsically 'technical', that is, they provide solutions to specific prob-lems defined by criminal justice agencies. For Ericson, therefore, those branches of the social sciences that concern themselves with issues of crime and order have largely engaged with issues of policy not least because such disciplines, by virtue of their largely normative nature, make technical research (which is concerned with improving existing institutional practices) a priority over critical research (which is concerned with critiquing institutional roles). This view, however, is met with some resistance from some UK academics, such as Reece Walters and Tim Hope. To Walters (2003), state authority in a variety of national contexts represents a means of suppressing criticality within criminology and ensures that criminological knowledge is largely shaped by those agencies that commission it. Similarly, Hope (2005) assesses the UK context of criminological research under the New Labour administration of Tony Blair and notes that even those forms of research that are essentially technical and policy driven are themselves subject to interference given the tensions between evidence-based knowledge and the highly charged and politicized nature of policy.

Methodological issues in police culture research

It is beyond dispute that the ethnographic tradition has provided a substantial part of the methodological impetus for researchers to explore the dynamics of the cultural world of the police. Indeed, authorities such as Reiner and Newburn (1997) and Westmarland (2008) lament the apparent demise of the police ethnography that has played such a pivotal role in our understanding. In the introduction to a chapter addressing the motivations that drive researchers towards studying the police, Van Maanen referred to the 'discrete illusion and growing mystique' (1978c, p. 310) that surrounded ethnographies of police work and which made them such important contributions to our knowledge. Whilst the ensuing years have also seen the publication of a number of works that have succeeded in extending this tradition (for example, Smith and Gray, 1983; Young, 1991; and Loftus, 2009), more recently there has been a trend towards the types of policy-driven work that Ericson (2003) saw as the primary role of police research and which Walters (2003) and Hope (2005) viewed in an altogether more negative light. One issue, however, which has arguably received insufficient attention from the research fraternity is that of rigorous and critical debate regarding the assumptions that underpin our understanding of police culture and which go on to influence the ways in which we conduct research into these areas.

Police culture, societal culture and interpretative over-reach

One key conceptual issue that hinders the effectiveness of much research into police culture is the ineffectiveness of sociological models in adequately accounting for the impact of social change on policing. The prevalence of the view, held by Manning and Van Maanen (1978a, p. vii), that 'the essence of police work was to be found at the ground level' has meant that our knowledge of policing is largely of policing at a micro-level. Accounts explain the nature of police–public interaction, officer discretion and the targeting of 'symbolic assailants' but fail to enlighten our understanding of the relationship between police work and the shifting social and cultural backdrops against which this occurs. Indeed, the UK literature appears to present a remarkable continuity in the accounts of British police relations with the working classes from the inter-war years (Brogden, 1991), to the 1930s (White, 1983), through the 1930s to the 1960s (Weinberger, 1995) and to the present day (Loftus, 2009). Whilst policing and the communities within which it takes place have experienced inestimable change, the world as presented by the literature of police culture reflects little of the blurring of boundaries or what Young (2007, p. 3) describes as the 'disembeddedness of everyday life'. Instead, police culture research and commentary seem to present a historically unchanging set of relationships that appear as mutually reinforcing affirmations of the unyielding culture that underpins police work. Research-derived depictions of police officers show them unceasingly complaining about bureaucracy, exploring the outer limits of their discretionary powers with young working-class males and espousing uncompromising views on minority groups. Whilst Loftus (2009) is correct to focus upon and highlight the persistence with which some of the cultural reference points of policing have survived throughout recent history, there is equally a case to be made that the nuances of the relationship between the police and wider society have necessarily shifted as a result of social changes that have occurred over recent decades. In a speech delivered at Leicester University in March 1976, Sir Robert Mark, former commissioner of the Metropolitan Police, suggested that 'We, the police, are in fact the most accurate reflection of British society, its tolerance, its strengths and its weaknesses' (1977, p. 33). Whilst some might question the exact shape and length of the reflection that Mark refers to, there is considerable support for the idea that police culture and wider societal culture are not mutually exclusive cultural categories and, furthermore, that many of the cultural properties common to policing are reflected in the values, behaviour and language of members of the public. The work of Waddington (1999a), for example, suggests that seemingly entrenched police cultural artefacts such as sexism are prevalent within wider culture and therefore not distinctive to the police environment. This prompted him to question the extent to which police scholars are correct to attribute distinctiveness to the behaviours and values that they see enacted and espoused by police officers. He goes on to present two explanations for this phenomenon. First, the absence of comparative data by which to establish the uniqueness of such behaviours to the police setting suggests that such conclusions are informed by the bias of the researcher rather than by any objective phenomenon. Second, the distinctiveness of a behavioural trait is ascribed not on the basis of its singularity but as a result of the context within which it takes place. In this way, the particular opportunities for interaction enabled by the police role may encourage us to see certain behaviours as culturally rather than organizationally facilitated. Similarly, the large degree of scrutiny which has been applied to police work over the last 40 years may lead to mistaken assumptions about the extent to which police officers are more prone to certain behaviours and attitudes than people who belong to other occupations that have not been subjected to the same degree of investigation. As Waddington (1999a) convincingly concludes, whilst reflecting on Chan's work into police racism against ethnic minorities in Australia, negative behaviours observed among these officers are not so much a reflection of personally held racial biases but a result both of the colonial traditions of the Australian police and of racial divisions in Australian society. In other words, we are witnessing an 'interpretative over-reach' (Waddington, 1999a, p. 91) whereby common behaviours and values are misconstrued as being 'distinctive' to the police setting.

Conceptual templates and cognitive burn-in

Increasingly, a number of writers have critiqued not so much the heritage of police culture research but the use of methodological, definitional and analytical approaches that are perceived as inappropriate to the contemporary study of police culture. For example, Sklansky (2007) introduces the concept of 'cognitive burn-in', whereby, over time, ideas become collectively imprinted and continue to resonate long after the original stimulus has subsided, and uses this as a means with which to challenge seemingly rigid approaches to investigating police culture. The result, he suggests, of this collective imprint is the 'police subculture schema', 'a cognitive burn-in not *caused* by that subculture but rather consisting in ideas *about* it' (2007, p. 20), and this is one explanation as to why, over a relatively short period, research into the orientation of lower-status police officers to street work has become the accepted orthodox account of the police organization. Like Loftus (2010), therefore, Sklansky questions the relevance of a 50-year-old conceptual template to twenty-first-century policing systems, which are increasingly subjected to widespread independent oversight and which consist of substantial numbers of recruits drawn from ethnic minority, female, homosexual and graduate populations. As the work, the composition and the role of the police have become ever more complex, so, arguably, has the culture, which is more divided and less unified than was previously thought. Manning (2007) is similarly critical of the failure to revisit the cultural template that has been used since the work of early luminaries such as Westley and Skolnick. The difficulty, primarily, with these pieces of research is that they are seen as failing to fully engage with the reality of police work. Early research describes an unproblematic and linear relationship between police culture and police action without addressing the role of superiors, supervision and bureaucracy in limiting the extent to which cultural values become realized at a physical level. In part, this can be seen as reflecting distinctions between 'etic' and 'emic' cultural research, where 'etic' research represents emblematic categories assigned on the basis of previous research and literature and where 'emic' refers to those which are assigned on the basis of their meaning and relevance to those being studied. This distinction is significant in that discussions regarding the tensions between these two approaches to research appear not to have been reflected in policing literature to date. It is probable that some might view the adoption of rigid cultural categories through an etic stance as unsuitable in all instances, owing to the potential to restrict the opportunity to uncover other equally suitable conceptual categories.

In an echo of Young's assertion that orthodox criminology leads to 'desiccated' accounts of human experience (2004, p. 14), even the dynamism of ethnographic police research has failed to provide a three-dimensional understanding of police experience. Instead, states Manning, we generate accounts in which officers are 'flattened, desiccated and displayed like insects pinned on a display board' (2007, p. 59). In this sterile caricature of the police world we seize upon the occupation and its cultural expressions but fail to acknowledge the intricacies of occupational structure and how this mediates both the culture and the practices through which it is articulated. Rather than focusing primarily on police attitudes, Manning makes a convincing case to argue that occupational culture encapsulates what happens, normative conceptions of what should happen and an idealized police world and, in doing so, asserts the importance of understanding the role that narration plays in perpetuating the symbolic dimensions of police work.

Culture, culture(s) and narration

One of the key arguments made by Waddington (1999a) is that police culture is, effectively, two separate cultures consisting of an operational culture (which relates to how police officers act) and an oral culture (which relates to how they narrate such actions). This provides distinct methodological challenges in a subject area where qualitative methodologies have been widely used yet where it has been generally assumed that narratives simplistically reflect behaviour. The notion of a divided, or bifurcated, culture raises some intriguing issues. Do the narratives of the canteen inform the operational culture of the street or reflect it? Do these narratives have a shifting role? Do they sometimes inform officers' operational behaviour and, conversely, sometimes provide officers with the presentational reference points to, for example, justify inappropriate operational behaviour? Whereas, previously, researchers studying police culture had to concern themselves only with the relationship between culture and behaviour, they are now being forced to consider a three-way relationship between culture, behaviour and language.

The 'vibrant oral tradition' (1999a, p. 111) that Waddington describes does not, as some might suppose, denote a blank canvas upon which officers present accurate representations of their day-to-day working lives. There is no seamless relationship between what happens and how it is later recounted. Instead, police culture is seen in rhetorical terms whereby the values that inform police work are exercised and reinforced. In some instances, for example when Waddington (1999a) refers to the persistent theme of 'crime-fighting', it becomes apparent that police 'talk' is often a means of highlighting an idealized component of the occupational identity. This is especially the case when that behaviour or role is largely symbolic rather than realized through day-to-day practice in officers' regular working life. Cultural practices that focus on the symbolic rather than grounded everyday experience are not solely related to police work but can become associated, for example, with specific geographical locations. For example, Hobbs describes 'the absurd posturing and delusions of "doing the business"' (1988, p. 144), which were a common symbolic feature of everyday East End life and which, at times, were significantly removed from the reality of many people's experience. In a similar way, the symbolic role of danger in the police officer's work will continue to shape attitudes, behaviours and commonly held assumptions regardless of the potential for that danger to be realized. At the same time, whilst Waddington (1999a) suggests, as does Loftus (2009), that some elements of police behaviour have been remarkably persistent over time and between areas, it should be stressed that this need not be taken as evidence to suggest that what we are witnessing is an isolated occupational structure. Indeed, Manning (2007) extrapolates this idea to suggest that the canteen culture is essentially a microcosm of wider Anglo-American values that are generally antagonistic towards social minorities. It is upon this basis that he declares the potential benefits to be had from exploring the relationships between the values that are articulated within police talk and police behaviour itself.

The complexity of this relationship between police narratives and police behaviour should not be understated. The work of the literary theorist Gérard Genette (1980), for example, envisages any narrative as having a relationship with both the event that it represents or symbolizes and the act of narration. The subtleties of the form and purpose of language, combined with the caprices of human perception and recall, suggest that an individual narrative often serves a different purpose to just one of informing as to what happened at a given time or location. Such a stance claims that narratives are not unproblematic representations of factual occurrences and that, accordingly, they are as valuable to police officers for the creativity which they offer as they are for the descriptivity. That is, their communicative value is largely symbolic.

The creative utility provided by narratives forms the basis of a 1991 paper by Shearing and Ericson entitled 'Culture as figurative action' in which they develop themes around the concept of the 'vocabulary of precedents' from an earlier paper by Ericson, Baranek and Chan (1987, p. 348). Their point is straightforward. The complexity of narratives allows police language to largely resemble a 'cultural tool-kit' (1991, p. 500). Police stories provide a symbolic guide to action through allowing for the construction of a 'police' version of the world whilst simultaneously retaining sufficient freedom to allow a certain degree of spontaneity. Police storytelling covers a wide variety of forms and purpose in this analysis, and police language subsequently takes on a multifaceted role, being able to direct language and cognition at different levels and for different purposes. Police narratives may therefore vary in purpose and form between those that are robust, persistent and cumulative and those that are fleeting, short and descriptive, depending on their intended purpose and the extent to which they are used as cultural or factual descriptors. The complexities that plague this relationship between police language, culture and behaviour, whilst intellectually intriguing, have largely failed to impact on police cultural research. Police accounts are largely taken at face value and tend to be used as an objective measure of behaviour rather than as a vehicle for communicating police values, assumptions and priorities at a largely symbolic level.

This issue is further compounded when placed in the context of 'interpretative over-reach'. Whilst we are happy to draw on police narratives as largely unproblematic transcriptions of physical events, and in so doing to reverse-engineer an often simplistic cultural backdrop to explain these occurrences, the allegorical layers of the same stories, paradoxically, are often lost. Furthermore, if Manning (2007) is correct to describe police culture as essentially a subculture of wider societal culture, then Punch's (1985) criticism of our eagerness to automatically view all police behaviours as artefacts of a specific and separate police culture looks even more robust. A failure to respond to these criticisms may, for example, lead to us viewing the targeting of members of ethnic minorities in police cultural terms of the 'symbolic assailant' rather than more general factors such as racial prejudice as a predisposition held regardless of occupation. By the same token, racially prejudiced talk by police officers becomes recast as something that is culturally supported only within police contexts rather than in wider society. Obviously such approaches fail to represent reality accurately, yet our failure to deal with interpretative over-reach reinforces such deterministic reasoning at the expense of potentially more rewarding conceptual approaches.

In part, these issues may reflect some of the inherent problems of trying to ascertain the properties of an intangible phenomenon (in this case, culture), where we can evidence its existence only through the ways in which it makes people behave, think or speak. Perhaps a logical progression to some of the questions of police narrative explored above is reflected in Waddington's claim that, rather than being a singular and universal occupational culture, police work revolves around two distinct and separate cultural frameworks. One of these relates to the physical operational environment of police work, and the other is a separate and predominantly oral culture, a 'canteen' culture, guided by a fundamentally different purpose. This idea of a bifurcated police culture with different cultural rules for 'doing policing' and 'talking policing' does appear to provide at least a partial resolution to some of the issues pertaining to police narratives and, as Waddington (1999a) suggests, explains the pronounced differentiation between policing in an operational sense and policing in a narrative sense. Whilst the operational police culture provides a framework of reference points that enables officers to negotiate the complexities of their interactions with the public, the 'canteen culture' fulfils a role that is both palliative and '*expressive*' (1999a, p. 287, italics in original). The canteen provides an environment where officers use rhetoric to make sense of their occupational experiences and to mutually reinforce collective understandings of policing and the world in which it takes place. Despite the fact that police work often takes place away from the supportive cushion of their colleagues, the oral tradition provides opportunities for officers to present experiences and in turn have their competence and membership of the occupational group reconfirmed.

At a more abstract level this suggests an inversion of the traditional conception of the relationship between culture, behaviour and language. Previously, police talk was viewed as reflecting attitudes and opinions and ways of seeing the world that also directed how police officers interacted with other social actors (both police and public). Waddington is suggesting that, in fact, the reverse is the case. The role of the oral, or canteen, culture of the police is predominantly directed at 'contextualizing occupational experiences, a way of emphasizing, and sustaining, the perceived "them" and "us" worldview of policing which disparages all who play down either the danger or the bureaucracy of the job' (Cockcroft, 2007, p. 97). The central factor to this oral culture is 'the glorification of violence over which they hold the legitimate monopoly' (Waddington, 1999a, p. 298), although, intriguingly, at the heart of this bifurcation of cultures also lies a fundamental contradiction. The strength of the occupational cultures of the police is derived not from the strength of the police institution but from its 'fragility' (Waddington, 1999a, p. 302), and it is the vulnerability of policing that ensures that its symbolism is often very different to its operational reality. The significance of Waddington's work regarding the purpose of these two cultural frameworks is to highlight the potential for the canteen culture to emerge as a reaction to police work, rather than as a guide. In this respect, therefore, the cultural narratives that emerge from within the police world represent an idealized reflection of police work that tells us more about its occupational values than its reality. In a similar way to how oral histories have shown how sometimes people recount their pasts by emphasizing actions that they ought to have taken rather than those which they actually took (Thomson, 1998), police narratives allow for cultural themes, integral to the police culture, to distort recollections of actual events. In short, the challenge for police researchers whose work draws on the narrative accounts of officers is of how to identify whether the phenomenon they are actually addressing is a factual account of what happened, where and to whom or a symbolically charged account aimed at perpetuating figurative themes.

Continuity, change and history

The challenge of making sense of police narratives becomes accentuated when one heeds Punch's (1985) appeal for police researchers to adopt a wider variety of methodological approaches with which to unpick the intricacies of their subject matter. In particular, a historical focus has been largely missing from analyses of police culture and, it can be argued, this may account for the somewhat polarized accounts that we have tended to witness over recent decades. These have tended to fall into one of two camps, be they the deterministic and prescriptive accounts of early police cultural theorists or the increasingly fluid accounts associated with the work of later writers such as Janet Chan. This tension between monolithic and fluid accounts provides the basis of an interesting paper by Paoline (2003), wherein he questions the conception of police culture as a singular phenomenon. Central to his paper is the idea that police scholars need to 'complicate the lines of culture enquiry' (p. 209) by moving beyond what he views as the simplistic dichotomy between diverse and monolithic cultural landscapes. His argument advocates that both sides of the debate are presenting views that are too polarized to aid our understanding of the reality of the police world. In this respect, he presents an approach that synthesizes the two positions through advocating that monolithic conceptions of police culture are being eroded but not dissolving. In other words, whilst wishing to distance himself from overly prescriptive understandings of police culture, he remains convinced of the relevance of police culture even in a world where policing represents a diverse and often contradictory grouping of roles, relationships and settings. The disputed frontier between these two positions remains, for Paoline, the real area for academic interest, and it is precisely these areas where cultural differentiation is witnessed that should provide future focuses for research. In particular, he encourages not just a description of these variations but an understanding of the factors which explain them and, in doing so, makes a strong case to argue for future research which differentiates between the 'mainstream' police culture and its subcultures. Fundamental to the achievement of this, he acknowledges, will be a broadening of methodological approaches.

Realistically, it appears that some aspects of police culture are embedded. This is shown by Loftus (2009), who found that class remained a continual symbolic element within the police world, whilst others may be considered more transient or fleeting. Accounts like these make ever more apparent the need to develop approaches to research that can accommodate the shifting relationship between the police and the policed, the residual importance of some factors and the temporal insecurity of others. If, as Skolnick suggests, police culture represents a set of 'cognitive lenses' (1994, p. 42) that provide a meaningful focus on the world, it appears reasonable to suggest that their focus will highlight particular issues, themes or narrative reference points at different times or under certain conditions. Particular aspects of cultural frameworks can, therefore, assume greater or lesser importance to the occupation in different eras, with the more fundamental cultural reference points experiencing the greatest amount of stability over time (Brown, 1995). The dynamics of class, and police orientation to class, does, as Loftus suggests, appear to embody an example of a cultural thread that successfully links accounts of police–public relationships from the earliest accounts to those of the present day. When Loftus refers to an 'underclass' which represents a (and perhaps the only) legitimate police target, we see parallels with social processes from 60 years earlier. The underclass of the inter-war years were formally controlled, first, by laws that protected the more wealthy citizenry from encountering loitering lower classes on street corners and, second, by laws which protected them from themselves by forbidding them from engaging in the gambling habits of the middle classes (Brogden, 1991). In what amounts to an apparently continual process, Loftus shows how the police focus on the poor exists to 'reproduce the exclusion and symbolic domination of this group' (2009, p. 197).

Whilst there is a wealth of research to suggest that authors like Brogden and Loftus are correct to highlight the seemingly entrenched importance of class to the police working personality, it does not, of course, represent a standalone factor, intersecting as it does with gender, race and a multitude of other variables. At the same time, an acknowledgement of the importance of class to police officer attitudes does little to tell us about the relationship between class and these other factors. Likewise, the assertion of a particular feature, in this instance class, having primacy over other factors appears to endanger the very notion of 'culture'. Potentially, we find ourselves in danger of reducing the study of police culture to the exploration of police orientations to individual issues without making a conceptual leap to explaining why and how these issues work as an interconnected and self-supporting cultural framework.

In part, the apparently embedded concept of class parallels the ideas of Abbott (1991), whose essay on the relationship between history and sociology provides a fascinating overview of some of the challenges of explaining social process through a historical perspective. His central argument is that many attempts to explain the social world fail to seek an appreciation of the way in which social change at a historical level adds a layer of complexity to those social processes which take place against this backdrop. In this respect, Cockcroft (2005) draws on the work of Samuel (1976) to highlight the ways in which critical historical stances (such as that of the oral history movement) allow for a more sophisticated assessment of complex social relationships that revolve around particular social agencies or structures. Many historical accounts of police work (such as that of Critchley, 1978) largely fail to present a critical portrayal of the working lives of police officers, or to engage constructively with the awkward reality that 'Policing is an inherently conflict-ridden enterprise' (Reiner, 2010, p. 69). However, the oral historical approaches used by White (1983), Brogden (1991), Weinberger (1995) and Loader and Mulcahy (2003) whilst describing the working lives and attitudes of officers also succeed in contextualizing such data in terms that bring to the fore 'the structural, slow-moving, determinants of police–working-class relations' (White, 1983, p. 39). Whereas the above advantages might, on their own, fail to convince some of the need to adopt new methodological approaches to understanding police cultures, it could be argued that change is needed for two further reasons. The first is that policing has become more complex and, as such, requires more sophisticated means of exploration. The second, as Loftus (2009) reminds us, is that police culture has become an essentially contested concept and there is much material that indicates that policing is no longer a culturally insulated occupation built upon the values and experiences of white, heterosexual, male officers from the upper working and lower middle classes. Police officers, according to Sklansky (2007), are no longer solely drawn from a relatively closed and homogenized set of classes, characteristics and experiences, and this has important implications for contemporary experiences of a range of cultural issues including police solidarity and prejudice. In part, this reflects the fact that policing has undergone a sustained and substantial amount of change over a relatively brief amount of time. These changes are outlined by Newburn (2003) in a chapter that shows how opinion is divided over the extent to which these changes represent evolution or revolution or continuity or change. What does become clear is that the power of the police, if not weakening, is beginning to change. At a symbolic level, in particular, that an institution so embedded in 'discourses of morality, tradition, and "Englishness"' (Loader and Mulcahy, 2003, p. 134) can undergo such substantive change demands not only a new way of understanding the core roles of the police, but, equally importantly, a more sophisticated understanding of the ways in which police identities are reconstructed through them.

Conclusion

Whilst it can be argued that the early pieces of research into cultural aspects of police work (for example, Westley, 1953) pre-dated the tumultuous social change of the 1960s, it is beyond doubt that the impetus for much of the work in this area is inextricably linked to the profound social and cultural changes that occurred during the second half of the twentieth century. This period, described by Sumner in his history of the sociology of deviance as one of 'a growing resistance on all fronts to the edifice of power and the one-dimensionality of hyper-consumerism' (1994, p. 200), largely defined the scope and focus of much of the work associated with the 'classic' era of police culture research. What is surprising here is that much of the work has failed to adequately recognize the ideological direction of such research, which often aimed to reform policing as much as to understand it. A case can be made, as for example Sklansky (2007) does, to advocate scholarly orientations to police culture that are more explicitly acknowledging of their historical precedent, biases and limitations. In particular, the restrictions of the 'normal diet of macho, racist, sexist thugs' (Waddington, 1999a, p. 291) does tend to obscure a very real need for research that engages with the 'undercurrents, inconsistencies and quirks' (Fielding, 1997) of police work and that prioritizes explanatory aims as much as descriptive or transformative ones.

In part these issues may reflect the trend, over recent decades, for academics to apply their knowledge to technical rather than systemic police issues through a buoyant market for what Zedner refers to as '"quick and dirty" policy-oriented research' (2003, p. 235). Whilst such work undoubtedly has a part to play in promoting effective and appropriate working practices, it generally does little to encourage debate or investigation into the more complex issues alluded to by Fielding (1997), which, whilst perhaps less likely to be of relevance to policy-makers, should be of central concern to those wishing to understand the cultural aspects of policing. Whilst Westmarland (2008) rightly advocates the need for a return to the ethnographic approaches of the latter part of the twentieth century, the symbolic interactionism that fuelled earlier accounts of police culture has surprisingly failed to foster an acceptance of the more biographical methods with which they are implicitly linked. To Goodey (2000) such methods hold many advantages for criminological researchers, not least in that they provide a means of exploring the convergence between the individual and the wider social world. It may be through the application of new means of exploring police culture, such as comparative, biographical, organizational, life history and oral history approaches, that police scholars manage to understand the cultural ramifications of sociological and historical analyses of police work.

At a more fundamental level, it has to be noted that the concept of police culture has largely failed to provide an adequately cultural account of the forces that are being investigated. A welcome reminder of the need for police culture to reflect policing as a 'cultural institution' is provided by Loader and Mulcahy (2003), who provide some potential guidance for future analyses of police culture by highlighting three central dimensions of symbolic power. The first suggests that policing exists as a collection of perceptual and professional assumptions that inform our understanding of threats and the way in which societies should appropriately respond to them. The second dimension refers to how policing assumes a central role in a hub of cultural knowledge that both 'produces and propagates meaning' (Cockcroft, 2010, p. 257), particularly in respect of our understanding of the social world, our position within it and the threats that face us. Finally, Loader and Mulcahy (2003), citing the work of Ericson and Haggerty (1997), make a case to suggest that policing has increasingly become predicated upon 'knowledge work'. The police, therefore, can be seen at one level as an institution whose role is largely symbolic in that they pronounce upon crime and risk and communicate the boundaries of moral acceptability. It is within this role that the cultural importance of police ideology resides, and it is hoped that future cultural analyses of police work will be sensitive to these symbolic aspects of policing.

It is fair to say that police culture is rarely dealt with empirically in the terms that Loader and Mulcahy suggest, and its symbolic aspects are generally ignored. Whilst police research has led to a general acceptance of the idea that numerous cultures may exist within policing institutions, insufficient attention appears to have been paid to the interplay between these different cultural enclaves. In particular, the subject area of police culture would benefit from sustained investigation of the extent to which overlap occurs between different cultural groupings, be they based on the distinction between street and management officers (for example, as in the work of Reuss-Ianni and Ianni, 1983) or on that of operational and canteen cultures (as in the work of Waddington, 1999a). In respect of the outward-facing dimensions of police culture, whilst it is evident that wider societal culture does not simply grind to a halt at the front door of the police station, we are left considering the best ways to assess the similarities and differences between the culture of the police and that of wider society. This interplay, whilst problematic enough at times of high levels of value consensus, becomes even more difficult to assess in the late modern period. Whilst the police, especially in England and Wales, tend to draw heavily on symbolic interpretations of policing from its 'Golden Age', it is becoming increasingly difficult to rationalize the symbolic presentation of the police with the 'disjointed world of hiatus and chasm' (Young, 2007, p. 9) that exists beyond it.

In conclusion, therefore, we need to be aware that research into police culture cannot just follow the tried and tested blueprints that were used with varying degrees of success during the last half of the twentieth century, as the social world has changed vastly over the intervening period. Furthermore, research would benefit immeasurably from a greater degree of reflection about the methods that we use and the conceptual assumptions upon which we base these methods. As far back as 1985, Punch called for a greater variety in the methodological approaches that we apply to the study of police culture by advocating that we utilize organizational, historical and comparative levels of analysis. Whilst Punch's suggestions remain valid, we should also adopt a degree of criticality regarding those methodological and conceptual approaches that we choose to employ. One observation that seems especially pertinent in respect of some of the issues raised in this chapter is attributed to Werner Heisenberg, the German theoretical physicist. In a collection of lectures delivered at the University of St Andrews, he remarked that 'what we observe is not nature itself, but nature exposed to our method of questioning' (Heisenberg, 1962, p. 58). Heisenberg's view, whilst originally directed at the natural rather than the social sciences, holds some stark reminders for those attempting research into policing, or any other phenomenon for that matter, namely that our concepts and methods should not be viewed as akin to a window on our research matter, but as a lens that highlights some contours of the natural or social world and diminishes others.

6   Managing police culture

Introduction

As we have seen from the previous chapter, discussions around police culture sometimes focus upon issues of conjecture and abstraction that, whilst stimulating both intellectually and as a means of generating new knowledge, may be less immediately helpful as a means of 'dealing' with police behaviour. For example, the work of Shearing and Ericson (1991) and Waddington (1999a) can be considered crucial additions to the literature of police culture, owing to their exploration of the relationship between police talk and police behaviour, yet may have seemingly little relevance to those exploring the challenges of changing police practice. This reflects, in part, the sheer breadth of work that has been produced under the banner of 'police culture' and which has, at different times, sought to describe, to explain or to change police attitudes and behaviour.

The literature of police occupational culture has been instrumental in increasing our understanding of what the police do, why they do it and how they present this behaviour to the outside world. Since the 1960s, when policing was first subjected to systematic cultural analysis, interest in the area has continued to grow, with events such as the Rodney King assault and the issues raised by the Stephen Lawrence murder inquiry reiterating or facilitating our commitment to explaining police behaviour in such terms. Several authors have noted that cultural explanations are, for the most part, used to describe negative police behaviours (Brown, 1981; Cohen and Feldberg, 1991), a point reiterated by Manning (2007) when he described how police culture had been customarily presented in terms that highlighted how the norms of the police were in conflict with their legal mandate.

This chapter will highlight the role that culture plays in enabling two very different forms of negative behaviour, corruption and absenteeism, within the police institution. These accounts will be contextualised within a discussion of police leadership, and the different forms that it takes, and its potential as a means of cultural and behavioural change. Particular attention will be paid to the uniqueness of policing and the ways in which its existing structures and cultural orientations may provide barriers to effective police reform.

Police corruption and the role of culture

Allegations of police corruption have been an intermittent but significant feature of the police forces of many societies since their inception, yet actually charting the extent, causes and impact of police corruption is a challenging task. As is often the case with matters pertaining to the more hidden aspects of policing, cause and effect are hard to assess and it becomes difficult to untangle the relative merits of journalistic, academic and policy responses to the issue. Focusing briefly on just one of these examples, journalism, it is possible to highlight the wide-ranging nature of corruption and its relationship to other external actors by showing how members of the media can work to highlight and combat police corruption whilst, at other times, becoming complicit in it. For example, in 2010, *Philadelphia Daily News* reporters Barbara Laker and Wendy Ruderman were awarded the 2010 Pulitzer Prize for investigative journalism for a ten-month series entitled 'Tainted justice' that led to allegations of theft, sexual assault and procedural irregularities against police officers and the subsequent re-examination of a large number of drug-related criminal cases. Conversely, in the United Kingdom, recent months have seen the arrests both of police officers and of journalists under two Metropolitan Police-led operations (Operation Weeting and Operation Elveden) which were set up to investigate allegations of phone hacking and inappropriate payments to police officers. Police corruption is, therefore, fluid and variable and takes different forms at different times and may or may not involve collusion with individuals from other professions. Likewise, the sheer extent of possible illicit behaviours (which may include unauthorized dissemination of information, illicit use of force, abuse of authority for financial or sexual favours, collusion with criminals and interference in proceedings against offenders) is extremely broad and may be caused by one or more of several factors. The picture is further complicated by acts which, whilst criminal, may not necessarily be suggestive of corruption. In other words, we need to differentiate between crimes committed by individuals who happen to be police officers (be they crimes, for example, of theft, fraud, drug offences or domestic violence) and those which are committed by police officers in relation to their role or their status or which are facilitated by their work.

Police culture has been presented as one possible means of explaining some forms of police corruption, from bribery and manipulation of evidence to illicit use of physical force. However, 'police corruption' is a term that covers a large array of behaviours, and attempts to describe its origins as sitting squarely within the culture of the police may be overly simplistic. Likewise, it is important to acknowledge that explanations of police corruption have undergone a significant shift during the twentieth century, as 'rotten apple' explanations (based on the notion of individual failings) have been replaced by those that advocate the 'rotten orchard' (which view police corruption as a result of more systemic failings). This shift is evidenced at a formal level by the findings of the Wood Royal Commission into the New South Wales Police. Any attempt to articulate the relationship between police corruption and the cultural worlds of the police demands, primarily, an explanation of what is meant by the term 'corruption'. Newburn (1999), in a review of the literature of police corruption, warns against the adoption of conclusive definitions of police corruption and, in doing so, hints at the complexities of the behaviours that the term seeks to cover. Instead, Newburn suggests that police corruption can be understood in terms of five dimensions. First, corruption can be assessed through looking at an officer's reasons for behaving in a particular way and by evaluating the outcomes of that behaviour. Second, the outcomes of corrupt behaviour might be considered wholly acceptable at an institutional level. Third, corrupt behaviour can be the result of both proper and improper use of police power. Fourth, police corruption can be internal to the organization and have no external impact. Fifth, and finally, police corruption is often associated with the desire to derive benefit at either an individual or an institutional level.

To evaluate the role that police culture plays in explaining these diverse behaviours it is necessary to fully explore the different ways in which we set about defining police corruption. In Newburn's review of the police corruption research, he identifies a number of definitional approaches, distinguishing between the broad approach forwarded by Roebuck and Barker (1974), which highlights corrupt behaviour as that which involves breaches of honesty, propriety, ethical considerations or, indeed, the criminal law, and that of Wilson (1968), which differentiates between police corruption (crimes linked to the inherent role, opportunities and authority of the police) and police crimes ('everyday' crimes that happen to be committed by police officers). Of significance here is that these conceptions of corruption are largely concerned with the benefits accrued by such behaviours (to an individual or force or unit) but need not necessarily involve financial recompense, illegality or even a breach of force policy. Newburn also raises the issue of whether or not all illegitimate behaviour (for example, dereliction of duty or use of illegitimate force) is corrupt, and it remains the case that police use of force can generally be considered corrupt if it furthers some occupational aim (be it, for example, asserting police authority or the extraction of a confession) but not if such ends are not served. Herein lies one aspect of the complexities surrounding definitions of corrupt behaviour, that corruption appears as much a quality of an officer's motivation or intention as an attribute of a particular physical act.

Police malpractice has been historically identified in numerous police forces throughout the world and has been found at all levels of the police hierarchy, although it does appear that particular roles provide greater opportunities or temptations for officers to indulge in corrupt behaviour. The broad basis of our understanding of police corruption is, however, to be explained not solely in terms of financial factors (where the rewards are monetary) or process factors (which provide benefits at an occupational level, for example through facilitating convictions), but also in terms of competency factors (where 'corrupt' behaviour has no specific motivation but is due to a skills deficit) and informal working practices (where officers may choose to interpret force policy in a particular way). This diversity provides some explanation as to Newburn's reluctance to commit to one particular definition of corruption, and this is compounded further by the fact that policing takes place in a number of different national and jurisdictional contexts where different stakeholders, oversight agencies and political groups all take an interest in police work.

Following widespread accusations in the UK of police collusion in media phone-hacking scandals during 2011, the Home Secretary approached the Independent Police Complaints Commission (IPCC) to report on police corruption within England and Wales. In the first of two scheduled reports, the IPCC highlighted the challenges of adequately defining the problem, gave examples of police corruption and identified some interim recommendations. In terms of defining 'corruption', the IPCC suggested that an accepted legal definition of the word had yet to be agreed upon, although the Association of Chief Police Officers (ACPO) had, within a policing and law enforcement context, defined it as 'the abuse of one's role or position held in the service for personal gain or gain for others' (cited in IPCC, 2011, p. 14). The IPCC itself provides a more rigorous definition of what it calls 'serious corruption' by identifying:

> any attempt to pervert the course of justice or other conduct likely seriously to harm the administration of justice, in particular the criminal justice system; payments or other benefits or favours received in connection with the performance of duties amounting to an offence in relation to which a magistrates' court would be likely to decline jurisdiction; corrupt controller, handler or informer relationships; provision of confidential information in return for payment or other benefits or favours where the conduct goes beyond a possible prosecution for an offence under Section 55 of the Data Protection Act 1998; extraction and supply of seized controlled drugs, firearms or other material; attempts or conspiracies to do any of the above.
>
> (IPCC, 2010, p. 65, para. 211)

The IPCC (2011) provided examples of such breaches of acceptable police behaviour by listing police sexual assault of vulnerable adults, inappropriate use of police databases to help external business concerns, the misuse of police position to unfairly progress applicants in the recruitment process, links to organized criminal groups, the use of improper practices to encourage prisoners to admit to unsolved offences and inappropriate use of corporate credit cards. Correspondingly, the IPCC has forwarded recommendations that advocate a strengthening of supervision, more vigorous leadership in the wake of 'whistle-blowing' incidents and the introduction of more robust safeguards in respect of computer systems and expenses procedures.

In a paper entitled 'Police investigations: practice and malpractice', Maguire and Norris (1994) confront one of the central dilemmas regarding the issue of police corruption, namely that the success of remedies to these apparently endemic issues is dependent on understanding the actual causes of the problem. For instance, better training of police officers is unlikely to reduce the threat of malpractice if there is still an unwritten expectation within a force that a particular illicit act (for example, fabrication of evidence) is the accepted way of dealing with a particular set of internal pressures (for example, pressure for results). Likewise, Maguire and Norris give the example that calls for greater supervision of staff by higher-ranking officers are deemed to be largely unhelpful if those same senior officers give greater priority to controlling crime than to ensuring due process. At the time of writing their paper, Maguire and Norris revealed, unsurprisingly, that research had yet to produce incontrovertible 'facts' regarding the nature of police corruption. This was due to a number of factors. First, police malpractice is difficult to research because of the challenges of developing a solid operational definition of the term. Although there are exceptions, police malpractice is largely a matter of incremental degrees of non-ethical behaviour in a work environment founded upon discretion. Behaviour is not always explicitly and unambiguously right or wrong. Second, police malpractice is a fringe activity that will, in almost all cases, take place beyond the scrutiny of the academic researcher and often beyond that of the line manager or supervisor. Third, when research does uncover evidence of corruption it does so usually in a way that grants us knowledge of 'specific' instances in a particular geographical and operational context but does little to tell us about the overall picture of the problem. We find ourselves in a position, according to Maguire and Norris, of having substantial amounts of case study data, none of which is generalizable to other areas or forces. As a result, we remain unaware of the extent of police corruption and of the degree to which the evidence that has come to light is typical of that which has not.

Whilst concerns in the United Kingdom over police corruption have undergone something of a resurgence during 2011 and 2012, largely as a result of allegations of police complicity in media scandals, recent attention has also been directed at different forms of police malpractice occurring in other national jurisdictions. In an article published in the *Observer* (2011), Paul Harris highlights a number of recent corruption scandals within North America, which he suggests are leading to mounting public anxieties over the discipline of police officers and the legality of their practices. For example, Michael Daragjati, a New York Police Department officer, arrested an African-American in Staten Island during April 2011 and recounted, during a telephone conversation with a female friend, that he had 'fried another nigger' and that it was 'no big deal' (his telephone calls at that time were being monitored by the FBI in connection with another matter). It transpired that Daragjati had arrested the individual involved and submitted faked evidence to implicate the person in question on grounds of resisting arrest. The result of Daragjati's actions was that an innocent man spent two days in jail. On the West Coast, in Los Angeles, accusations have been levelled against officers working for the Sheriff's Department regarding acts of abuse allegedly committed against some inmates. Officers within the same police force also face allegations of having conducted sexual relations with prisoners. In a case concerning the Pittsburgh police, an 18-year-old student, Jordan Miles, was beaten by police officers with such force that a dreadlock was removed from his head, resulting in a medical referral for neurological treatment. He had been stopped on suspicion of having a concealed gun (which later transpired to be a soft drink bottle) and charged with aggravated assault, a charge that was later dismissed by a judge. Harris's article continues by citing findings reported by the New York Civil Liberties Union that, in 60 per cent of cases where Tasers were used, the incident did not meet the threshold required for the deployment of such a tactic. According to the report, a number of such cases involved individuals who were already restrained through handcuffs and who belonged to vulnerable groups such as the young, the elderly and the mentally ill.

One of the growing trends being witnessed in the United States, notes Harris, is the growing use of mobile phone technology to capture images of such examples of apparent police malpractice. One of his sources, Chris Calabrese of the American Civil Liberties Union, states that this has resulted in an increase in cases where police officers have intimidated bystanders into not filming police operations. Another source, Diop Kamau, of the Police Complaint Center, noted that, despite the intrusive nature of widespread digital camera technology, the 'culture of secrecy' within police departments meant that officers believed that the chances of being caught acting inappropriately were narrow. Moreover, even if they were discovered, they believed that there was little chance of their being formally punished. Harris concluded his article by highlighting the essentially hidden nature of these behaviours. These, in part, he saw as being enabled by the localized policing arrangements common to American policing, which lead to a scarcity of data regarding the extent of these problems at a national level.

Maurice Punch's extensive research and commentary on the subject of police corruption helps us to understand variations in the patterns and forms that it takes between national jurisdictions. One such example is that of the different types of corruption that occur in European and North American settings. Whilst Punch suggests that all forms of corruption tend to occur to varying extents within most areas, certain types have become more predominant and embedded in particular locales. Punch (2003) shows how, for example, 'grafting' (police involvement in illicit financial arrangements) and police violence have been the key characteristics of police corruption in the United States, whilst professional negligence and noble cause corruption have been key themes within a European context. Within American settings, 'grafting' has long been considered a problem. As far back as 1935, Key referred to the payments made to police officers, in return for protection, by brothels and other illicit businesses in New York that were in breach of gambling and alcohol legislation. In Europe much greater emphasis has been placed on corruption as either a consequence of the pressure for results experienced by officers or dubious professional practices, although, as Punch (2009) suggests, the last 30 years or so have seen a shift within the UK to forms of corruption that are increasingly less visible. In terms of understanding this variation in forms of police corruption between Europe and North America, Punch (2009) provides an engaging account not only of the more lowly pay and status of American police officers but, significantly, of the American trend towards decentralization of power and the associated importance of 'machine politics' at the local level. Importantly, this process encouraged, and indeed relied upon, a system of favours in return for political support, thus perpetuating a system based on vested interests. One example of this is the Democrat-affiliated New York City organization Tammany Hall, which provided widespread Irish-American influence on public appointments between the 1790s and 1960s and which was based upon a system of:

> machine politics lubricated by 'graft'. The incumbents of office in the cities and their ward bosses induced people to vote for them and to contribute to their coffers by the distribution of favours and jobs to faithful supporters. The police chief, commanders in the wards and often ordinary officers owed their positions to patronage and even paid for the appointment as in pre-modern times.
>
> (Punch, 2009, p. 54)

Substantial amounts of literature have attempted to explain the reasons why corruption occurs through the identification of core variables. For example, Sherman (1974) draws a distinct line between constant and variable factors. The constant factors that he describes relate to those aspects of the police role that are linked to the core roles, responsibilities and actions of police officers and include discretion, the limited visibility of police work, secrecy, the pay and status of police work and the opportunities presented by it. The variable factors include organizationally contingent factors such as the level of police cynicism, the extent and nature of leadership and subcultures in the organization, controls against corruption and the extent of moral and regulative work undertaken by the police (for example, through the policing of vice and traffic). They also, however, relate to the politics, cohesion and conflict of wider society.

Typically, of older work in the area, the focus falls primarily upon those aspects of the police role that appear also to support the culture of the police. What is debatable is the extent to which this can be taken as evidence of a direct causal relationship between police corruption and police culture. Perhaps one of the most relevant pieces of literature exploring police corruption and its relationship with contemporary police organizational cultures was produced by Miller (2003) in a piece of research that drew on data from professional standards units in eight English and Welsh police forces and the National Crime Squad. Not only did the research reiterate the breadth of behaviours that could constitute police corruption but it astutely unpicked the importance of different types of explanatory factor. Drawing attention to the role played by police organizational culture, Miller suggested that three particular aspects of it could contribute to police corruption. First, he highlighted the issue of 'poor security awareness'. Officers were criticized for paying insufficient attention to the need for discretion in their sharing of sensitive information with their colleagues, and information-sharing on a 'need-to-know' basis was not generally the norm. In some areas, this issue appeared to have been exacerbated by the use of computerized systems of data management. Second, the performance-driven culture of the police was identified as a significant contributory factor, historically, although one that was slowly declining in importance. The part played by efficiency was highlighted as a key factor by earlier work, such as that of Skolnick (1994), and there remains room for debate surrounding the impact of managerialist pressures as a driver for corrupt behaviour. The third and final factor described by Miller refers to the role of culturally sustained solidarity in providing barriers to police officers who might otherwise report the illicit behaviours of their colleagues. In words that reflect Manning's notion of a 'sacred canopy' (1977, p. 5), Miller refers to the 'protective layer' (2003, p. 22) that inhibits officers from whistle-blowing in cases of 'internally-networked corruption' (2003, p. 22). Whilst the solidarity of the police might ensure that illicit behaviour was tolerated, it could not always be taken as evidence of outright endorsement of it. (A related point is made by Westley, 1953, who differentiates between speaking out against colleagues' behaviour and openly supporting it.) These three explanations can be drawn on to suggest that a specific connection exists between the culture of the police and police corruption. In addition, Miller, significantly, identifies the importance of another neglected category of explanation, that of non-occupational factors. He suggests that some police corruption is informed, not by the cultural factors of the organization, but by the interplay between personal difficulties experienced by officers (be they, for example, relationship problems, financial problems or drug or alcohol use) and opportunities for corruption presented by social networks. In conclusion, Millar draws attention to the broad range of factors that can contribute to police corruption and, by doing so, perhaps undermines the long-standing wisdom that illicit police behaviour is essentially just a police cultural problem.

Many accounts of police corruption do present somewhat polarized explanations, which portray police corruption as the result either of personal deviance ('bad apple' theories) or of systemic organizational failing at a cultural or operational level ('rotten orchard' theories). These, in turn, reflect wider ideological tensions between the rights and responsibilities of individuals in the former and those of the state and its agencies in the latter. Importantly, and as Crank (1998) notes, policing represents a paradoxical balance between the individualism of specific officers set against the backdrop of an occupational environment steeped in hierarchy, tradition and ideology. For this reason, it is natural for there to exist accounts that stress one set of explanations at the expense of the other. Whilst a diversity of accounts of the variables responsible for police corruption are likely always to exist, Punch (2009) suggests that only those attempts at reform that acknowledge the *institutional* basis of corruption (rather than the *individual*) are likely to be successful.

A slightly different account and one that veers away from the traditional dichotomy of individual and institutional (or cultural) explanations sees police corruption as driven by the relation of the police to institutions within wider society. An example of such an explanation can be found in the work of Brogden (1982), who suggests that the uniqueness of the police comes not from the legitimation of their use of force but through what he terms their 'legal relation' (p. 121), which results in senior officers being significantly less likely to be subjected to political interference, and therefore more fully accountable. According to Brogden, this legal relation consequently promotes an ideologically driven view of the police that fails to reflect the reality of police practice. He notes that:

A criterion of reasonableness permits significant police freedom of action in the process of arrest, in the presentation of court-room evidence, in the legal form itself, and in the decision to prosecute. In turn, that latitude reflects the unique position of the police as arbiters of legal relations within the class relations embodied in the spirit of legality.

(1982, p. 123)

To Brogden, therefore, the reality of police corruption extends beyond the personal inclinations of officers, or the way in which groups of officers respond to embedded expectations of values and behaviour. Furthermore, such an analysis maintains that it is wrong to suggest that the legal relation of the police, whilst guaranteeing political independence, is merely an extension of those powers granted to all citizens. The police's legal position grants them sufficient freedoms, under the guise of legality, to maintain a sense of legitimacy surrounding their key role, which is that of maintaining order in a divided society. Waddington (1999b) expands upon this stance by noting that police corruption exists within 'a context of tolerance' (1999b, p. 175) whereby the particular legal relation of the police described above means that courts are often inclined to accept or even encourage the creative application of the 'Ways and Means Act' as long as it is undertaken for 'noble' causes. The underlying idea here is that discretion, which seems so critical to numerous accounts of 'negative' police behaviour, may be as much a legal as a cultural issue.

We should also remain aware that implicit support for improper police practice is not just an issue pertaining to the institution, its legal relation and the courts. Skolnick and Fyfe (1993) note the extent to which the public support the police in their role as specialists in discerning between behaviour that is tolerable and that which is not. Indeed, the social contract under which we secede our claims to freedom in return for state protection explicitly entitles us to expect the police not only to make such distinctions but, note Skolnick and Fyfe (1993), to act upon them. We, in other words, demand that the police are suspicious and, whilst not the most appealing of traits, suspicion is fundamental to the work of the police in dealing with those who constitute their legitimate targets (Crank, 1998). As members of the public we expect the police to stop criminals and are not exceptionally concerned by the methods that they employ to achieve this. Furthermore, we complain about police action, according to Skolnick and Fyfe, only when 'innocent' people are presumed guilty, and mistakes are acceptable when they are made against those with certain social characteristics. This sits slightly at odds with a description of what constitutes acceptable use of police force articulated by Bittner:

the fundamental maxim of the methodical exercise of coercion by the police is that, just as society as a whole attempted to restrict the legitimate use of force by creating a special institution, so, in turn, resorting to it in police practice must be restricted to an unavoidable minimum. Above all, force must not be used for any other purpose except to effect restraint.

(1970, p. 106)

Thirty years after the likes of Westley (1970) and Bittner (1970) addressed the subject, some of their contemporaries continued to debate these issues. Skolnick (2000), for example, explains conflicting attitudes towards police use of unauthorized force in terms of a 'culture war' between those who believe that police officers should adhere both to the law and to prescribed police procedures at whatever cost and those who believe that law-breakers should lose any automatic entitlement to redress against unauthorized use of force. Crucially, this 'culture war' is not being played out merely amongst police officers but also between politicians and members of the voting public. This point echoes that of Sparrow, Moore and Kennedy (1990), namely that unspoken public approval of police use of unauthorized force has been instrumental in, if not legitimizing it, then at least thwarting its disappearance. In other words, if the culture of the police has a role to play in facilitating the continued existence of corrupt behaviour, that role is one made easier by the discretion of the police role and a tendency for these behaviours to be supported by both the public and the work of the courts.

The above point is further contextualized by the work of Waddington (1999b), who questions the extent to which some examples of police corruption are actually 'corrupt' given the ways in which the courts, juries and public opinion have failed, historically, to robustly condemn police malpractice. Waddington draws on the Rodney King incident, specifically the failure of the jury to accept that King's beating constituted an illegal use of police force, to make a number of important points in this respect. First, he proposes that in cases like these the power or authority to determine what does or does not constitute police brutality rests solely with the jury. Second, given that the jury concluded that King was not the victim of assault, they disregarded potential objections to police use of force against African-Americans with criminal records. This leads us to question the extent to which it is appropriate to consider some apparently illegal police practices as 'deviant'. Third, the officers who were exonerated in terms of the assault charges were subsequently charged with violating King's civil rights. This implies that, at a legal level (in respect of the original jury concluding that police brutality had not occurred), the criminal case had been effectively concluded. The civil trial therefore became a means of mollifying public opinion, which had been inflamed by the video evidence surrounding the original events. This draws into focus the problem of defining what constitutes deviant police behaviour. The police have to make quick, conclusive and potentially life-changing decisions as situations present themselves, whilst the legal analysis of such actions is always undertaken with hindsight. To Waddington, 'What is acceptable and unacceptable policing is profoundly uncertain. This arises from the fact that policing entails using methods of intrinsically marginal legality and acceptability' (Waddington, 1999b, p. 180). Importantly, the police are largely judged on the outcomes, rather than the processes, of their decision-making.

Little real formal consensus exists, therefore, about the extent to which the police can or should be controlled. In part this is due to the situational context, which dictates whether police action is correct and appropriate. Two different instances of police use of force might meet with very different public reactions dependent solely on the characteristics of the people being subjected to it. Simultaneously, it appears that political, legal and public opinion is unwilling to engage in debate regarding which contours of such behaviour should be accepted and which should not. It might indeed be the case, as Brogden (1982) suggests, that police corruption, whilst often accommodated by the courts, the police hierarchy and the public, is more fully facilitated by its relation to the legal structure. In this respect police legitimacy is not so much politically as legally ascribed and, as a result, serves to imbue police work with a neutrality that fails to reflect its reality.

Police culture and police reform

The issue of reform in the face of corruption is one addressed by Punch (2009), who notes that approaches that focus on corruption at an individual rather than at an institutional level have generally failed to prove effective. Punch's work shows how contemporary police reform has been largely shaped by the move towards a more centralized policing model, in the United Kingdom, and that this has skewed police deviance to the extent that it now effectively has become a response to external rather than internal pressures. This process is amply evidenced by the emergence of new public management in policing (Johnston, 2000a; Waters, 2000; Cockcroft and Beattie, 2009), and it is this, according to Punch (2009), which has led to the rise of a number of novel forms of police discourse. The first, evident during the 1970s and 1980s, was concerned with the scrutiny of the internal effectiveness of police responses to new police challenges. A more externally facing challenge also emerged during the same period in response to revelations concerning well-documented police corruption. During the 1990s accountability was further redefined, in accordance with the managerialism of the time, to encompass police performance. In this way attention was shifted away from the shortcomings of street-level officers to a focus upon the ability of police managers to evidence effectiveness through measurable outputs. Finally, according to Punch, most recently the official discourse of accountability has altered to emphasize the 'new professionalism' (Punch, 2009, p. 196) of police work, which highlights leadership and transparency to stakeholders against a changing context of competing priorities. Under this model, accountability is ensured, not through interventions aimed at the cultural dynamics of the police world, but through liaison at a community level and through the regulation provided by a succession of external bodies. What soon becomes apparent through the more contemporary literature of police corruption is that the convergence of police culture with the market orientation of policing reveals a complex amalgamation of factors that fail to unanimously confirm the extent to which police culture promotes deviant behaviour. Whilst early work tended to promote the view that police culture could be considered a significant factor, more recent work by Miller (2003) appears to show that non-work factors may also encourage police corruption. Punch (2009) also addresses some of the more contemporary factors that may aid our understanding of the role that culture now plays in explaining corrupt behaviour. Whilst acknowledging the shift, over recent years, towards a plurality of forms of external oversight in British policing, he questions the extent to which this represents a 'new *culture* of accountability' (2009, p. 198), whilst noting that, at present, rhetoric outweighs reform. Likewise, he refers to recent evidence that suggests that a 'performance culture' (2009, p. 202) may be considered a major driver for some forms of corruption. However, Punch notes the rather contradictory way in which Her Majesty's Inspectorate of Constabulary, whilst partially responsible for driving police forces towards greater efficiency, also acknowledged in one report the potential for performance cultures to encourage some corrupt behaviour. This potential link between pressure to evidence effectiveness and illicit police practices represents a politically sensitive area that further complicates our cultural understanding of police corruption.

Whilst it has become de rigueur to acknowledge the existence of multiple cultures, references to cultures of performance and accountability probably tell us little about police culture in the terms within which it is generally understood. This, in turn, necessitates a questioning of the assumptions with which we underpin our understanding of culture. Furthermore, it is not unreasonable to argue that police culture research's real strength lies in the breadth of its explanatory vigour, not in its selective application to areas such as accountability and performance. This is not to suggest that police culture theories cannot help our understanding here, but that the 'emotional and logical *consistency*' (Crank, 1998, p. 26) that is integral to police culture appears too complex to make sense when applied to specific types of culture. This is especially the case when these cultures are defined not through the organization itself but through the application of generic external pressures. Performance cultures therefore have come to represent an artificial driver motivated not by the ideology of the occupation and its participants but by managerial incentives aimed at modifying existing ways of doing policing. Similarly, measures to enhance police accountability, in many cases, do little to deal with issues at a cultural level but focus on how cultural values become manifest at a behavioural level. This is perhaps unsurprising and, as Chan (1997) notes, police reform at a cultural level is difficult to achieve without structural change to the police environment. Chan (2003) also notes how one source of frustration, and subsequently cynicism, amongst police recruits centres upon what are viewed as disproportionate mechanisms of accountability. In itself, this provides us with some useful information regarding the nature of police culture, namely that it appears to be a bottom-up response to conditions beyond the control of the rank and file. Rowe develops this idea further by identifying how the culture of the police represents the defiance of the lower ranks to 'politically driven management initiatives' (2004, p. 54) and, if true, this suggests that initiatives to instil new forms of control will encounter difficulties in provoking anything but new forms of resistance from officers.

By way of conclusion to this discussion of police corruption, I want to return to the work of Maguire and Norris (1994), as it provides us with some potential strategies for modifying police behaviour through cultural change. Ultimately, they believe that there has to be a convergence between both structural and cultural factors within police agencies for behavioural change to occur. They recommend that, to counter police malpractice, a number of areas have to be addressed, including the acknowledgement by higher-ranking officers that corruption is an issue worthy of address, the establishment of clear lines of management within investigations, the monitoring of case materials by independent force quality units, the reduction of a 'results' ethos that leads to unnecessary pressure upon police officers, the introduction of rewards for high-quality investigative work and reform of the structures and work of detective units. These reforms can be effective only if there is a modification of the existing cultures within the police force. In conclusion, they noted that the consistent message that they had received throughout their research was that informal communications from senior officers were more important than formal policies in determining how policy was implemented and, moreover, that those senior officers themselves receive informal direction from the government, regulatory bodies and the media. These findings therefore emphasize the importance of appreciating the tensions between formal communication of policy and the mediation of those policies via the cultural lens of the police service. The latter point, Maguire and Norris suggest, has largely gone unacknowledged by previous attempts at reform.

Leadership and police culture

As can be seen from the previous section, policing, at operational, strategic and political levels, remains a perplexing and conflict-ridden endeavour aggravated by the challenge not only of articulating a vision of policing but of implementing it at a practical level. The management of police behaviour has emerged as a persistent theme over recent years, with traditional culturalist views presenting the police institution as being enslaved to a set of cultural reference points that leave little opportunity for effective change to police officer attitudes and behaviour. More recently, writers like Savage (2007) have identified the emergence of cultural groupings within the police organization that have more in common with the values, language and orientation of private sector management than the insular *esprit de corps* described within earlier scholastic works in policing. Given the unlikeliness for this set of new cultural values to fully replace more traditional value sets, there remains a substantial challenge for police leaders in communicating a concept of policing that will have resonance within both managerialist and traditional cultures. Whilst, in many respects, this distinction may reflect the split between street officers and police managers described by Reuss-Ianni and Ianni (1983), there is a historical precedence to be found in Niederhoffer's (1969) work, which remains of interest for its portrayal of a divided police force long before the advent of public sector managerialism. His work shows that, as far back as the 1940s, the New York City Police Department was recruiting applicants more than half of whom had received a college education and that the resulting diversity of workforce had led to officers driven by competing sets of values and for whom policing meant different things. He wrote: 'Dissension has reached serious proportions, verging on internecine class conflict between the lower-class conservatives and the upwardly mobile middle-class radicals' (1969, p. 18).

The tensions that arose between street officers and management were the result of class-based differences becoming manifest in a tension between conservative 'common-sense' policing and radical 'professional' policing. However, whilst the professionalization of the police may be founded upon friction between beat officers and their managers, experiences in the UK also highlight the importance of the relationship between police and government as dictating the direction and governance of the process. For example, Savage (2007) identifies the ways in which the performance culture of the English and Welsh police can be seen as going through three distinct phases, the first being the general nudging of the police by the government towards greater efficiency and economy under the 'Financial Management Initiative' of the early 1980s. As Savage notes, this represented a preoccupation with inputs and the way that police resources were used most successfully, although, importantly, at this stage the government did not generally involve itself in taking an active role in setting police priorities. This development was largely driven by the growing perception in policy circles that, despite increases in police pay, numbers and resources, police performance (when measured in terms of crime reduction and increased clear-up rates) was apparently declining (Morgan and Newburn, 1997). By the mid-1990s, however, the gentle nudges of previous administrations had given way to an increasingly formalized focus upon police outputs or, in other words, the quantity and quality of what police services delivered to their communities. With the emergence of key performance indicators and performance league tables individual forces still retained substantial autonomy. Simultaneously, however, government assumed responsibility for broadly articulating major operational priorities and for facilitating the generation of data with which to judge police forces' performance. The third and final phase of this gradual strengthening of the state role within the orientation of police strategy and practice, according to Savage, resulted in a performance culture that veered towards the 'oppressive' (2007, p. 213) and was achieved through three main developments. First, the ratcheting up of state expectation from 'objectives' to 'plans' allowed for greater centralized control over the work of the police. Second, police performance at force level came under the scrutiny of newly formed agencies imbued with powers to intervene in forces, or parts of forces, that were deemed to be underperforming. Finally, targets were introduced by which performance could be quantified and assessed. These changes, whilst representing an extensive rewriting of the ways in which the police role was defined and their success measured, also impacted at an altogether more cultural level, with Savage describing the management culture of the police as increasingly analogous to that of the corporate boardroom. It is against this backdrop of managerialism and politicization that recent decades have seen a growing emphasis on the importance of leadership as a catalyst for organizational change. In particular, leadership styles have increasingly come into focus as potential solutions to the cultural 'problems' of police work.

Of note here is the increasing popularity (at both conceptual and practical levels) of the concept of 'leadership', which has had a crucial role to play in framing much of the debate surrounding organizational behaviour and effectiveness.

Over recent decades, as a result, we have seen a growing trend for police leadership to attract the kind of scrutiny previously reserved for lower-level officers and, in particular, research has tended to concentrate on the operational impacts of different forms of leadership style. For example, Krimmel and Lindenmuth (2001), in a piece of research exploring varieties of police leadership in Pennsylvania, attempted to identify positive and negative police leadership styles. In common with previous research into police leadership (by, for example, Kuykendall and Unsinger, 1982; Bruns and Shuman, 1988; and Girodo, 1998), the authors identified the existence of a variety of police leadership styles, noting that these tend to occupy a limited spectrum from 'Machiavellian' (based on unscrupulous manipulation to achieve favoured results) to 'participatory' (based on inclusive management practices). Research findings also suggest that police leadership is, in many cases, problematic. Girodo (1998), for example, surveyed senior officers from police organizations throughout the world in an attempt to understand the different ways in which leaders exercised control over their staff, and found that leadership approaches could be categorized as 'bureaucratic', 'social contract', 'transformational' or 'Machiavellian'. Interestingly, he found that the majority of police leaders appeared to adopt the negatively perceived Machiavellian style of leadership, a finding reinforced by Krimmel and Lindenmuth (2001). Likewise, the work of Bruns and Shuman (1988) highlighted favourable attitudes, amongst middle-ranking police managers, for participatory styles of police leadership, but found that these failed to be widely implemented, as police organizations were ultimately unwilling to support such managerial strategies.

Whilst participatory leadership has not always been championed within the police, the tide of public opinion has, suggest Krimmel and Lindenmuth (2001), moved against bureaucratic styles of leadership, which are perceived as leading to unproductive, unmotivated and undynamic work practices. Furthermore, bureaucratic police forces are perceived as being disadvantaged by a host of other factors, including poor workplace relations between managers and staff, divisive and divided workforces due to unionization, a proliferation of self-interest amongst individual workers and, finally, high turnover rates amongst staff. Whilst it is clear that bureaucratic styles of police management have been subject to criticism over recent years, Mastrofski (2004) notes how a variety of preventive and corrective options are available within them, through which police managers can exert control over their officers. These strategies may range from preventive approaches, such as modifications to recruitment, training and beat assignment policies, to corrective ones that focus on new forms of disciplinary code. What must be borne in mind, however, is that policing is a complex set of actions restricted not only by elements of bureaucracy but also by the influence of organizational culture (Crank, 1998). Densten (1999), for example, charts some of the further complexities for effective police leadership by highlighting a number of key issues. First, whilst police leadership is necessarily located in the hierarchical rank structure of the police, the external environment, or individuals located within it, can also influence how street officers act. This point inevitably highlights the importance of discretion as a factor alongside police hierarchy in determining police behaviour.

(However, Mastrofski, 2004, is careful to suggest that focusing on the relative strengths of situational, officer and organizational factors should be considered a lower priority than charting differentiation in 'patterns of influence' (p. 103) in the use of police discretion.) Second, policing, owing to its nature, involves an inevitable degree of failure, and this necessitates reflection on the respective definitions of success and failure within the police organization. Third, Densten (1999) suggests that a 'paradox of accountability' (p. 46) exists whereby police officers are held accountable for their actions even when there is no defined expectation of what constitutes appropriate behaviour. This point has previously been acknowledged by Reiner (1998), who noted the absence, within debates of policing, of constructive dialogue regarding what constitutes good performance and how it might be measured.

All these issues are viewed as potential barriers to the implementation of effective leadership within the police service and, furthermore, may prompt us to question what exactly constitutes effective police leadership. Often it may appear sufficient to define good leadership through reference to examples of bad leadership, characterized by Densten (1999, p. 46) as 'frequent empty and ritualistic gestures, conservative, cautious, and authoritarian management styles, poor communication skills, and lack of managerial support'. Silvestri (2007, p. 39), alternatively, provides a succinct and unambiguous definition of good leadership as being, simply, 'the ability to bring about sustained organizational change'. Attempts to unpick the individual components of successful leadership have tended to focus on a limited range of factors, with Krimmel and Lindenmuth (2001), for example, highlighting the beneficial impact upon performance of individual officers having been mentored and prepared for their leadership role and of them having worked their way up through the ranks, having worked in a unionized workplace and having received a college education. Whilst they were unable to explain why the unionization of police organizations coincided with positive perceptions of the quality of police leadership, they state that the importance of education has long been identified as a determining factor in perceptions of good leadership in a variety of management contexts. Although such findings may be superficially appealing, there are some methodological challenges associated with them, not least in terms of the internal validity of such work. For example, Mastrofski (2004) notes that it is incredibly difficult to assess where exactly the 'added value' lies in police officer education, as research rarely differentiates between the actual experience of attending an educational programme and the effects of passing the selection procedure.

Perhaps the most helpful way of distinguishing between types of leadership and their effectiveness is to use the distinction between 'transactional' and 'transformational' styles. Transactional styles have generally come to be associated with negative or problematic leadership and are founded upon 'explicit and implicit contractual relationships' (Bass and Avolio, 1993, p. 116), which motivate workers to act in accordance with their own feelings of self-interest rather than to identify with the needs of the organization. Such leadership tends to take one of two forms, 'contingent reward' (reward for appropriate behaviour) and 'management by exception' (intervention when performance does not meet expectation), and it is the latter that has been most commonly observed in police organizations (Densten, 1999). Despite transactional approaches generally being considered unproductive and potentially damaging (Silvestri, 2007), members of police organizations appear to be largely uncritical of them as management styles (Densten, 1999). Similarly, and as Densten acknowledges, professions like policing that have traditionally encompassed reactive roles and that involve comprehensive procedural systems are largely suited to transactional methods such as management by exception.

In direct contrast to the autocratic transactional approach to leadership, 'transformational' leadership has come to represent, to some, a more favoured, and effective, means of controlling staff within organizations. Where transactional leadership sees the management role as oriented towards staff who have successfully or unsuccessfully followed instructions, transformational leadership is characterized by 'participation, consultation and inclusion' (Silvestri, 2007, p. 39) and a commitment to effecting organizational change legitimately rather than through reacting to staff on the basis of their actions (Mastrofski, 2004). Consequently, Mastrofski views the potency of transformational approaches as being in their ability to encourage a convergence of followers' values with those of their leaders rather than through the 'transaction of compliance' (2004, p. 104) associated with a linear reward–punishment system (Densten, 1999). In effect, therefore, such approaches 'transform' followers through effective role modelling and ensure that they behave in a particular way, not as a means of avoiding or ensuring particular consequences, but because they believe it to be appropriate. Whilst proponents such as Bass and Avolio (1993) identify the approach's features in terms of influence, motivation, stimulation and consideration, it is open to criticism on the grounds that it might be considered a method that relies on the personal characteristics of one person to inspire a workforce rather than constituting a fully strategic approach. Supporters of transformational leadership point to a number of particular benefits associated with its implementation within an organizational context. It is seen to facilitate communication, especially in regard to the ways in which an organization articulates success and failure (Densten, 1999), to encourage a more motivated workforce (Pillai and Williams, 2004; Silvestri, 2007), to improve performance (Pillai and Williams, 2004), to create synthesis between strategy and culture (Bass and Avolio, 1993), to make followers more goal oriented (Pillai and Williams, 2004) and to stimulate greater workplace solidarity (Pillai and Williams, 2004).

Whilst garnering substantial support within management circles, transformational leadership has a tendency to be portrayed as a panacea to the challenges of leadership (Currie and Lockett, 2007; Neyroud, 2011) and is often depicted as the only viable option for management. However, the enthusiastic support that the concept has received from some quarters has been countered by those who believe that its implementation at an operational level would prove difficult.

Transformational leadership in the public sector

When assessing the impact, or potential for impact, of transformative leadership on policing and its occupational cultures, we must be aware that transposing transformative leadership from a private to a public sector context represents a not altogether seamless process. In particular, it is important to realize that the importing of concepts from the private sector to the public sector is often problematic, owing to a failure to appreciate the extent of the differences between the two (Williams, 1985). Not least, providing simple measures of success and failure may be more difficult to achieve in public sector institutions with broader roles. Similarly, whilst Densten (1999) suggests that transformational leadership facilitates the articulation of what constitutes success and failure within organizational contexts, the work of Jackson (1993) prompts reflection upon the extent to which failure can become normalized within public sector institutions where the stated aims often appear to be undermined by financial constraints. Finally, one might consider Williams's (1985) assertion that, in the public sector, key knowledge is usually held by those who are excluded, intellectually and organizationally, from engaging at a strategic level.

Currie and Lockett (2007) addressed the appropriateness of transformational leadership to public sector organizations by studying its introduction within an English secondary school. What the research found was that policies aimed at introducing transformative leadership to public sector contexts were largely ineffective and that the reasons for this failure could be explained as follows. First, when transformative leadership was introduced it was implemented in a limited and managerially oriented way that failed to engage with staff of all levels. Second, the managerialistic elements of transformative leadership tended not to be welcomed amongst those whose conception of leadership in the educational context was more aligned with moral and pedagogic values, and in this case meant that the particular organizational context of the environment had not been fully recognized. In an educational setting characterized by professional values some of the more managerial forms of transformational leadership may appear improper to practitioners. Third, the very complexity of public sector institutions, and the roles that they undertake, means that, unlike within the commercial sector, leaders are usually unable to develop the solution to an institution's challenges unaided. Finally, leaders have insufficient power to effect change within the context in which they exercise leadership, owing to the overriding influence of central government. This effectively constrains their ability to lead in a transformative manner. In conclusion, therefore, whilst this idea of 'generic transfer' (Currie and Lockett, 2007, p. 345) of transformational leadership from the private to the public sectors remains popular, some barriers need to be overcome before it provides a fully appropriate response to the challenges and contexts posed by public sector organizations like the police.

The preceding sections have explained the importance of leadership, the different forms that it can take and the application of transformative leadership styles to the public sector context. One important aspect of leadership, however, has been neglected. Despite the suggestion that successful leadership was predominantly concerned with effecting change within an organizational setting, little mention has been made of what exactly was in need of change. In most cases, it can straightforwardly be assumed that the target or focus of effective leadership should be to change the values held by followers and their resultant actions so that they more closely support the overall strategic direction of the organization. In this respect, therefore, leadership, especially within a policing context, becomes largely concerned with effecting cultural change.

Whilst police culture has become synonymous with a range of negative behaviours, in the wider literature pertaining to organizational culture there is a tendency for workplace cultures to be viewed in more positive terms. For Bass and Avolio the organizational culture is integral to the processes of transformational leadership, as it represents 'the setting within which the vision takes hold' (1993, p. 112) and reflects the shared values of the workplace. They also note that where such cultural backdrops become problematic is when they begin to constrain innovation through being backward rather than forward focused. In itself this reflects a challenge for the successful application of transformational leadership theories to police organizations where the organizational culture of the police is more likely to be influenced by an essentially reactive police role rather than the proactive orientation of senior officers.

Furthermore, despite most police culture research focusing on the behaviour of street-level officers, Rowe (2006) charts the intermittent concerns that have arisen regarding the leadership qualities of senior police officers in the UK, from the corruption scandals of the 1950s (when, for example, the Chief Constable of Worcester was imprisoned for fraud) through to the criticisms of police leadership made by the Lawrence Enquiry. Home Office proposals published in 2004 highlight the importance attached to the idea that organizational change within the police was essentially a leadership issue. They suggested that 'The leadership of managers and chief officers in valuing customer service and communicating this to frontline staff will be critical to delivery of a new culture of customer responsiveness' (Home Office, 2004, p. 61). Importantly, Rowe notes perhaps the major challenge regarding police leadership. It is not solely an issue of individual 'qualities and performance' (2006, p. 759) but one affected greatly by the broader cultural issues of policing. The personal qualities of senior officers will have little impact if lower-ranking officers fail to consider the leaders, or their reforms, legitimate and, logically, Rowe suggests that the forms of leadership that followers will be responsive to will be those that reinforce traditional perceptions of the occupation. Understandably, this poses some fundamental obstacles to the implementation of far-reaching change within police organizations. As long as practical experience remains an embedded theme in police narratives of effective leadership (Rowe, 2006), 'radical' proposals (for example, to make senior positions open to individuals from other professions) will be met with resistance. This recurrent theme of the importance of practical experience to police work can be viewed at some levels as constituting a tautological device for perpetuating what Reuss-Ianni and Ianni (1983) saw as the entrenched divisions separating street and management cops.

For example, Rowe (2006) subtly shows how the practical elements of policing are used rhetorically at two levels. First, they are used as a means of highlighting the inappropriateness of having non-warranted officers in senior operational positions. Second, the same device is used to denigrate the ways in which senior officers have 'forgotten' about the realities of policing the street since embarking upon their managerial career paths. Similarly, Rowe's work demonstrates that the perceived erosion of discretion (integral to the tenets of practical policing) has become cast as an attack on traditional police work, with a resultant ratcheting up of tensions between officers in operational and managerial roles. The growing prevalence of risk-averse behaviour (which has accompanied decreases in police discretion) has led to police forces evolving into 'punitive bureaucracies' (Mastrofski, 2004, p. 104). These represent a narrowing of the police role and occur in situations where police leaders have succeeded in eradicating certain types of behaviours but failed to instil sufficient confidence for officers to perform new ones.

The practical nature of police work poses yet further challenges for transformative leadership as a catalyst for cultural change, not least because leaders and followers alike remain contributing players in the same cultural milieu. Senior officers tend to be cut from the same cultural cloth as lower-ranking officers. Whilst Foster (2003) acknowledges this factor as a potential inhibitor to cultural change, she remains optimistic that policies to reform police organizational culture can be successful if supported by appropriate leadership strategies. Other authors have made strong cases to suggest that police reform is, in many cases, less of a leadership issue than a political one. Numerous external factors hold sway over issues of police use of discretion, according to Mastrofski (2004), and these include police professional associations, civil rights groups and legal systems. Furthermore, in a paper assessing the success of police reform in the New South Wales Police Service, in the light of the Wood Royal Commission Report of 1997, David Dixon (2001) argues that police reform cannot be understood without reference to the political and social forces which shape policing and its position within political arenas. Dixon's analysis largely places blame for the limited success of reform initiatives on the politicized nature of policing contexts whereby the intricacies of the criminal justice system are misrepresented by politicians and succeed in diverting attention away from the complexities of police administration. In part, the police are culpable for this. Dixon (drawing on Manning, 1977) suggests that the police have, in reality, become hostages to fortune by allowing their effectiveness to be assessed in relation to crime, a phenomenon that research has largely shown they have limited control over. This identification with crime-fighting (rather than with, for example, community service) has effectively left them facing considerable challenges in respect of evidencing their effectiveness. As a result, Dixon suggests that policing, whilst inevitably a political issue, has become far more sensitive to partisan political squabbles than necessary. Dixon ends by highlighting that the rhetoric of leadership reform has masked the fact that 'command and control' forms of leadership remain in use and, by way of example, shows how the auditors of the New South Wales reform process concluded that 'management-by-fear' continued to be a leadership strategy of choice for some senior officers.

Police culture, absenteeism and transformational leadership

The issue of police absenteeism provides an interesting focal point with which to assess some dynamics of the relationship between the culture of the police and the impact of transformational leadership. Police absenteeism, on health grounds, is generally associated with mental health conditions such as stress (Summerfield, 2011). Whilst there may be a temptation to link the concept of police stress to the emotional impact of their operational experience, research findings suggest that we should exercise caution in this respect. The literature has consistently shown that a central motivating factor for many individuals planning to join the police is the opportunities it presents for undertaking demanding operational work in situations of conflict (Cain, 1973; Smith and Gray, 1983; Wessely, 2011). However, research conducted by Collins and Gibbs (2003) proposes that organizational issues rather than operational events are most likely to lead to incidents of stress. Furthermore, they hypothesize that culturally located pressures may make police officers more liable to suffer from stress-related illnesses, a sentiment echoed by Wessely (2011). This apparent connection between workplace absenteeism or ill health and police culture is a telling one, not least in that it highlights the impact of police culture as reaching beyond the parameters generally accepted within the literature. Moreover, research by Derek Summerfield (2011), a consultant occupational psychologist working within London's Metropolitan Police, indicates how clinical diagnoses of officer psychiatric ill health are often patient led, take place against a context of workplace discord and are increasingly conducted within the presence of representatives of professional associations (for example, in a UK context, the Police Federation). While workplace stress amongst police officers was generally caused by a convergence of issues, the origins of which might be work based, home based or a combination of the two, officers articulated their health issues within a narrative of disillusionment with the police organization and their role within it. The patients themselves often led the diagnostic process, and retirement on the grounds of ill health, to some, became a career option to be worked towards and one which occupational health workers became complicit in. The report describes one consultant for whom 'the wear and tear of an officer's entire police career' (Summerfield, 2011, p. 92) was the key event accounting for the post-traumatic stress disorder diagnosis that would lead to a recommendation for retirement on the grounds of ill health. Few officers undergoing this diagnostic process exhibited the degree of disability that Summerfield deemed appropriate for retirement on psychiatric grounds, and the main criterion of determining whether an officer returned to work was whether or not he or she wanted to. Summerfield's conclusion was straightforward, that ill health had become a cultural tool in an organization where extended absence was associated with both work disputes and perceptions of the police organization as indifferent to officers' needs. What this suggests, therefore, is that police culture may pervade occupational life to such an extent that it negatively influences police officers' mental and emotional well-being, provides a means through which to ascribe the causes of health problems and, importantly, leads to health professionals 'buying in' to these cultural accounts of what constitutes ill health.

Recent years have seen a gradual realization, not only that occupational culture may influence the extent and presentation of staff sickness and absenteeism, but also that there is potential for transformational leadership to play a role in combating this process. For example, research by a UK national independent regulator for health, safety and illness issues, the Health and Safety Executive (HSE) (2008), investigated the extent to which transformational leadership could reduce absenteeism in four public sector organizations (including the police). In part, the research was prompted by the aim of the Ministerial Task Force for Health, Safety and Productivity to enforce 'culture change' (Cabinet Office *et al.*, cited in HSE, 2008, p. 1), therefore framing the problem as a cultural one. The report concluded that transformational leadership had a positive but unexceptional impact on rates of absenteeism. In an echo of the findings of Currie and Lockett (2007), the Health and Safety Executive explained these findings by concluding that the inflexibility of centrally controlled public organizations restricted them from articulating new 'visions', thus limiting the potency of any transformational leadership initiatives.

Culture, leadership, continuity and change

The challenge of police leadership was amply articulated by Pat Murphy, a former New York Police Department commissioner from the 1970s, who was charged with cleaning up the department in the face of public scandal and entrenched structural and cultural predispositions towards corruption. To Murphy, the politicization of police work (in its North American context) allowed for compromise, corruption and political control, leaving police chiefs 'simpering like a court jester in the halls of the mighty' (Murphy and Plate, cited in Punch, 2009, p. 55). Police leadership is increasingly seen as the solution to organizational problems. Importantly, it is seen as a potential means of resolving all manner of institutional challenges regardless of the nature of the problem, be it the 'graft' associated with big city policing in North America, the 'systemic incompetence and chronic non-performance' (Punch, 2003, p. 173) of some European police institutions or culturally induced ill health and absenteeism. The concept of transformational leadership appears to be well received in many policing contexts, a point perhaps reinforced, during the summer of 2011, when William Bratton, widely credited as bringing much needed change to the police services of Los Angeles, Boston and New York and touted as a potential commissioner of the London Metropolitan Police Force, stated that 'I think of myself as a transformational leader who changes cultures' (Dodd and Stratton, 2011). Despite such proclamations, some dissent has been voiced regarding the extent to which transformational leadership represents the silver bullet with which to resolve the complexities of managing police values, behaviour and performance. More specifically, some have raised doubts as to the extent to which transformational leadership is wholly appropriate for, or effective within, policing organizations. Neyroud (2011), himself a former chief constable, describes the awkwardness with which transformational leadership can be applied to an organizational hierarchy that relies on elements of command. This point is reinforced by Densten's (1999) assertion that policing is reactive and reliant upon procedure, thus making it more readily suited to transactional as opposed to trans-formational leadership styles.

The structure and culture of the police may therefore have a defined role to play in ensuring that transactional leadership continues to be used within police organizations. Given the way in which many police forces have a clearly defined internal career structure where police leaders are essentially drawn from officers who have walked the beat, it is logical to suggest that leaders and followers alike belong to the same occupational cultures (Foster, 2003) or, at the very least, are influenced by them. At the same time, and somewhat ironically, the intrusion of management into the largely unsupervised work of street officers is one of the key drivers that sustains the predominantly lower-rank outlook of police culture (Crank, 1998). Furthermore, the structures of police forces may do little to provide a fertile environment for transformational leadership. In a piece of research that aimed to explore both public perceptions and expectations of the London Metropolitan Police and the experiences of officers, FitzGerald, Hough, Joseph and Qureshi (2002) found criticisms of police management that had originally surfaced close to 20 years ago (see, for example, Smith and Gray, 1983) and that had largely failed to be resolved over subsequent years. These were further compounded by a top-down, management-driven performance culture that encouraged short-term strategic responses, owing to the fact that performance criteria were subject to regular change. Whilst, at one level, this might be considered broadly beneficial and taken as evidence that performance indicators evolve and adapt in response to changes in public opinion and local need, evidence from the report suggests that formal indicators fail to reflect those issues upon which the public make their judgements. In many cases, performance measurement defaults towards measuring processes (activities) rather than outcomes (achievements) (Reiner, 1998; Cockcroft and Beattie, 2009), and this, unsurprisingly, can lead to uncertainty regarding the true role of the police and, importantly, the effectiveness with which they undertake it.

The authors continue by identifying shortcomings in the Metropolitan Police's approach to management, citing the two key themes of 'poor management' and 'staff morale'. 'Poor management' was evidenced through both a lack of consideration towards career development and constraints that were placed upon police managers. In terms of the former, weaknesses in career development could be traced back to initial training, which was seen as failing in its core function of preparing new officers for the situations that they would face during their working lives. When career development issues were engaged with, it was generally in respect of officers who sought promotion. Officers who were not seeking promotion but who also wanted to experience different types of role within the organization were viewed as being at odds with the expectations of the police force. Career development policies, therefore, applied only to those seeking promotion and focused simply upon demonstrating an aptitude for implementing change. This system, according to FitzGerald, Hough, Joseph and Qureshi (2002), led to a perception that a process of change for change's sake had become a legitimate career development strategy, which did little to ease tensions between those working under constantly changing regimes and those who were responsible for them.

Likewise, managers were restricted in the extent to which they could actually lead staff effectively. In an environment where economy had become the overriding priority, managers had scarce resources with which to reward 'good' policing, leading to a transactional system that can only bring sanctions against those whose work is unacceptable, rather than reward those whose work exceeds expectation. The lack of managerial options available to supervisory staff was, note FitzGerald, Hough, Joseph and Qureshi (2002), further exacerbated by the expansion of roles that police managers were expected to undertake. Senior officers reported that they were increasingly unlikely to know their staff, with one officer recalling the difficulties he encountered both in ensuring that officers who deserved credit for their work received it and in making sure that he could remember which officers had been praised and for what reason.

'Staff morale', the other major theme used to explain problematic management, was apparently compromised at all levels of service. Whilst higher-ranking officers voiced concern at barriers to implementing an effective rewards system, lower-level staff considered themselves failed in terms of reward, support and resources. Officers felt that senior members of the service failed to appreciate the work they did and, on the occasions that senior officers attempted to engage with the lower ranks, such attempts at bridge-building were viewed as both patronizing and misguided. Information technology infrastructures created practical challenges for officers, as they were either insufficient to deal with demand or increasingly being used for purposes beyond their original remit. One example of this was the increasing use of such systems as a means of producing data for management purposes rather than their intended use as an operational tool. Importantly, this piece of research identified some sources of tension and conflict as being so widespread within the policing institution that they might be considered culturally embedded. The pressures described by FitzGerald, Hough, Joseph and Qureshi (2002) appear to mirror those previously described by Reuss-Ianni and Ianni (1983). At the same time, however, this research does appear to highlight a number of more contextual factors that have a part to play in aggravating existing cultural tensions within the police. While Reuss-Ianni and Ianni's work details the differentiation of role and belief systems experienced between street and management cops and warns against management attempts to replace rather than adapt work practices in the work context, such issues are portrayed in a way that does little to acknowledge political pressures or the tendency for private sector management techniques to cross over into the public sector. Two factors may partially explain this. First, Reuss-Ianni and Ianni's research largely preceded the introduction of new public management and, second, British policing has traditionally been centrally controlled whereas American policing is more localized. It is the centralized nature of British policing that has provided the key means by which new public management could become so fundamental to UK police practice over the last 25 years. As a consequence, the symbolic aspects of police work have been made more complex by the interplay between traditional police cultures and cultural changes associated with the import of new public management methods and ideologies.

Another issue highlighted in the work of Fitzgerald, Hough, Joseph and Qureshi

(2002) is the emphasis upon the growing discourse of 'change management' as a desirable aptitude in officers looking for elevation to more senior ranks. Change management represents a novel and unprecedented driver for police values, attitudes and behaviours, representing, as it does, the values of the free market rather than the traditions of policing. This provides some intriguing options with regard to police culture. For example, the work of Monique Marks (2007) charts the contrasting visions of police work advocated by the managerialist agenda and the police unions and questions the extent to which the advent of new managerialist agendas represents a change to the established cultural code of police officers. Her work suggests that, for the time being at least, it does not. Whilst managerialism may have become part of the everyday lives of police officers, the transactional leadership styles of old remain intact, owing in no small part to the role that they play in providing 'the foundation for efficiency and accountability' (Marks, 2007, p. 238). Concurrently, management discourses and practices reflect little of the shared occupational heritage of police officers but advocate a generic organizational blueprint for effectiveness. Police leaders are tasked with promoting innovation, which, by its very nature, suggests changes to ideas and practices that may be firmly embedded. Despite managerialism offering a new focus for policing within circumstances that demand ever greater efficiencies, it is unlikely to find any sustained cultural resonance for many officers, as it represents a value set that has been projected on to policing rather than developed *through* policing. Similarly, the essentially 'palliative' nature (Waddington, 1999a, p. 295) of traditional culture (for lower-status officers at least) is not reflected within managerialist cultures, where the benefits will hypothetically be reaped by police leaders and supervisors. When we assess the relative characteristics of traditional and managerialist views of policing, it is important to note the apparent convergence between the symbolic identity of the police as charted by traditional views of police culture and that forwarded by the police unions. Marks suggests that it is largely the conservative outlook, rather than any pronounced tendency towards labour activism, that allows police unions to retain their popularity with large swathes of police officers. She notes: 'Police unions are made up of police workers whose identities are very powerfully shaped by their occupation, which, despite organisational overhauls, is still steeped in entrenched traditional police cultural norms' (Marks, 2007, p. 242).

Furthermore, that police unions have focused largely on the traditional attributes of the police officer suggests that managerialist attempts to redefine core elements of policing will be unlikely to enjoy sustained success at all levels. A second issue to consider here is the extent to which the constraints of police structures effectively inhibit the effectiveness of transformational techniques, most notably in the absence of a reward system. A substantial amount of policing is effectively rooted in a transactional system as a result of its relationship to the state, its focus on procedure and the stringent financial controls that are applied to public sector services. In the UK context, therefore, the introduction during the early 1980s of the government's Financial Management Initiative ensured that there was only a partial realization of the market doctrine that was being proposed. It essentially meant that the police, whilst being encouraged to greater levels of parsimony in respect of the mantra of the '3 Es' of effectiveness, efficiency and economy (Morgan and Newburn, 1997), were essentially denied the opportunity, pivotal to the market economy, of exploring new markets, generating new streams of income or incentivizing individual officers through financial reward. In this sense the market has never been allowed to fully flourish in the police economy, as successful police forces do not generate profit, have financial independence or offer financial rewards for high levels of performance. Furthermore, the notion of what constitutes 'performance' is problematic here, and whilst police forces may have broadly defined aims, articulated through mission statements and local policing plans, the 'paradox of accountability', identified by Densten (1999, p. 46), suggests that these fail to remove the ambiguities surrounding what constitutes 'good practice'.

This meeting of the peculiarities of the police world with those of market economies does provide an emerging area of scholarly work, that of 'entrepreneurial policing' (see Smith, 2008, 2009a). However, there remains some potential for development and clarification of this subject area. Whilst the nexus of 'policing' and 'entrepreneurialism' can be traced back to Hobbs (1988, cited in Smith, 2008) we have little idea, at present, of how this variable is realized in different settings and eras. Ultimately, when one takes into account the convergence of the 'paradox of accountability' (Densten, 1999), the strict procedural requirements of the police, a history of transactional leadership styles (based on management by exception rather than on contingent reward) and a growing tendency towards 'risk aversion' (Flanagan, 2008; Heaton, 2010) there appear grounds to argue that there is little opportunity, appetite or indeed reward for entrepreneurial police work.

A further issue is that there remains some area for discussion of what constitutes 'success' within the police working personality. The *esprit de corps* that characterizes early work into policing, for example in Skolnick's (1994) coverage of police solidarity and Smith and Gray's (1983) examples of camaraderie, suggests that movement beyond the strict cultural tenets of routine police or detection work was viewed distastefully by others (see, for example, Young, 1991). While the competitive nature of the traditional 'thief-taker' is evidenced through the cultural divisions between detectives and beat officers (Cain, 1973), it rarely appeared to manifest itself in a culturally driven desire to aspire to leadership roles. There is some evidence, however, to suggest that the emergence of police managerialism has had some impact on the values of officers in this regard. Research suggests that promotion has become the accepted means of measuring individual achievement within police forces (Smith, 2009b), with eligibility largely being judged through success in the implementation of change (FitzGerald, Hough, Joseph and Qureshi, 2002). This, in itself, may indicate a tension between correlates of success being operational or managerial in origin. Interesting, as well, is the fact that, whilst officers remain largely critical of managerial performance measurement systems, some officers tend to buy into the success measurement ethos that rewarded competitive edge rather than public service (Loftus, 2009) whilst others chose not to (Cockcroft and Beattie, 2009).

Conclusion

Whilst the intellectual and theoretical aspects of police occupational culture present a number of challenges, for many it is at the operational level that the majority of concern lies. As highlighted throughout this book, the manifestations of police culture have provided a primary focus for many pieces of research. However, we should never forget the breadth of problematic behaviours that have come to be associated with police culture, and these range from high-profile and well-reported instances of corruption and scandal through to altogether more mundane issues like staff absenteeism. Furthermore, the work of Miller (2003) draws attention to the ways in which the causes of often undesirable police behaviours may be partially explained by factors beyond those of the cultural aspects of the police role. Whilst this is of interest at a theoretical level (not least in that it might draw us towards considering the convergence of occupational and societal cultures and how they impact on individual predisposition), such findings also have implications for how police institutions try to control such behaviours.

The challenge of leadership within police institutions can, at one level, be understood in the tension between the police hierarchy and the culture. Whilst the hierarchy provides a way of distinguishing between low-, middle- and high-status officers, the core values of the police are based upon and reinforced by the experiences of lower-ranking officers interacting with the public. Furthermore, in many countries, all police officers have at some part of their service undertaken such work, and it is these experiences, and the cultural framework within which they are understood, that provide a unifying factor to all members of the hierarchy, regardless of status. The core disposition of the average police officer therefore will be based on values associated with street work and not with externally generated values regarding organizational management. Underpinning this tension is the discretion that is an inevitable part of the officer's working role and which appears to contradict demands, from above, for greater control over the work of lower-ranking officers.

Conclusion

The intention of this book has been to provide an informed overview of the themes and concepts of police culture. The term's popularity belies the fact that it can tend to obscure as much as it explains, and behind a rather plain façade can be found multiple layers of understanding which themselves reflect academic, political and institutional tensions. Moreover, recent works have suggested that police culture has an increasingly limited relevance to our understanding of police work in a world where both policing and its social environment continue to change. From the vantage point of the twenty-first century much of the research into police culture, and the concepts that have subsequently emerged from it, portray policing and its cultures as distinct and hermetic packages operating in a vacuum far removed from the shifting landscapes of everyday life. This should not be construed as a criticism. The social worlds described by the likes of Skolnick (1994), Westley (1953), Holdaway (1983) and Cain (1973) were fundamentally more stable than later eras, which have become defined by fragmentation as much as by consensus. At the same time, whilst some earlier works, such as that of Niederhoffer (1969), described cultural tensions between working- and middle-class police officers, it is generally correct to assume that police officers today represent a significantly more diverse group in terms of a range of social characteristics than was previously the case. It is now no longer possible, if it ever was, to portray the cultural orientation of the police as synonymous with that of white, working-class males.

Whilst we may find a degree of comfort in cultural depictions of police and police work that remain anchored in the traditions and values of the previous century, Loader and Mulcahy show how these 'affective seductions of policing' (2003, p. 125) have increasingly become 'desacralized' and lost their symbolic meaning to many members of the public. Many of the discussions around police culture, ironically, tend to present culture as a crude process through which police officers become cultural adepts as they learn the operational side of their role (Manning, 2007; Sklansky, 2007). Consequently, much of the work that has been explored in this book has drawn us towards acknowledging that the cultural elements of the police world operate at a deeper and more symbolic level than this, and it is these areas that may produce the next generation of classic police cultural research. One way of countering the more superficial accounts of the police world that we sometimes encounter is to return to ethnographic analyses of policing, a point previously articulated by Westmarland (2008) amongst others. In an account of the purpose of ethnography from his seminal 1922 study of the Trobriand of the Kiriwina Islands, Malinowski highlights vividly the ways in which such explanations may go well beyond the less expansive accounts provided by other methodological orientations. He states:

> This goal is, briefly, to grasp the native's point of view, his relation to life, to realise *his* vision of *his* world. We have to study man, and we must study what concerns him most intimately, that is, the hold life has on him. In each culture, the values are slightly different; people aspire after different aims, follow different impulses, yearn after a different form of happiness. In each culture, we find different institutions in which man pursues his life-interest, different customs by which he satisfies his aspirations, different codes of law and morality which reward his virtues or punish his defections. To study the institutions, customs, and codes or to study the behaviour and mentality without the subjective desire of feeling by what these people live, of realising the substance of their happiness – is, in my opinion, to miss the greatest reward which we can hope to obtain from the study of man.
>
> (2005, p. 19)

Whilst advocating a solely ethnographic approach to understanding police culture would be impractical and unbalanced, there is undoubtedly a case to suggest that the sheer depth of understanding that emerges from such research would provide a welcome addition to our knowledge of contemporary police work. Furthermore, it would provide a much needed balance to reformist accounts that aim to identify and react to 'problematic' policing rather than, quite simply, to *understand* the cultural dimensions of police work. The level of understanding that ethnographic accounts can generate allows us to see police culture as more than a collection of mere informal 'trade' rules that carry police officers from one day to the next. Furthermore, given the sustained popularity of the classic works of this particular academic field, the prospects must be positive for research that seeks nothing more than to understand the relationship between police culture, behaviour and talk.

The police culture, or cultures, of the mid- to late twentieth century, whilst undoubtedly intricate, represented a period when the terms of reference for policing were significantly less fragmented than today. This recognition leads us towards some incredibly challenging conceptual and practical barriers, and it is these areas of our understanding, where ideas are contested, changeable and conditional, that the concept of 'culture' proves of real worth. I therefore want to draw on some of the elements that have been addressed throughout this book to briefly highlight some of the key concepts and themes that may facilitate our future understanding of police culture.

The role of culture is integral to our understanding of organizations, occupations and institutions. However, the literature of police occupational culture appears at variance with that of scholars from other fields who study the role of culture in other occupational settings, especially in respect of the core assumptions and understandings upon which knowledge is generated. In particular, the work of organizational theorists, such as Schein (2004), does much to depict a fully cultural institutional world. When culture is investigated within a police setting, distinctions between cultural belief and associated behavioural manifestations (such as those articulated by Schein in respect of 'artefacts', 'espoused beliefs and values' and 'underlying assumptions') tend to attract little if any attention from criminologists and police scholars. Whilst we often fail to appropriately articulate the complexity of the relationship that links culture and behaviour we still tend to invoke culture as a key causal factor. In other words, we stubbornly cling to the concept of police culture but fail to articulate how, for example, it might differ from, say, police socialization. At the same time, organizational cultures need to be understood in respect of other variables that are particular to that individual profession. Therefore, whilst we need to analyse, for example, the role of police discretion at the cultural and symbolic levels, we tend not to take into account the essentially legal dimensions of the discretion in the police role (see Brogden, 1982). In part, these tendencies may be a result of much police research focusing upon ways of managing rather than understanding police culture. The distinction made by Downes and Rock (2003) between social problems and sociological problems remains relevant. Recent years have seen police culture cast largely as a social problem rather than a sociological one, and it is hoped that this balance might be redressed by future research.

The symbolic world of policing is as important as the operational world for those exploring police culture. Waddington (1999b) introduces his book *Policing Citizens* by exploring the exact purpose of the police. He notes that, despite variations in role, there appear to be notable parallels of opinion and behaviour amongst officers even between countries. Regardless of the breadth of roles undertaken by the police, it is perhaps law enforcement that is, to many, their key priority. Despite this, research makes a convincing case to argue that the discretionary basis of police work ensures that, rather than pursuing policies of law enforcement, officers tend to pursue strategies of under-enforcement. Correspondingly, the importance of detection to the police role has seemingly been overstated not least by the influence of fiction and filmmaking, where, as Reiner (2007) notes, crime detection rates fail to reflect real life by remaining remarkably high. Despite the emergence of the 'new criminologies of everyday life' (Garland, 2001, p. 127) that normalize both crime and the police institution's difficulties with dealing with it, public conceptions of policing largely continue to converge on these central myths. This highlights the incredible importance of symbolism to our understanding of police work, the acknowledgement of which led Reiner (2003) to suggest that support for the police is as much a result of the symbolism which shrouds the institution as it is a consequence of its employees' actions. Whilst this serves to emphasize what he terms 'police fetishism', through which the police are unquestioningly assumed to be a 'functional prerequisite of social order' (2007, p. 259), we have to realize that this condition is one that is subject to variation. As Loader and Mulcahy (2003) point out, the symbolism of the police varies over time and between locations and is further differentiated by factors such as age, class and ethnicity. To some members of the public, therefore, the symbolism of the police will equate with the sentiments explicit in accounts such as that of Sir Harold Scott, commissioner of police of the Metropolis, who wrote, whilst describing the wartime contribution of the Metropolitan Police, that:

> Londoners have long taken their police for granted, but during these years they came to know them as never before. Lending a hand at every sort of job, encouraging, helping and rescuing the citizen under the grimmest conditions, the Metropolitan policeman won for himself a place in the hearts of Londoners which we may hope he will always retain.
>
> (Hargrove-Graham, 1947, p. vii)

For others, the testimony of James Brazier, an African-American who eventually died in the US state of Georgia in 1958 as a result of injuries allegedly sustained through police brutality, will provide a more recognizable depiction of the nature of police–public relations. In a statement presented by the Commission on Civil Rights, he recounted the following treatment at the hands of a police officer following arrest for a motoring charge:

> When I first entered the door of the jail, ['Y'] hit me on the back of the head and knocked me down and said, 'You smart son-of-a-bitch, I been wanting to get my hands on you for a long time.' I said, 'Why you want me for [*sic*]?' ['Y'] said, 'You is a nigger who is buying new cars and we can't hardly live. I'll get you yet.'
>
> (United States Commission on Civil Rights, 1961, p. 10)

These accounts, of course, portray a polarized scale of experience that varies along temporal, socio-economic, racial and geographical variables. They remind us that policing and portrayals of policing arouse instinctual fears regarding stability and physical safety whilst, simultaneously, reinforcing the power that the police wield. From this basic symbolic framework, individual and group social positions, histories and trajectories will lead to a multiplicity of 'meanings, associations, and vocabularies' (Loader and Mulcahy, 2003, p. 45) that we use to describe the police, what they do and what they represent. It is for these reasons that the relationship between the police and the public remains central to our understanding of police values and behaviour (Waddington, 1999b), as, in turn, these symbolic representations of the police become reinforced by the ongoing acting out of these positions in the physical world.

One recurrent theme in this book has been the theoretical and methodological impasse that occurs between sociological and historical accounts of police culture, and this tension between continuity and change is of great importance. Despite a growing appreciation and acknowledgement of the fluidity of culture, little attempt has been made to actually understand, or to research, police culture at a historical level. Historical events and factors tend to be underplayed, and the environments in which the police–public relationship is situated appear to be presented with little or no mention of the ways in which local cultural dynamics can distort the prescriptive tendencies that many cultural accounts suggest. As the works of Emsley (2005), Brogden (1991) and Hobbs (1988) amply demonstrate, police culture and its impact on police officers are largely mediated through the filtering properties of a given environment. In Emsley's work, the mixture of sleaze and wealth that characterized 1920s Soho provided the ultimate motivation for the corruption case of Sergeant George Goddard. For Brogden, the maritime tradition of Liverpool impacted directly on the local nature of secondary economies and industrial and race relations. To Hobbs, the entrepreneurial edge that characterized working-class life in the East End of London was mirrored in the creativity displayed by detectives navigating the gap between 'policing by the book' and 'getting the job done'. The limited and outdated templates that we sometimes adopt to understand police culture (see Manning, 2007; Sklansky, 2007) are, in part, a result of this apparent reluctance to accept that geography and history collide when explaining the cultural foundations of the police–public relationship. Until the artificial barriers that separate sociology and history are removed, suggests Abbott (1991), there is little scope for a full understanding of the temporal changes that punctuate our social realities. Mastrofski (2004) reiterates this argument by suggesting that the treatment of police culture as a constant, rather than as a variable, has effectively curtailed the development of meaningful theoretical models to explain police behaviour.

However, despite the dearth of explicitly historical accounts, there is some room for optimism regarding the exploration of change and continuity in police culture research. Recent work by Loftus (2009) has articulated this idea that certain core aspects of police culture are apparently subject to change whilst others remain firmly embedded. Sensitivities to gender and race have become officially recognized, and a lack of tolerance towards associated stereotyping or pejorative language is enshrined in policy and regulation. Whilst not always 'bought into' at an individual level these changes have resulted in a substantial reduction of overtly discriminatory behaviour and talk. What Loftus suggests is that perhaps the central cultural constant in terms of police stereotyping is that of class, not least because it remains the one key differentiating factor that has yet to become 'politicized'. The 'class contempt' observed by Loftus is not generally an explicit factor in earlier accounts of police culture, but it is one, interestingly, that is easily observable in many of the accounts that have been generated over the years. This is significant for a number of reasons. Structural differentials, whilst not always articulated in terms of 'class', remain a constant within most societies and therefore allow for a fixed variable to be identified against an undercurrent of change. It is this very idea that led Paoline (2003) to note that it will be the investigation of these areas of cultural persistence that will allow us to properly assess the balance between fragmented and monolithic cultures. They also allow us to tentatively assess the ways in which police culture intersects with the social changes associated with late modernity. For example, Jock Young (2007) in *The Vertigo of Late Modernity* draws us again to this idea of class and the role it plays in our articulations of social hierarchy. In particular, he argues against the idea that class ceases to have relevance in late modernity, instead suggesting that cultural explanations serve as a means of justifying class-based inequality. For Young, therefore, differences in life chances caused by class are explained in terms of cultural deficit. This immediately raises questions regarding the extent to which police cultures reflect these changing conceptions of class and difference. Furthermore, he also draws our attention to an accompanying feature of the late modern society. In the midst of such a blurring of cultural and structural concepts, we search for certainty and distinction most notably through an increasing need for the divisions between correct and incorrect behaviour to be articulated and enforced. These aspects of social change are of such relevance to policing and the police relationship with the public that cultural analyses that remain rooted in the conceptual templates of 40 years ago are likely to pastiche rather than to appreciate the police world.

The grey area between police culture and that of wider society remains an important one for police cultural scholars and holds real interest as a means of exploring the extent to which police culture and that of wider society may converge on some issues and diverge on others. Whilst it appears sensible to propose that wider culture does not end at the front door of the police station, a more precise knowledge of the conditions that influence this relationship would be welcome. Obviously, whilst police cultures do not represent an inversion of wider societal ideas, or a counter-cultural position, the relationship between the two might not be as straightforward as implied by Sir Robert Mark's assertion, in 1978, that the police merely reflect the values of the public.

The extent to which police cultures are different from wider 'outside' cultures remains largely unexplored and, increasingly, it appears the case that there is scope for accepting that some police behaviours previously associated with police culture may find partial explanation outside of the police world. With a determinism that reflects that inherent in Reiner's (2003) notion of 'police fetishism', where the role of the public in enforcing social control (albeit informally) was effectively rejected, the 'interpretative over-reach' described by Waddington similarly negates the influence of non-police cultural forces on police behaviour. In one of the clearer examples of how these rigid conceptions may successfully become eroded, we find that Miller's (2003) work into police corruption has started to chip away at the received wisdom on this matter by highlighting the partial role played by non-occupational factors. Significantly, such accounts do not signal a return to individualized or 'rotten apple' explanations of police behaviour but, simply, show that people's non-work lives sometimes become implicated in their work lives.

In conclusion, it is possible to identify some exciting prospects for future research, analysis and commentary. All of these, however, necessitate an altogether more complex reading not only of the terms 'culture' and 'police' but also of the processes that reflect and reinforce the relationship between the two. Correspondingly, an acknowledgement of police culture as a variable rather than as a static feature will allow for the use of methodological approaches that are sensitive to the presently under-explored relationships between geographical, socio-economic and historical contexts of police work.

References

Abbott, A. (1991), 'History and sociology: the lost synthesis', *Social Science History*, 15 (2): 201–328.

Ajzenstadt, M. (2009), 'Moral panic and neo-liberalism: the case of single mothers on welfare in Israel', *British Journal of Criminology*, 49 (1): 68–87.

Audit Commission (1990), *Effective Policing: Performance Review in Police Forces*, London: Audit Commission.

Baldwin, J. and Moloney, T. (1992), *Supervision of Police Investigation in Serious Criminal Cases*, Royal Commission Research Study No. 4, London: HMSO.

Banton, M. (1964), *The Policeman in the Community*, London: Tavistock.

Bass, B.M. and Avolio, B.J. (1993), 'Transformational leadership and organizational culture', *Public Administration Quarterly*, 17: 112–122.

Baudrillard, J. (1994), *Simulacra and Simulation*, trans. S.F. Glaser, Ann Arbor: University of Michigan.

Bayley, D.H. (1979), 'Police function, structure, and control in Western Europe and North America: comparative and historical studies', in N. Morris and M. Tonry (eds), *Crime and Justice*, Vol. 1: *An Annual Review of Research*, Chicago, IL: University of Chicago Press.

Bayley, D.H. (1994), *Police for the Future*, New York: Oxford University Press.

Bayley, D.H. and Mendelsohn, H. (1969), *Minorities and the Police*, New York: Free Press.

Beal, C. (2001), 'Thank God for police culture', *Police Journal Online*, 82 (12). Online. Available at: http://www.policejournalsa.org.au/0112/39a.html (accessed 20 December 2011).

Beck, U. (1992), *Risk Society: Towards a New Modernity*, London: Sage.

Becker, H. (1963), *Outsiders*, New York: Free Press.

Berger, P.L. and Luckmann, T. (1967), *The Social Construction of Reality*, Garden City, NY: Doubleday.

Berry, J. (2009), *Reducing Bureaucracy in Policing: Final Report*, London: Home Office.

Bittner, E. (1970), *The Functions of the Police in Modern Society*, Washington, DC: US Government Printing Office.

Bittner, E. (1983), 'Legality and workmanship: introduction to control in the police organization', in M. Punch (ed.), *Control in the Police Organization*, Cambridge, MA: MIT Press.

Black, D. (1971), 'The social organization of arrest', *Stanford Law Review*, 23: 1087–1111.

Black, D. (1980), *The Manners and Customs of the Police*, New York: Academic Press.

Bogg, J. and Cooper, C. (1995), 'Job satisfaction, mental health, and occupational stress among senior civil servants', *Human Relations*, 48 (3): 327–341.

Bowling, B. and Phillips, C. (2003), 'Policing ethnic minority communities', in T. Newburn (ed.), *Handbook of Policing*, Cullompton, Devon: Willan.

Broderick, J. (1973), *Police in a Time of Change*, Morristown, NJ: General Learning Press.

Brodeur, J. (1983), 'High policing and low policing: remarks about the policing of political activities', *Social Problems*, 30 (5): 507–521.

Brogden, M. (1982), *The Police: Autonomy and Consent*, London: Academic Press.

Brogden, M. (1991), *On the Mersey Beat: An Oral History of Policing Liverpool between the Wars*, Oxford: Oxford University Press.

Brogden, M., Jefferson, T. and Walklate, S. (1988), *Introducing Policework*, London: Unwin Hyman.

Brown, A. (1995), *Organisational Culture*, London: Pitman Publishing.

Brown, J. (1997), 'European policewomen: a comparative research perspective', *International Journal of the Sociology of Law*, 25: 1–19.

Brown, J. (2000), 'Discriminatory experiences of women police: a comparison of officers serving in England and Wales, Scotland, Northern Ireland and the Republic of Ireland', *International Journal of the Sociology of Law*, 28: 91–111.

Brown, J. (2007), 'From cult of masculinity to smart macho: gender perspectives on police occupational culture', in M. O'Neill, M. Marks and A. Singh (eds), *Police Occupational Culture: New Debates and Directions*, New York: Elsevier.

Brown, M.K. (1981), *Working the Street: Police Discretion and the Dilemmas of Reform*, New York: Russell Sage Foundation.

Bruns, G.H. and Shuman, I.G. (1988), 'Police managers' perception of organizational leadership styles', *Public Personnel Management*, 17 (2): 145–157.

Bryant, L., Dunkerley, D. and Kelland, G. (1985), 'One of the boys?', *Policing*, 1 (4): 236–244.

Bureau of Justice Statistics (2010), *Crime Data Brief: Women in Law Enforcement 1987–2008*, Washington, DC: US Department of Justice, Office of Justice Programs, Bureau of Justice Statistics.

Butler, A.J.P. (2000), 'Managing the future: a chief constable's view', in F. Leishman, B. Loveday and S. Savage (eds), *Core Issues in Policing*, 2nd edn, Harlow: Pearson Education.

Cain, M. (1973), *Society and the Policeman's Role*, London: Routledge.

Carlin, J.E. (1966), *Lawyers' Ethics: A Survey of the New York City Bar*, New York: Russell Sage Foundation.

Chan, J. (1997), *Changing Police Culture: Policing in a Multicultural Society*, Cambridge: Cambridge University Press.

Chan, J. (with Devery, C. and Doran, S.) (2003), *Fair Cop: Learning the Art of Policing*, Toronto: University of Toronto Press.

Chatterton, M.R. (1979), 'The supervision of patrol work under the fixed points system', in S. Holdaway (ed.), *The British Police*, London: Edward Arnold.

Chibnall, S. (1979), 'The Metropolitan Police and the news media', in S. Holdaway (ed.), *The British Police*, London: Edward Arnold.

Cockcroft, T. (2001), 'An investigation into the cultures of the Metropolitan Police Force between the 1930s and the 1960s', Unpublished Ph.D. thesis, Brunel University.

Cockcroft, T. (2005), 'Using oral history techniques to investigate police culture', *Qualitative Research*, 5 (3): 365–384.

Cockcroft, T. (2007), 'Police culture(s): some definitional, contextual and analytical considerations', in M. O'Neill, M. Marks and A. Singh (eds), *Police Occupational Culture: New Debates and Directions*, New York: Elsevier.

Cockcroft, T. (2010), 'Vers une reconnaissance de la valeur de l'histoire orale de la police en criminologie', in J. Berlière and R. Lévy (eds), *L'historien, le sociologue et le témoin. Archives orales et récits de vie: usages et problèmes*, Paris: Nouveau Monde Éditions.

Cockcroft, T. and Beattie, I. (2009), 'Shifting cultures: managerialism and the rise of "performance"', *Policing: An International Journal of Police Strategies and Management*, (32) 3: 526–540.

Cohen, H.S. and Feldberg, M. (1991), *Power and Restraint: The Moral Dimension of Police Work*, New York: Praeger.

Cohen, S. (1972), *Folk Devils and Moral Panics*, London: MacGibbon & Kee.

Collins, P.A. and Gibbs, A.C.C. (2003), 'Stress in police officers: a study of the origins, prevalence and severity of stress-related symptoms within a county police force', *Occupational Medicine*, 53 (4): 256–264.

Colman, A.M. and Gorman, L.P. (1982), 'Conservatism, dogmatism, and authoritarianism in British police officers', *Sociology*, 16: 1–11.

Crank, J.P. (1998), *Understanding Police Culture*, Cincinnati, OH: Anderson.

Critchley, T.A. (1978), *A History of the Police in England and Wales*, 2nd edn, London: Constable.

Currie, G. and Lockett, A. (2007), 'A critique of transformational leadership: moral, professional and contingent dimensions of leadership within public services organizations', *Human Relations*, 60 (2): 341–370.

Dahl, R.A. and Lindblom, C.E. (1953), *Politics, Economics and Welfare: Planning and Politico-economic Systems Resolved into Basic Social Processes*, New York: Harper & Brothers.

Davis, K.C. (1969), *Discretionary Justice*, Baton Rouge: Louisiana State University Press.

Davis, K.C. (1975), *Police Discretion*, St. Paul, MN: West.

Davis, M. (1991), 'Do cops really need a code of ethics?', *Criminal Justice Ethics*, 10 (2): 14–28.

Davis, M. (1992), *City of Quartz: Excavating the Future in Los Angeles*, New York: Vintage.

Denison, D.R. (1990), *Corporate Culture and Organizational Effectiveness*, New York: John Wiley & Sons.

Densten, I.L. (1999), 'Senior Australian law enforcement leadership under examination', *Policing: An International Journal of Police Strategies and Management*, 22 (1): 45–57.

Dixon, D. (2001), '"A transformed organisation"? The NSW Police Service since the Royal Commission', *Current Issues in Criminal Justice*, 13 (2): 203–218.

Dodd, V. and Stratton, A. (2011), 'Bill Bratton says he can lead police out of "crisis" despite budget cuts', *Guardian*, 14 August. Online. Available at: http://www.guardian.co.uk/uk/2011/aug/14/bill-bratton-police-crisis-cuts (accessed 26 February 2012).

Domberger, S. and Hall, C. (1996), 'Contracting for public services: a review of antipodean experience', *Public Administration*, 74: 129–147.

Downes, D. and Rock, P. (2003), *Understanding Deviance*, 4th edn, Oxford: Oxford University Press.

Emsley, C. (1991), *The English Police: A Political and Social History*, 1st edn, London: Harvester Wheatsheaf.

Emsley, C. (1996), *The English Police: A Political and Social History*, 2nd edn, London: Longman.

Emsley, C. (2005), 'Sergeant Goddard: the story of a rotten apple, or a diseased orchard?', in A.G. Srebnick and R. Lévy (eds), *Crime and Culture: An Historical Perspective*, Aldershot: Ashgate.

Ericson, R.V. (2003), 'The culture and power of criminological research', in L. Zedner and A. Ashworth (eds), *The Criminological Foundations of Penal Policy*, Oxford: Oxford University Press.

Ericson, R.V., Baranek, P.M. and Chan, J.B.L. (1987), *Visualizing Deviance: A Study of News Organization*, Toronto: University of Toronto Press.

Ericson, R.V. and Haggerty, K.D. (1997), *Policing the Risk Society*, Oxford: Clarendon Press.

Etzioni, A. (1975), *A Comparative Analysis of Complex Organizations*, Glencoe, IL: Free Press.

Farrell, A. (1993), *Crime, Class and Corruption: The Politics of the Police*, London: Bookmarks.

Fielding, N.G. (1988), *Joining Forces: Police Training, Socialization, and Occupation*, London: Routledge.

Fielding, N.G. (1994), 'Cop canteen culture', in T. Newburn and E.A. Stanko (eds), *Just Boys Doing Business: Men, Masculinities and Crime*, New York: Routledge.

Fielding, N.G. (1997), Review of J. Chan, *Changing Police Culture: Policing in a Multicultural Society* (1997), *Sociological Research Online*, 2 (2). Online. Available at: http://www.socresonline.org.uk/2/2/fielding.html (accessed 26 February 2012).

FitzGerald, M., Hough, M., Joseph, I. and Qureshi, T. (2002), *Policing for London*, Cullompton, Devon: Willan.

Flanagan, R. (2008), *The Review of Policing: Final Report*, London: HMSO.

Foster, J. (1989), 'Two stations: an ethnographic study of policing in the inner city', in D. Downes (ed.), *Crime and the City*, London: Macmillan.

Foster, J. (2003), 'Police cultures', in T. Newburn (ed.), *Handbook of Policing*, Cullompton, Devon: Willan.

Friedson, E. (1983), 'The theory of the professions: the state of the art', in R. Dingwall and P. Lewis (eds), *The Sociology of the Professions*, London: Macmillan.

Garland, D. (2001), *The Culture of Control*, Oxford: Oxford University Press.

Genette, G. (1980), *Narrative Discourse*, Oxford: Basil Blackwell.

Girodo, M. (1998), 'Machiavellian, bureaucratic, and transformational leadership styles in police managers: preliminary findings of interpersonal ethics', *Perceptual and Motor Skills*, 86: 419–427.

Goffee, R. and Jones, G. (1998), *The Character of a Corporation*, New York: Harper Collins.

Goldson, B. (2000), 'Whither diversion? Interventionism and the new youth justice', in B. Goldson (ed.), *The New Youth Justice*, Lyme Regis: Russell House.

Goldstein, H. (1979), 'Policing: a problem-oriented approach', *Crime and Delinquency*, 25 (2): 236–258.

Goodey, J. (2000), 'Biographical lessons for criminology', *Theoretical Criminology*, 4 (4): 473–498.

Graef, R. (1989), *Talking Blues*, London: Collins.

Greene, J.R. (2010), 'Pioneers in police research: William A. Westley', *Police Practice and Research*, 11 (5): 454–468.

Gregory, K.L. (1983), 'Native-view paradigms: multiple cultures and culture conflicts in organizations', *Administrative Science Quarterly*, 28 (3): 359–376.

Grimshaw, R. and Jefferson, T. (1987), *Interpreting Policework*, London: Unwin Hyman.

Hall, S., Critchley, C., Jefferson, T., Clarke, J. and Roberts, B. (1978), *Policing the Crisis*, London: Macmillan.

Harris, P. (2011), 'Police brutality charges sweep across the US', *Observer* (Kindle edn), 23 October.

Harris, R.N. (1978), 'The police academy and the professional self image', in P. K. Manning and J. Van Maanen (eds), *Policing: A View from the Street*, Santa Monica, CA: Goodyear.

Haylett, C. (2001), '"Illegitimate subjects": abject whites, neoliberal modernization and middle-class multiculturalism', *Environment and Planning D: Society and Space*, 19: 351–370.

Health and Safety Executive (HSE) (2008), *The Effects of Transformational Leadership on Employees' Absenteeism in Four UK Public Sector Institutions*, Research Report RR 648, Norwich: HMSO.

Heaton, R. (2010), 'We could be criticized! Policing and risk aversion', *Policing: A Journal of Policy and Practice*, 5 (1): 75–86.

Heidensohn, F. (1985), *Women and Crime*, Basingstoke: Macmillan.

Heidensohn, F. (1992), *Women in Control? The Role of Women in Law Enforcement*, Oxford: Clarendon Press.

Heisenberg, W. (1962), *Physics and Philosophy: The Revolution in Modern Science*, New York: Harper & Row.

Her Majesty's Inspectorate of Constabulary (1999a), *Police Integrity: Securing and Maintaining Public Confidence*, London: Home Office.

Her Majesty's Inspectorate of Constabulary (1999b), *Winning the Race – Revisited: A Follow-up to the HMIC Thematic Inspection Report on Police Community and Race Relations (1998/1999)*, London: HMSO.

Hobbs, D. (1988), *Doing the Business: Entrepreneurship, Detectives and the Working Class in the East End of London*, Oxford: Clarendon Press.

Hobbs, D. (1989), 'Policing in the vernacular', in D. Downes (ed.), *Crime and the City*, London: Macmillan.

Holdaway, S. (1983), *Inside the British Police*, Oxford: Blackwell.

Holdaway, S. and Parker, S.K. (1998), 'Policing women police: uniform patrol, promotion and representation in the CID', *British Journal of Criminology*, 38 (1): 40–60.

Home Office (1983), *Manpower, Effectiveness and Efficiency in the Police Service*, Circular 114/83, London: Home Office.

Home Office (1988), *Civilian Staff in the Police Service*, Circular 105/88, London: HMSO.

Home Office (1993), *Police Reform: A Police Service for the Twenty-First Century*, Cm 2281, London: HMSO.

Home Office (2000), *Home Office Statistical Bulletin: Police Service Strength England and Wales 30th September 2000*, London: Home Office.

Home Office (2004), *Building Communities, Beating Crime: A Better Police Service for the 21st Century*, London: HMSO.

Home Office (2008), *Improving Performance: A Practical Guide to Police Performance Management*, London: Home Office.

Home Office (2010), *Home Office Statistical Bulletin: Police Service Strength England and Wales 31st March 2010*, London: Home Office.

Hope, T. (2005), 'Things can only get better', *Criminal Justice Matters*, 62: 4–39.

Howgrave-Graham, H.M. (1947), *The Metropolitan Police at War*, London: HMSO.

Hunt, J. (1984), 'The development of rapport through the negotiation of gender in field-work among police', *Human Organization*, 43: 283–296.

Hunte, J. (1966), *Nigger Hunting in England?*, London: West Indian Standing Conference.

Independent Police Complaints Commission (IPCC) (2010), *Statutory Guidance: Statutory Guidance to the Police Service and Police Authorities on the Handling of Complaints*, London: IPCC.

Independent Police Complaints Commission (IPCC) (2011), *Corruption in the Police Service of England and Wales – Part 1*, London: IPCC.

Innes, M. (2003), *Investigating Murder: Detective Work and the Police Response to Criminal Homicide*, Oxford: Clarendon Press.

Jackson, P.M. (1993), 'Public service performance evaluation: a strategic perspective', *Public Money Management*, 13: 19–26.

James, D. (1979), 'Police–black relations: the professional solution', in S. Holdaway (ed.), *The British Police*, London: Edward Arnold.

Johnson, S.D., Koh, H.C. and Killough, L.N. (2009), 'Organizational and occupational culture and the perception of managerial accounting terms: an exploratory study using perceptual mapping techniques', *Contemporary Management Research*, 5 (4): 317–342.

Johnston, L. (2000a), 'Private policing: problems and prospects', in F. Leishman, B. Loveday and S. Savage (eds), *Core Issues in Policing*, 2nd edn, London: Longman.

Johnston, L. (2000b), *Policing Britain: Risk, Security and Governance*, Harlow: Longman.

Jones, T. (2008), 'Discretion', in T. Newburn and P. Neyroud (eds), *Dictionary of Policing*, Cullompton, Devon: Willan.

Jones, T. and Newburn, T. (1998), *Private Security and Public Policing*, Oxford: Clarendon Press.

Jordan, J. (2001), 'Worlds apart? Women, rape and the police reporting process', *British Journal of Criminology*, 41 (4): 679–706.

Judge, T. (1994), *The Force of Persuasion: The Story of the Police Federation*, Surbiton: Police Federation.

Key, V.O., Jr (1935), 'Police graft', *American Journal of Sociology*, 40 (5): 624–636.

Kitzinger, J. (1999), 'The ultimate neighbour from hell? Stranger danger and the media framing of paedophiles', in B. Franklin (ed.), *Social Policy, the Media and Misrepresentation*, London: Routledge.

Kleinig, J. (1996), *The Ethics of Policing*, Cambridge: Cambridge University Press.

Klockars, C. (1985), *The Idea of Police*, Beverly Hills, CA: Sage.

Kraska, P.B. and Kappeler, V.E. (1995), 'To serve and pursue: exploring police sexual violence against women', *Justice Quarterly*, 12 (1): 85–111.

Krimmel, J.T. and Lindenmuth, P. (2001), 'Police chief performance and leadership styles', *Police Quarterly*, 4 (4): 469–483.

Kuykendall, J.L. and Unsinger, P. (1982), 'The leadership styles of police managers', *Journal of Criminal Justice*, 10: 311–321.

LaFave, W. (1962a), 'The police and nonenforcement of the law – part I', *Wisconsin Law Review*, 1: 104–137.

LaFave, W. (1962b), 'The police and nonenforcement of the law – part II', *Wisconsin Law Review*, 2: 179–239.

Levi, R. (2008), 'Auditable community: the moral order of Megan's law', *British Journal of Criminology*, 48 (5): 583–603.

Loader, I. and Mulcahy, A. (2003), *Policing and the Condition of England: Memory, Politics and Culture*, Oxford: Oxford University Press.

Loader, I. and Sparks, R. (2005), 'For an historical sociology of crime policy in England and Wales since 1968', in M. Matravers (ed.), *Managing Modernity: Politics and the Culture of Control*, London: Routledge.

Loftus, B. (2009), *Police Culture in a Changing World*, Oxford: Oxford University Press.

Loftus, B. (2010), 'Police occupational culture: classic themes, altered times', *Policing and Society*, 20 (1): 1–20.

Long, M. (2003), 'Leadership and performance management', in T. Newburn (ed.), *The Handbook of Policing*, Cullompton, Devon: Willan.

MacAlister, D. (2004), 'Canadian police subculture', in S. Nancoo (ed.), *Contemporary Issues in Canadian Policing*, Mississauga, Ontario: Canadian Educators' Press.

McLaughlin, E. and Muncie, J. (2006), 'Editor's introduction', in J. Muncie and E. McLaughlin (eds), *The Sage Dictionary of Criminology*, 2nd edn, London: Sage.

Macpherson, W. (1999), *The Stephen Lawrence Inquiry*, Cm 4262, London: HMSO.

Maguire, M. and Norris, C. (1994), 'Police investigations: practice and malpractice', *Journal of Law and Society*, Special Issue: *Justice and Efficiency? The Royal Commission on Criminal Justice*, 1: 72–84.

Malinowski, B. (2005), *Argonauts of the Western Pacific: An Account of Native Enterprise and Adventure in the Archipelagoes of Melanesian New Guinea*, London: Taylor & Francis.

Manning, P. K. (1977), *Police Work: The Social Organization of Policing*, Cambridge, MA: MIT Press.

Manning, P.K. (1978a), 'The police: mandate, strategies and appearances', in P.K. Manning and J. Van Maanen (eds), *Policing: A View from the Street*, Santa Monica, CA: Goodyear.

Manning, P.K. (1978b), 'Rules, colleagues, and situationally justified actions', in P.K. Manning and J. Van Maanen (eds), *Policing: A View from the Street*, Santa Monica, CA: Goodyear.

Manning, P.K. (1989), 'Occupational culture', in W.G. Bailey (ed.), *The Encyclopedia of Police Science*, New York: Garland.

Manning, P.K. (2007), 'A dialectic of organisational and occupational culture', in M. O'Neill, M. Marks and A. Singh (eds), *Police Occupational Culture: New Debates and Directions*, New York: Elsevier.

Manning, P.K. and Van Maanen, J. (1978a), 'Preface', in P.K. Manning and J. Van Maanen (eds), *Policing: A View from the Street*, Santa Monica, CA: Goodyear.

Manning, P.K. and Van Maanen, J. (1978b), 'Part IV – practice of policing', in P.K. Manning and J. Van Maanen (eds), *Policing: A View from the Street*, Santa Monica, CA: Goodyear.

Mark, R. (1977), *Policing a Perplexed Society*, London: Allen & Unwin.

Mark, R. (1978), *In the Office of Constable*, London: Collins.

Marks, M. (2007), 'Police unions and their influence: subculture or counter-culture?', in M. O'Neill, M. Marks and A. Singh (eds), *Police Occupational Culture: New Debates and Directions*, New York: Elsevier.

Martin, J. (2002), *Organizational Culture: Mapping the Terrain*, Thousand Oaks, CA: Sage.

Mastrofski, S.D. (2004), 'Controlling street-level police discretion', *Annals of the American Academy of Political and Social Science*, 593 (1): 100–118.

Matravers, A. and Maruna, S. (2005), 'Contemporary penality and psychoanalysis', in M.

Matravers (ed.), *Managing Modernity: Politics and the Culture of Control*, London: Routledge.

Miller, J. (2003), *Police Corruption in England and Wales: An Assessment of Current Evidence*, Online Report 11/03, London: Home Office, Research, Development and Statistics Directorate.

Mooney, J. and Young, J. (2000), 'Policing ethnic minorities: stop and search in North London', in B. Loveday and A. Marlow (eds), *Policing after the Stephen Lawrence Inquiry*, Lyme Regis: Russell House.

Morgan, R. and Newburn, T. (1997), *The Future of Policing*, Oxford: Oxford University Press.

Narayanan, G. (2005), 'Theorizing police response to domestic violence in the Singaporean context: police subculture revisited', *Journal of Criminal Justice*, 33 (5): 429–439.

Newburn, T. (1999), *Understanding and Preventing Police Corruption: Lessons from the Literature*, London: Home Office.

Newburn, T. (2003), 'The future of policing', in T. Newburn (ed.), *Handbook of Policing*, Cullompton, Devon: Willan.

Neyroud, P. (2003), 'Policing and ethics', in T. Newburn (ed.), *Handbook of Policing*, Cullompton, Devon: Willan.

Neyroud, P. (2011), *Review of Police Leadership and Training*, London: Home Office.

Neyroud, P. and Beckley, A. (2001), *Policing, Ethics and Human Rights*, Cullompton, Devon: Willan.

Niederhoffer, A. (1969), *Behind the Shield: The Police in Urban Society*, New York: Anchor.

Noaks, L. and Wincup, E. (2004), *Criminological Research: Understanding Qualitative Approaches*, London: Sage.

O'Malley, P. and Hutchinson, S. (2007), 'Converging corporatization? Police management, police unionism, and the transfer of business principles', *Police Practice and Research*, 8 (2): 159–174.

O'Malley, P. and Palmer, D. (1996), 'Post-Keynesian policing', *Economy and Society*, 25 (2): 137–155.

O'Neill, M. and Holdaway, S. (2007), 'Black police associations and the police occupational culture', in M. O'Neill, M. Marks and A. Singh (eds), *Police Occupational Culture: New Debates and Directions*, New York: Elsevier.

O'Neill, M., Marks, M. and Singh, A. (eds) (2007), *Police Occupational Culture: New Debates and Directions*, New York: Elsevier.

O'Neill, M. and Singh, A. (2007), 'Introduction', in M. O'Neill, M. Marks and A. Singh (eds), *Police Occupational Culture: New Debates and Directions*, New York: Elsevier.

Paoline, E.A. (2003), 'Taking stock: towards a richer understanding of police culture', *Journal of Criminal Justice*, 31 (3): 199–214.

Parker, R. and Bradley, L. (2000), 'Organisational culture in the public sector: evidence from six organisations', *International Journal of Public Sector Management*, 13 (2): 125–141.

Pearson, G. (1983), *Hooligan: A History of Respectable Fears*, London: Macmillan.

Pillai, R. and Williams, E.A. (2004), 'Transformational leadership, self-efficacy, group cohesiveness, commitment and performance', *Journal of Organizational Change Management*, 17 (2): 144–159.

Punch, M. (1979), 'The secret social service', in S. Holdaway (ed.), *The British Police*, London: Edward Arnold.

Punch, M. (1983), 'Officers and men: occupational culture, inter-rank antagonism, and the investigation of corruption', in M. Punch (ed.), *Control in the Police Organization*, Cambridge, MA: MIT Press.

Punch, M. (1985), *Conduct Unbecoming: Social Construction of Police Deviance and Control*, London: Tavistock.

Punch, M. (2003), 'Rotten orchards: "pestilence", police misconduct and system failure', *Policing and Society*, 13 (2): 171–196.

Punch, M. (2007), 'Cops with honours: university education and police culture', in M. O'Neill, M. Marks and A. Singh (eds), *Police Occupational Culture: New Debates and Directions*, New York: Elsevier.

Punch, M. (2009), *Police Corruption: Deviancy, Accountability and Reform in Policing*, Cullompton, Devon: Willan.

Quinton, P., Bland, N. and Miller, J. (2000), *Police Stops: Decision-making and Practice*, Police Research Series, Paper No. 130, London: Home Office.

Rawlings, P. (2002), *Policing: A Short History*, Cullompton, Devon: Willan.

Reiner, R. (1978), *The Blue-coated Worker*, Cambridge: Cambridge University Press.

Reiner, R. (1985), 'The police and race relations', in J. Baxter and L. Koffman (eds), *Police: The Constitution and the Community*, London: Professional Books.

Reiner, R. (1992), *The Politics of the Police*, 2nd edn, London: Harvester Wheatsheaf.

Reiner, R. (1997), 'Policing and the police', in M. Maguire, R. Morgan and R. Reiner (eds), *Oxford Handbook of Criminology*, 2nd edn, Oxford: Oxford University Press.

Reiner, R. (1998), 'Process or product? Problems of assessing individual police performance', in J. Brodeur (ed.), *How to Recognize Good Policing*, London: Sage and Police Executive Research Forum.

Reiner, R. (2003), 'Policing and the media', in T. Newburn (ed.), *Handbook of Policing*, Cullompton, Devon: Willan.

Reiner, R. (2007), 'Media made criminality: the representation of crime in the mass media', in M. Maguire, R. Morgan and R. Reiner (eds), *The Oxford Handbook of Criminology*, 4th edn, Oxford: Oxford University Press.

Reiner, R. (2010), *The Politics of the Police*, 4th edn, Oxford: Oxford University Press.

Reiner, R. and Newburn, T. (2007), 'Police research', in R.D. King and E. Wincup (eds), *Doing Research on Crime and Justice*, 2nd edn, Oxford: Oxford University Press.

Reiss, A.J., Jr (1974), 'Discretionary justice', in D. Glaser (ed.), *Handbook of Criminology*, Chicago, IL: Rand McNally.

Reuss-Ianni, E. and Ianni, F. (1983), 'Street cops and management cops: the two cultures of policing', in M. Punch (ed.), *Control in the Police Organization*, Cambridge, MA: MIT Press.

Risk and Regulation Advisory Council (RRAC) (2009), *Response with Responsibility: Policy-making for Public Risk in the 21st Century*, London: Department for Business, Enterprise and Regulatory Reform.

Roebuck, J.B. and Barker, T. (1974), 'A typology of police corruption', *Social Problems*, 21 (3): 423–437.

Rowe, M. (2004), *Policing, Race and Racism*, Cullompton, Devon: Willan.

Rowe, M. (2006), 'Following the leader: front-line narratives on police leadership', *Policing: An International Journal of Police Strategies and Management*, 29 (4): 757–767.

Royal Commission on the Police (1961), *Minutes of Evidence 15*, London: HMSO.

Sacks, H. (1978), 'Notes on police assessment of moral character', in P.K. Manning and J. Van Maanen (eds), *Policing: A View from the Street*, Santa Monica, CA: Goodyear.

Sahlins, M. (1995), *How 'Natives' Think: About Captain Cook, for Example*, Chicago, IL: University of Chicago Press.

Samuel, R. (1976), 'Local history and oral history', *History Workshop: A Journal of Socialist Historians*, 1 (1): 191–208.

Savage, S.P. (2007), *Police Reform: Forces for Change*, Oxford: Oxford University Press.

Scarman, G. (1982), *The Scarman Report: The Brixton Disorders 10–12 April 1981*, London: Pelican.

Schein, E.H. (1992), *Organizational Culture and Leadership*, San Francisco, CA: Jossey-Bass.

Schein, E.H. (2004), *Organizational Culture and Leadership*, 3rd edn, San Francisco, CA: Jossey-Bass.

Schraeder, M., Tears, R.S. and Jordan, M.H. (2005), 'Organizational culture in public sector organisations: promoting change through training and leading by example', *Leadership and Organization Development Journal*, 26 (6): 492 502.

Scott, H. (1947), 'Foreword', in H.M. Howgrave-Graham, *The Metropolitan Police at War*, London: HMSO.

Shearing, C. (1981), 'Deviance and conformity in the reproduction of order', in C. Shearing (ed.), *Organisational Police Deviance*, Toronto: Butterworth.

Shearing, C. (1997), 'Unrecognised origins of the new policing: linkages between public and private policing', in M. Felson and R.V. Clarke (eds), *Business and Crime Prevention*, Monsey, NY: Criminal Justice Press.

Shearing, C. and Ericson, R.V. (1991), 'Culture as figurative action', *British Journal of Sociology*, 42 (4): 481–506.

Sheehy Report (1993), *Report of the Enquiry into Police Responsibilities and Rewards*, Cm 2280, I, II, London: HMSO.

Sherman, L.W. (1974), 'Introduction: toward a sociological theory of police corruption', in L.W. Sherman (ed.), *Police Corruption: A Sociological Perspective*, New York: Doubleday.

Sherman, L.W. (2004), 'Research and policing: the infrastructure and political economy of federal funding', *Annals of the American Academy of Political and Social Science*, 593: 156–178.

Silvestri, M. (2003), *Women in Charge: Policing, Gender and Leadership*, Cullompton, Devon: Willan.

Silvestri, M. (2007), '"Doing" police leadership: enter the "new smart macho"', *Policing and Society*, 17 (1): 38–58.

Sinclair, A. (1991), 'After excellence: models of organizational culture for the public sector', *Australian Journal of Public Administration*, 50 (3): 321–332.

Singh, A. and Kempa, M. (2007), 'Reflections on the study of private policing cultures: early leads and key themes', in M. O'Neill, M. Marks and A. Singh (eds), *Police Occupational Culture: New Debates and Directions*, New York: Elsevier.

Skidelsky, R. (1975), *Oswald Mosley*, London: Macmillan.

Sklansky, D.A. (2007), 'Seeing blue: police reform, occupational culture, and cognitive burn-in', in M. O'Neill, M. Marks and A. Singh (eds), *Police Occupational Culture: New Debates and Directions*, New York: Elsevier.

Skolnick, J.H. (1994), *Justice without Trial: Law Enforcement in Democratic Society*, 3rd edn, London: Wiley.

Skolnick, J.H. (2000), 'Code blue', *American Prospect*, 11 (10): 49–53.

Skolnick, J.H. (2008), 'Enduring issues of police culture and demographics', *Policing and Society*, 18 (1): 35–45.

Skolnick, J.H. and Fyfe, J.J. (1993), *Above the Law: Police and the Excessive Use of Force*, New York: Free Press.

Smith, D. and Gray, J. (1983), *Police and People in London*, Vol. 4: *The Police in Action*, London: Policy Studies Institute.

Smith, R. (2008), 'Entrepreneurial policing: developing a new mindset', Paper presented to the British Society of Criminology Conference, July 2008.

Smith, R. (2009a), 'Entrepreneurial policing', *Police Professional*, 12 February. Online. Available at: http://www.sipr.ac.uk/downloads/Smith_Entrepreneurial_Policing.pdf (accessed 27 February 2012).

Smith, R. (2009b), 'Entrepreneurship, police leadership and the investigation of crime in changing times', *Journal of Investigative Psychology and Offender Profiling*, 5: 209–225.

Southgate, P. (1985), 'Police output measures: past work and future possibilities', in J. Burrows, K. Heal and R. Tarling (eds), *Policing Today*, London: Home Office.

Sparrow, M.K., Moore, M.H. and Kennedy, D.M. (1990), *Beyond 911: A New Era for Policing*, New York: Basic Books.

Spradley, J.P. (1980), *Participant Observation*, London: Harcourt Brace Jovanovich.

Stablein, R. (1996), 'Data in organization studies', in S. Clegg, C. Hardy and W. Nord (eds), *Handbook of Organization Studies*, London: Sage.

Steer, D. (1970), *Police Cautions: A Study in the Exercise of Police Discretion*, Oxford: Blackwell.

Storch, R. (1976), 'The policeman as domestic missionary: urban discipline and popular culture in Northern England 1850–1880', *Journal of Social History*, 9 (4): 481–509.

Summerfield, D. (2011), 'Metropolitan Police blues: protracted sickness absence, ill health retirement, and the occupational psychiatrist', *British Medical Journal*, 342: 950–952.

Sumner, C. (1994), *The Sociology of Deviance: An Obituary*, Buckingham: Open University Press.

Telegraph Online (15 September 2008), 'Obituary: Harold "Tanky" Challenor'. Online. Available at: http://www.telegraph.co.uk/news/obituaries/2965282/Harold-Tanky-Challenor.html (accessed 25 February 2012).

Temkin, J. (1997), 'Plus ça change: reporting rape in the 1990s', *British Journal of Criminology*, 37 (4): 507–528.

Temple, R. (1995), 'The Metropolitan Police and the anti-fascists 1934–40', *Journal of the Police History Society*, 10: 34–44.

Thomson, A. (1998), 'Anzac memories: putting popular memory theory into practice in Australia', in R. Perks and A. Thomson (eds), *The Oral History Reader*, London: Routledge.

Tierney, J. (2006), *Criminology: Theory and Context*, 2nd edn, Harlow: Pearson.

United States Commission on Civil Rights (1961), *1961 U.S. Commission on Civil Rights Report Book 5: Justice*, Washington, DC: US Commission on Civil Rights.

Van Maanen, J. (1978a), 'The asshole', in P.K. Manning and J. Van Maanen (eds), *Policing: A View from the Street*, Santa Monica, CA: Goodyear.

Van Maanen, J. (1978b), 'Observations on the making of policemen', in P.K. Manning and J. Van Maanen (eds), *Policing: A View from the Street*, Santa Monica, CA: Goodyear.

Van Maanen, J. (1978c), 'On watching the watchers', in P.K. Manning and J. Van Maanen (eds), *Policing: A View from the Street*, Santa Monica, CA: Goodyear.

Van Maanen, J. and Barley, S. (1985), 'Cultural organization: fragments of a theory', in P. Frost, M. Louis and L. Moore (eds), *Organization Culture*, Newbury Park, CA: Sage.

Vollmer, A. (1936), *The Police and Modern Society*, Berkeley: University of California Press. Reprinted 1971 by Patterson Smith, Montclair, NJ.

Waddington, P.A.J. (1999a), 'Police (canteen) sub-culture: an appreciation', *British Journal of Criminology*, 39 (2): 287–309.

Waddington, P.A.J. (1999b), *Policing Citizens*, London: UCL Press.

Waddington, P.A.J. (2008), 'Police culture', in T. Newburn and P. Neyroud (eds), *Dictionary of Policing*, Cullompton, Devon: Willan.

Wakefield, A. (2003), *Selling Security: The Private Policing of Public Space*, Cullompton, Devon: Willan.

Walklate, S. and Mythen, G. (2008), 'How scared are we?', *British Journal of Criminology*, 48 (2): 209–225.

Walsh, J.L. (1977), 'Career styles and police behaviour', in D.H. Bayley (ed.), *Police and Society*, Beverly Hills, CA: Sage.

Walters, R. (2003), *Deviant Knowledge: Criminology, Politics and Policy*, Cullompton, Devon: Willan.

Waters, I. (2000), 'Quality and performance monitoring', in F. Leishman, B. Loveday and S. Savage (eds), *Core Issues in Policing*, 2nd edn, London: Longman.

Weber, M. (1949), *The Methodology of the Social Sciences*, ed. and trans. E. Shils and H.A. Finch, New York: Free Press.

Weinberger, B. (1995), *The Best Police in the World: An Oral History of English Policing*, Aldershot: Scolar.

Wessely, S. (2011), 'A police officer's lot is not a happy one', *British Medical Journal*, 342: 953.

Westley, W.A. (1953), 'Violence and the police', *American Journal of Sociology*, 59 (1): 34–41.

Westley, W.A. (1970), *Violence and the Police: A Sociological Study of Law, Custom, and Morality*, Cambridge, MA: MIT Press.

Westmarland, L. (2001), *Gender and Policing: Sex, Power and Police Culture*, Cullompton, Devon: Willan.

Westmarland, L. (2008), 'Police cultures', in T. Newburn (ed.), *Handbook of Policing*, 2nd edn, Cullompton, Devon: Willan.

Whitaker, B. (1964), *The Police*, Harmondsworth, Middlesex: Penguin.

White, D. (2006), 'A conceptual analysis of the hidden curriculum of police training in England and Wales', *Policing and Society*, 16 (4): 386–404.

White, J. (1983), 'Police and people in London in the 1930s', *Oral History*, 11 (2): 34–41.

Whitehead, T. (2008), 'More laws but no more order, say academics', *Telegraph Online*, 13 November. Online. Available at: http://www.telegraph.co.uk/news/newstopics/politics/lawandorder/3454450/More-laws-but-no-more-order-say-academics.html (accessed 27 April 2012).

Whitfield, J. (2004), *Unhappy Dialogue: The Metropolitan Police and Black Londoners in Post-war Britain*, Cullompton, Devon: Willan.

Williams, A. (1985), 'Performance measurement in the public sector: paving the road to hell?', Seventh Arthur Young Lecture, University of Glasgow, 19 March.

Williams, H. and Murphy, P.V. (1990), 'The evolving strategy of the police: a minority view', *Perspectives on Policing*, 13, Washington, DC: National Institute of Justice.

Wilson, J.Q. (1968), *Varieties of Police Behavior: The Management of Law and Order in Eight Communities*, Cambridge, MA: Harvard University Press.

Wisniewski, M. and Olafsson, S. (2004), 'Developing balanced scorecards in local authorities: a comparison of experience', *International Journal of Productivity*, 53 (7): 602–610.

Wood, D. and Tong, S. (2009), 'The future of initial police training: a university perspective', *International Journal of Police Science and Management*, 11 (3): 294–305.

Young, J. (1994), 'Incessant chatter: recent paradigms in criminology', in M. Maguire,

R. Morgan and R. Reiner (eds), *The Oxford Handbook of Criminology*, Oxford: Oxford University Press.

Young, J. (1999), *The Exclusive Society*, London: Sage.

Young, J. (2004), Voodoo criminology and the numbers game', in J. Ferrell, K. Hayward, W. Morrison and M. Presdee (eds), *Cultural Criminology Unleashed*, London: Glass-House Press.

Young, J. (2007), *The Vertigo of Late Modernity*, London: Sage.

Young, J. (2009), 'Moral panic: its origins in resistance, ressentiment and the translation of fantasy into reality', *British Journal of Criminology*, 49 (1): 4–16.

Young, M. (1991), *An Inside Job*, Oxford: Clarendon Press.

Zedner, L. (2003), 'Useful knowledge? Debating the role of criminology in post-war Britain', in L. Zedner and A. Ashworth (eds), *The Criminological Foundations of Penal Policy*, Oxford: Oxford University Press.

Zurn, C.F. (2005), 'Recognition, redistribution, and democracy: dilemmas of Honneth's critical social theory', *European Journal of Philosophy*, 13 (1): 89–126.

Index

accountability 105, 106, 143; legal dimensions of 18; and managerial reform 13, 129–130; 'paradox of accountability' 134, 144; and police discretion 51; political dimensions of 17; and professionalism 52

Banton, M.: cynicism 54; police and ethnic minorities 70, 74, 76; police role 3; suspicion 56; under-enforcement 23–24
Bass, B. M. and Avolio, B. J. 134, 135, 137
Baudrillard, J. 96
Bourdieu, P. 33
Brogden, M.: discretion 18, 47, 50, 51, 56; ethnic minorities 70, 72; external environments 36, 42–43; occupational isolation 60; political relation 17; victims of sexual and domestic violence 66

Cain, M.: 'easing' behaviours 25–27; police attitudes to ethnic minorities 73; rural v. urban policing 25–26; symbolic importance of events 53
Challenor, H. 19–20
Chan, J.: critique of early work 32–33; cynicism 54, 55; 'field' and 'habitus' 34; multiple cultures 35–36; re-conceptualization of police culture 33–34
Chibnall, S. 20
class 92–93; class-based nature of police work 105; composition of police service 115–116; embedded class relations 108, 114–115; and late modernity 151; as legitimate target 101–102; Liverpool,

England 42–43; policing middle class communities 81–82; presentational codes 30–31; tensions between officers 131–132; working class culture 32
corruption: camaraderie and 59–60; definition of 120–122; 'graft' 28, 124, 125, 140; historic examples of 19–20, 43–44; as individual v. systemic 44, 120, 126; 'machine politics' and 124–125; media expose and involvement 120; national contexts 124; noble cause 124, 127; non-occupational factors 126; reform 129–131; tolerance of 127–128
Crank, J. P.: conservatism 76–77; individualism and ideology 126; management 141; police and ethnic minorities 72, 73, 76; 'sense of mission' 52
criminology 1, 19, 106–107, 110
culture: cultural typologies 7–8; as figurative action 111–112; late modernity and 93; level of 'artefact' 6, 10–11, 148; level of 'espoused belief and value' 5, 6–7, 148; level of 'underlying assumption' 6, 8, 10–11, 148; organizational and occupational cultures 12; organizational culture 4–6; police culture and wider culture 35, 36, 76, 108–109, 111, 112, 151; public and private sector 12–14

danger 40, 80; and the 'symbolic assailant' 57; symbolism of 57, 111, 113; 'working personality' 24–25, 26, 38, 53, 56
detectives: alcohol 63–64; creativity of 150; gender divisions amongst 68;

detectives: alcohol (*cont.*):
solidarity amongst 60; strategies for paperwork 55; uniform officers attitudes towards 29, 55; use of presentational codes 31
discretion 46–52, 108; barrier to reform 145; centrality to police culture 18, 22, 27, 104; decision-making 20, 28, 41; delegated and unauthorized 48; detectives 77; differential use of 65; factors impacting upon the use of 44–45, 138; as a legal issue 127; and 'legalistic' styles 81; and managerialism 96; as an occupational universal 38; problematic use of 102, 106, 123, 128; and risk aversion 98–99, 138; and under-enforcement of law 23–24, 43
divisions between police officers: class 131–132, 42; detective and uniform 30, 41, 60, 77; division 29, 32; gender 67–68; between 'street' and 'management' roles 86–87, 96, 137
Dixon, D. 138

Emsley, C.: corruption 20, 43–44, female officers 61–62, 62–63; minority groups 69–70; orthodox police histories 50; pro-protestant police bias 43
equal opportunity legislation, agendas and politics 97, 100, 101, 102
Ericson, R.V.: 'knowledge work' 96–97, 117; police storytelling 54; purpose of criminology 107; risk 92–93

Garland, D. 17, 38, 90, 91, 148
Goddard, G. 20, 43–44, 150

higher education 28, 87–89, 100, 131, 134
Hobbs, D., CID 30–31; East End of London 32, 111; paperwork 55; police relationship with community 30, 31

identity politics 101–102
IPCC (Independent Police Complaints Commission) 122

Keynesian and post-Keynesian policing 94
King, R. 128
Kleinig, J. 49–50
Klockars, C. 47, 49, 50, 51
Knapp Commission 28, 59

labelling theory 104, 105, 106
LaFave, W. 23, 48, 51, 104
late modernity 24, 90–95, 151
Loader, I. and Mulcahy, A.: complexity of police symbolism 148–149; police 'desacralization' 146; political orientation of police officers 77, 78; responses to race relations agenda and legislation 74; symbolic power of the police 117
Loftus, B.: class 102, 115, 150; contemporary fields of policing 101; identity politics 101, 102; relevance of early work 46; single and multiple cultures 3
London Metropolitan Police: alcohol 63; corruption 19–20, 43–44; Ethnic Minority Staff Association 85; introduction of female officers to 61–62; management of 141; relationship with ethnic minorities 73, 74–75; wartime contribution 149
Los Angeles 17–18, 93, 123, 140

Macpherson Report 75, 85
Manning, P. K. conservatism 76; cynicism 55; hidden nature of policework 54; police and wider culture 112; relevance of early work 46, 110, 150; ritual 59; 'threat-danger-hero' concept 57; 'unauthorized' discretion 48; variations in behaviour 79–80
Mark, Sir R. 30, 76, 77, 108, 151
Media 20, 28, 91, 120, 122, 123
Miller, J. 125–126, 129, 145
Mollen Report 59
morality 23, 52, 54, 59

neo-conservatism 91
neo-liberalism 91, 93, 94, 101
New South Wales Police 120, 138
New York City 27, 123
New York Times 60
Newburn, T.: context of police research 104, 105, 106; corruption 121; pluralization 90, 94, 100; politicization of social issues 17
Neyroud, P. discretion 50, 51; status of policework 51; transformational leadership 135, 140
Niederhoffer, A. 54, 131
NYPD (New York Police Department) 28, 59–60, 123, 131, 140